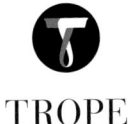

TROPE

TROPE MOBILE EDITION

VOLUME 2

NEAL KUMAR

TROPE MOBILE EDITION

VOLUME 2

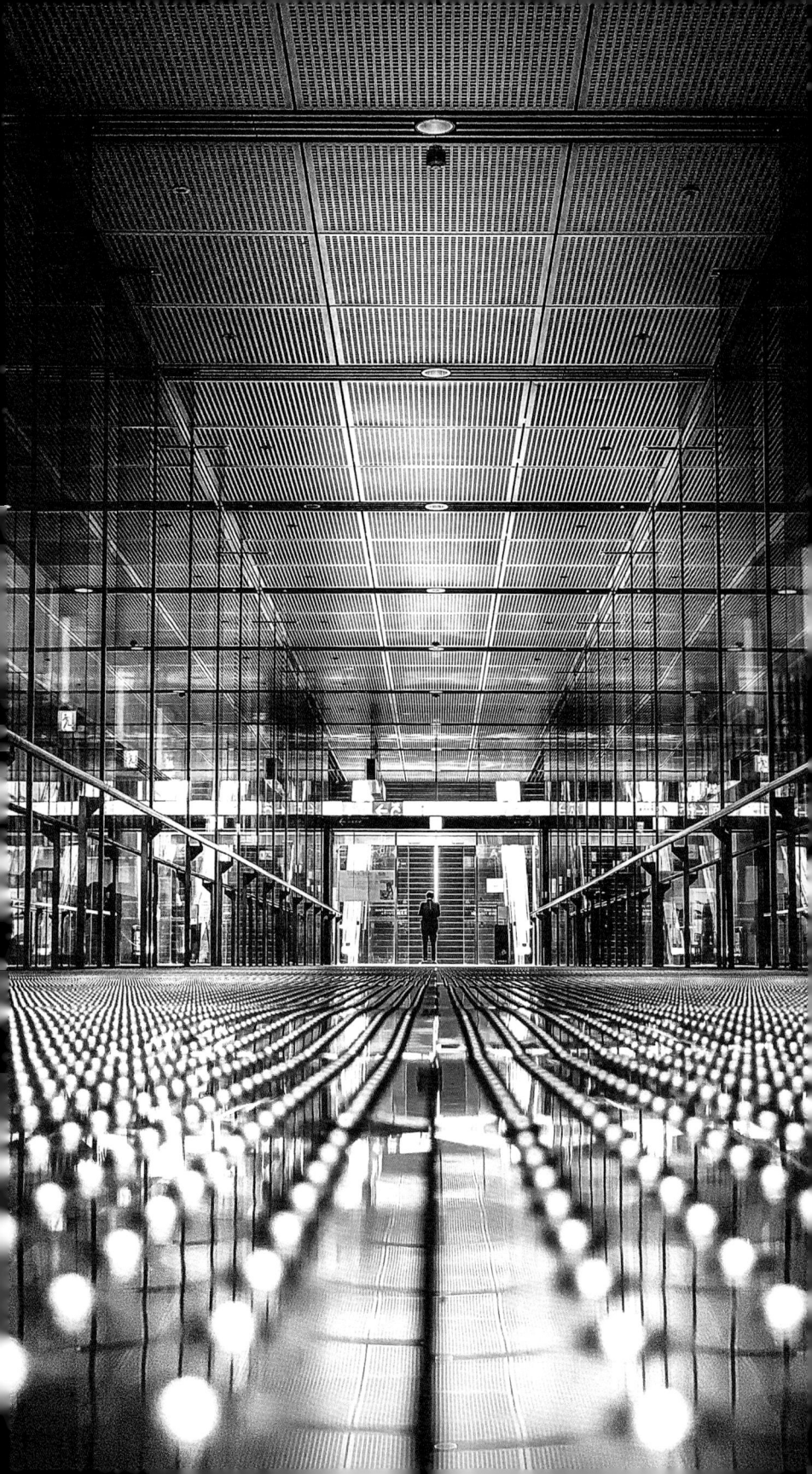

The hype surrounding the release of the very first iPhone in 2007 was focused on the fact that it had a camera, period. Those two megapixels may have been impressive in the context of a phone, and made taking snaps of family & friends more accessible, but it certainly wasn't turning the heads of any self-proclaimed photographers. Within just a few years, though, new iPhones were touting eight megapixels, and minting new photography buffs by the thousands. A revolutionary way to take pictures was born.

I initially became acquainted with photography while in Madrid, as an undergraduate student at the University of North Carolina. Just prior to my trip, I bought a small point-and-shoot camera to document my memories studying abroad. As soon as I arrived, however, I was stunned by Europe's old world, cityscapes, cultures and people. I couldn't resist documenting every moment of my trip. Looking back through my hundreds (and hundreds) of photos, I was surprised to find that a few of them truly captured a moment in time, exactly as I remembered seeing it through my own eyes. It was a means to share my vision of the world. Upon my return home, I was inspired to learn about the basic techniques of photography, which led to my first official opportunity as a UNC yearbook photographer.

I became pressed for time to dedicate to my newfound hobby as I started medical school. I had only used SLR cameras for so long, but despite the challenges of mobile photography at the time, it became the most efficient way to continue exploring photography. As iPhone features improved with each subsequent version, I found myself upgrading my personal iPhone every year. With each evolution, I challenged myself to see what kind of photos I could create with the limited capabilities of those tiny cameras.

My time became even more finite as medical school progressed and residency started, but with the rise of Instagram, the photography bug really got me again. Instagram offered a community with whom to share, from whom to get feedback and, even more, by whom to get inspired. Rather than posting all of my images, I challenged myself from the beginning to only post mobile shots to my feed - a restriction that I still hold to. Instagram inspired me to get out and shoot every week again; it brought me back to photography and, in many ways, back to life.

Now, I find that I love both mobile and SLR photography, each for different reasons. When shooting events, portraits, or large prints I will typically grab my SLR. But as mobile technology has evolved, paired with apps and tripods, I have become impressed with how well a mobile phone can capture light trails, night shots, and slow shutter. Zoom and wide-lens attachments add even further versatility. I can now reach into my pocket for my iPhone to capture shots that once would have made me wish for my SLR instead.

I love to travel, and I do it every chance I get; being comfortable with mobile photography means I can document the moment anytime inspiration strikes. I do a lot of urban and city travel, which means a lot of walking. Many of the places I go have narrow, historic streets where I would not want to lug around a bunch of camera equipment (though admittedly, it's not uncommon for me to walk around with both my phone and my SLR; I do like having two camera setups readily accessible). And big lenses tend to make people uncomfortable. A mobile camera is more discreet; using my iPhone means I can capture more intimate and natural street shots. Plus, instead of constantly switching lenses on my camera for different zoom lengths, I can have my iPhone on hand to capture a variety of shots in a short period of time.

I mostly work on instinct, but there are patterns in my approach. I often find myself first looking for an interesting frame, using anything from urban structures to nature. From there, the scene has to capture my attention in another way; with depth, details, or colors. Finally, if possible, I scan around for any possible subject to have inside the frame, which may be a person or an element that can create a foreground. This can mean waiting patiently for a subject to line up with the background.

Beyond that, I also try to be mindful of the time of day and weather patterns that can affect the lighting. For example, early in the morning or before sunset the sun is closer to the horizon, which leads to more diffusion and less intensity of direct light. This helps to cast the scene in a softer, more golden light. With harsh direct sunlight, details can sometimes get overblown and potentially lost.

The ability to capture "the moment" at any time, all the time, is a result of people having mobile phones; however, I think it is your particular "eye" for capturing everyday moments that makes those images your own.

NEAL KUMAR
@nealkumar

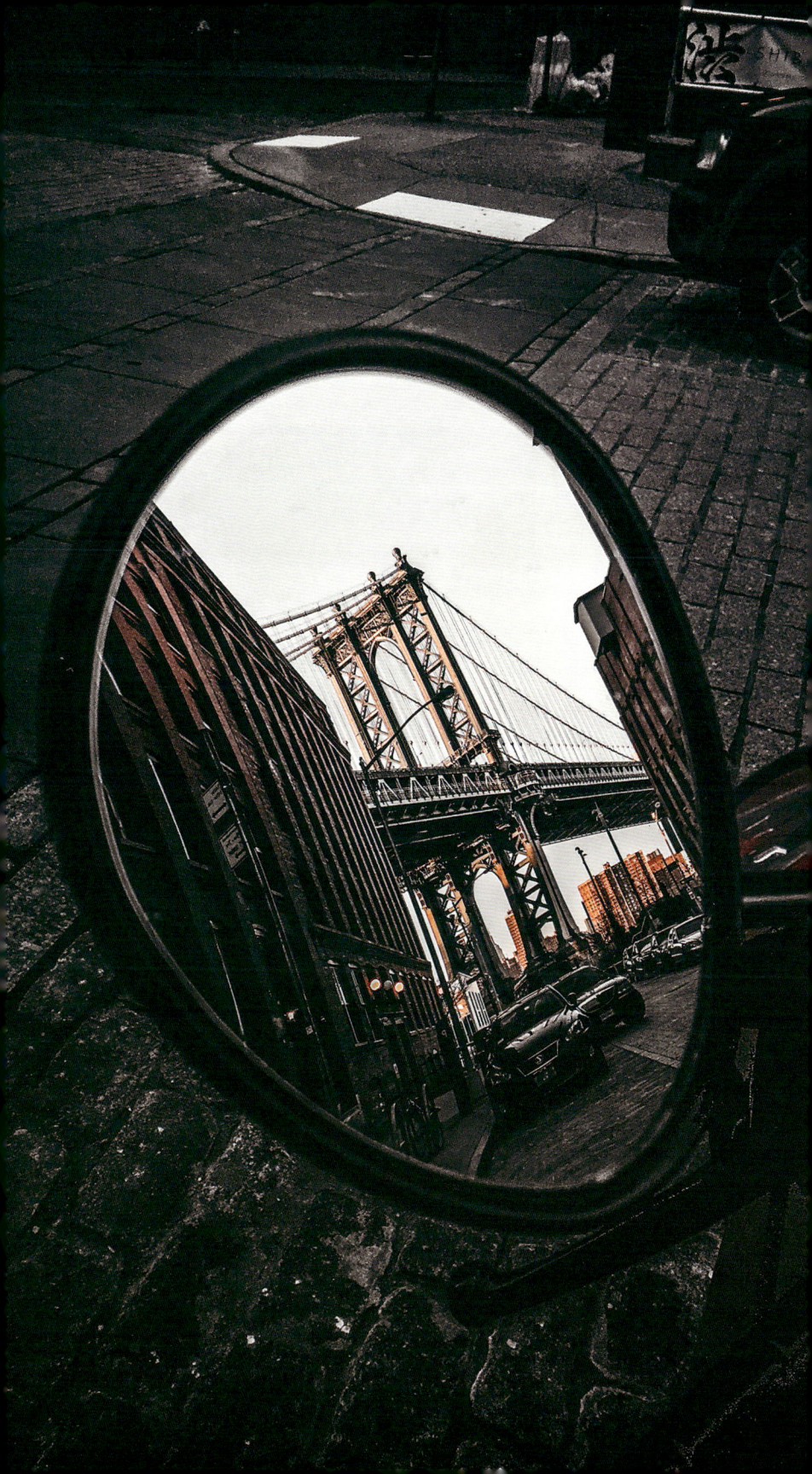

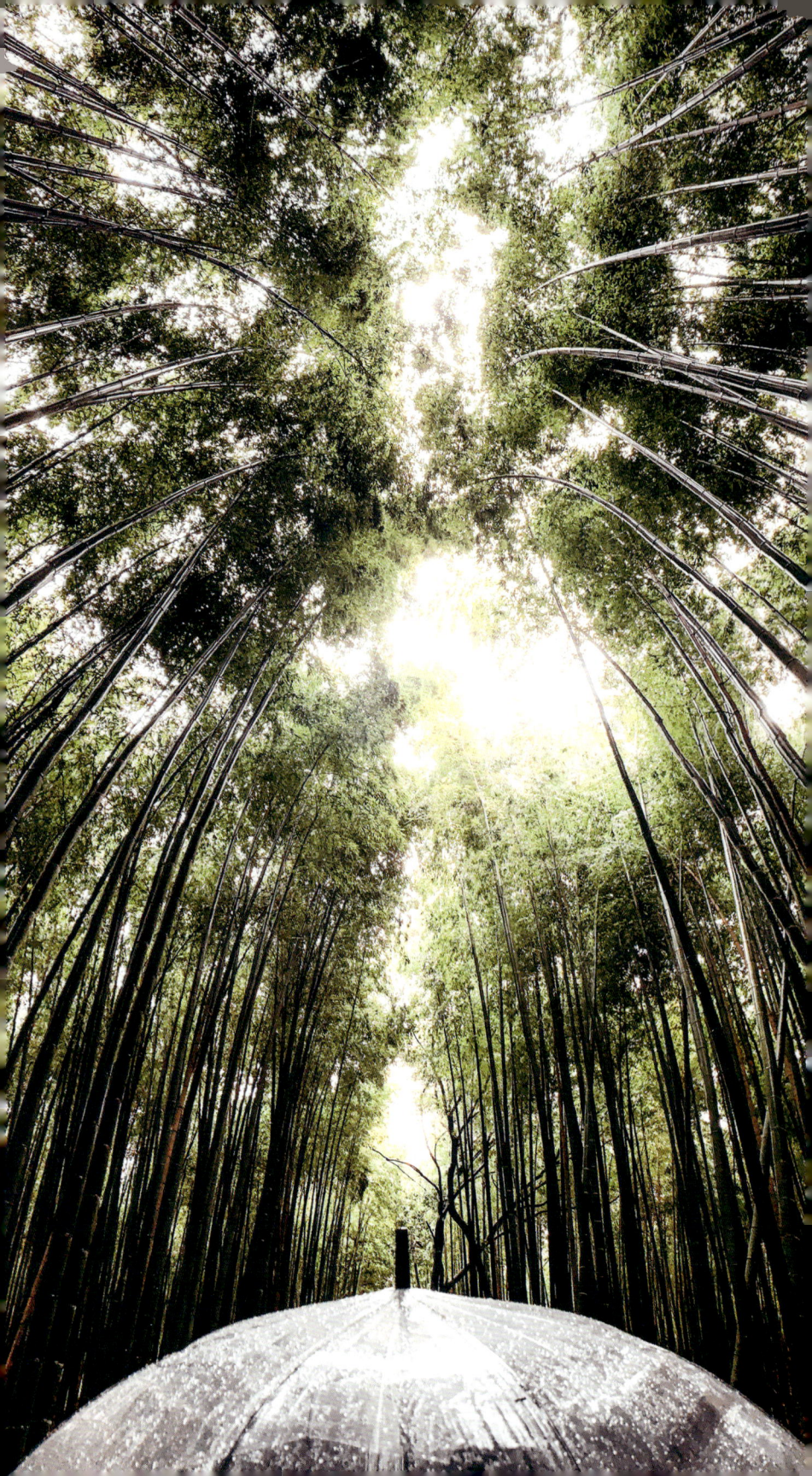

NEAL KUMAR

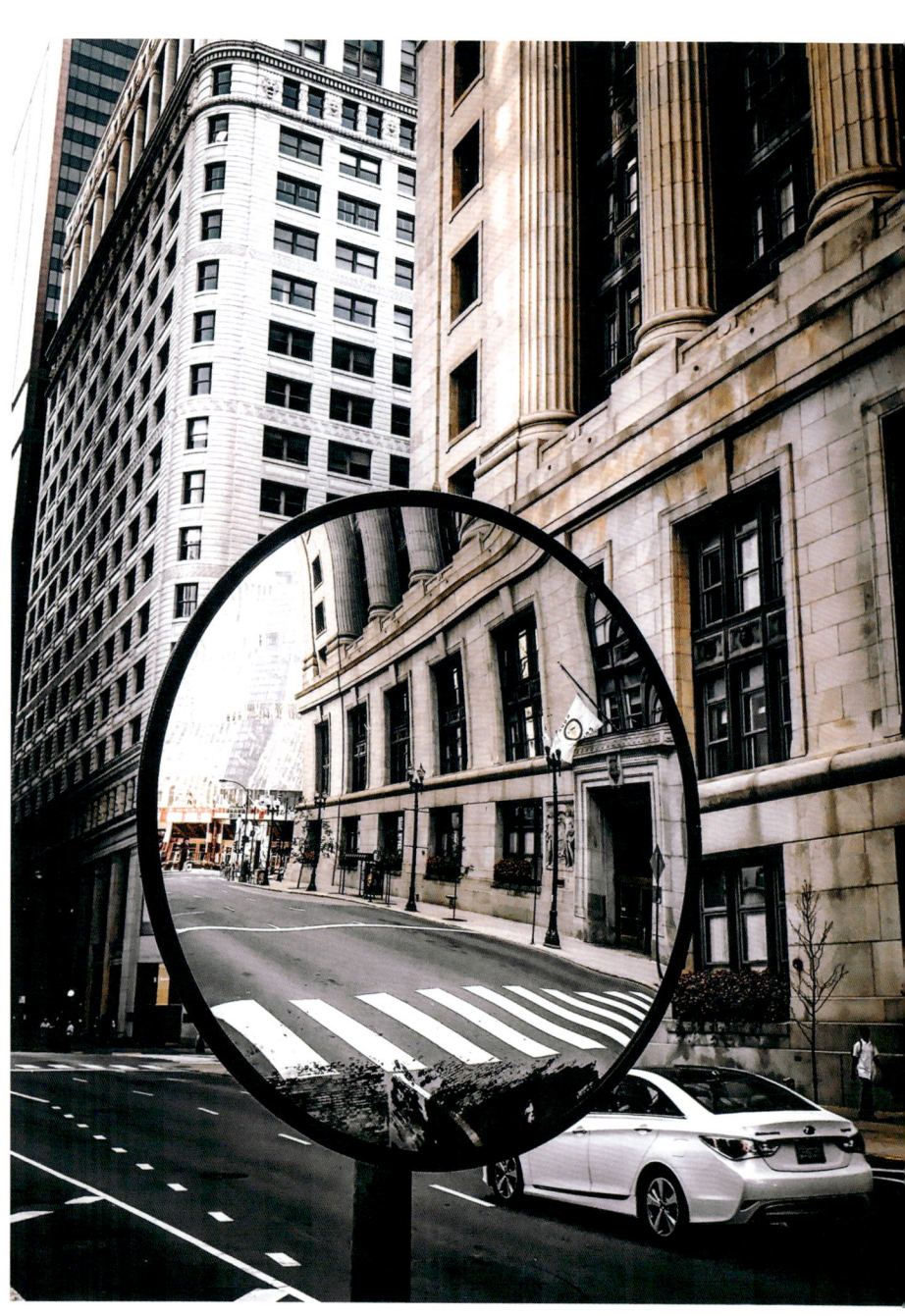

The iPhone 6 had a much sharper display than earlier iterations, but it was the 6S that was really the game-changer. The camera made a big leap from 8MP to 12MP, which made a huge difference in lower light. The 7 Plus a year later included the dual camera, opening up a lot more possibilities for zoom and field depth. Shots weren't nearly as grainy, and details were sharper. It made me want to go out and take shots I wouldn't have been able to capture before without my "real" camera.

During this time I was doing my residency in Chicago, and that cityscape became an incredible backdrop. I could take advantage of the architecture and elevated train to frame my shots, providing me with natural leading lines. Chicago's river winds its way through downtown, overlaid with tons of steel bridges – a contrast in shape and geometry. I could find a great perspective, set up my framing, and then just wait for a boat or a taxi to provide some dynamic motion.

I could play with light. The city's streetlights illuminate when it rains, even during the day, which is atypical of most cities. I used puddles as mirrors, reflecting the lamps for more depth in the shot. Moreover, Chicago's distinct seasons provided me with options for color year-round - the rich green of a short but intense summer, loads of red and yellow hues in fall, and, of course, the bright white of snowfall. I used the city's spectrum of colors as my focus point against the somber black and gray shades of the steel and concrete.

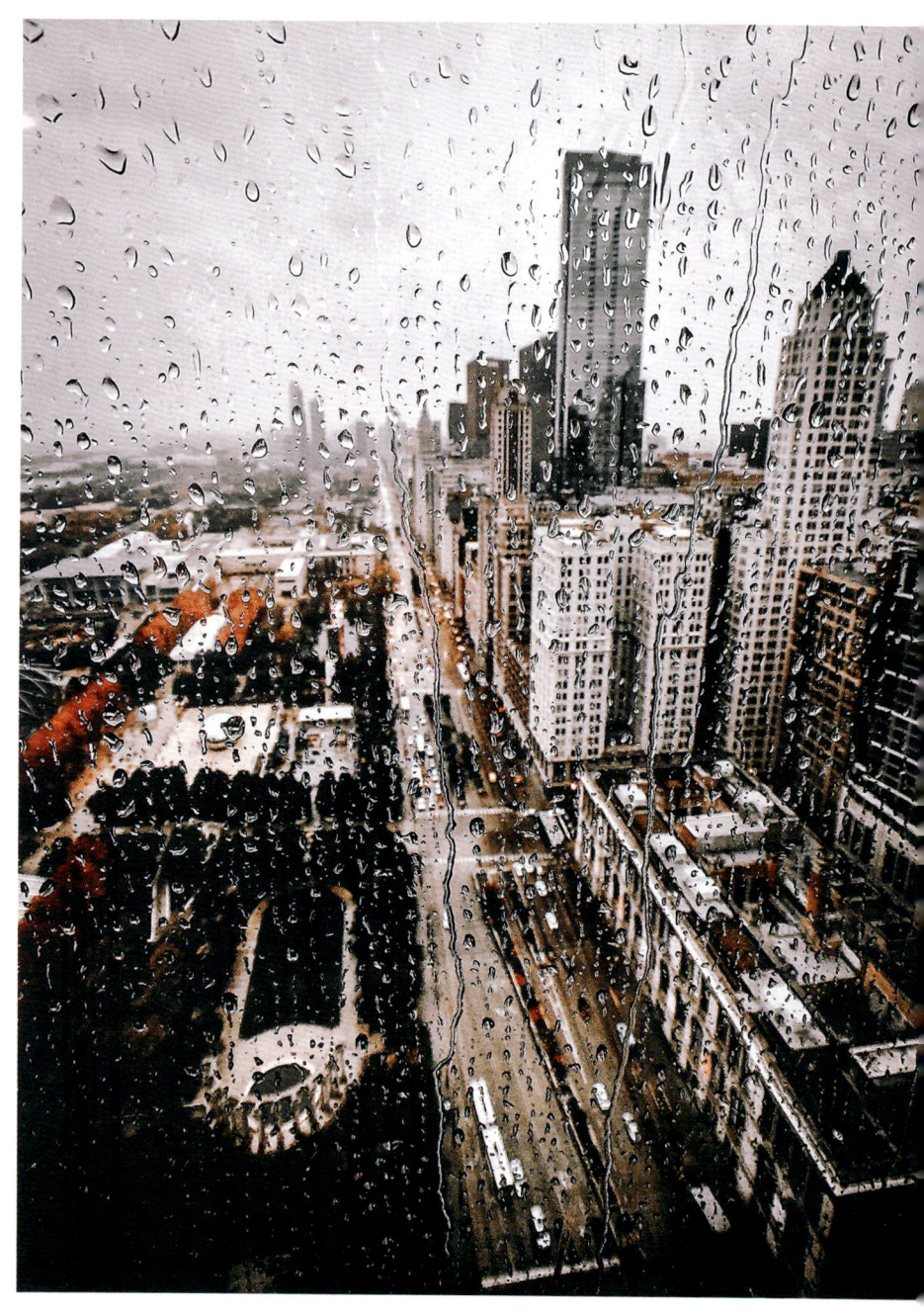

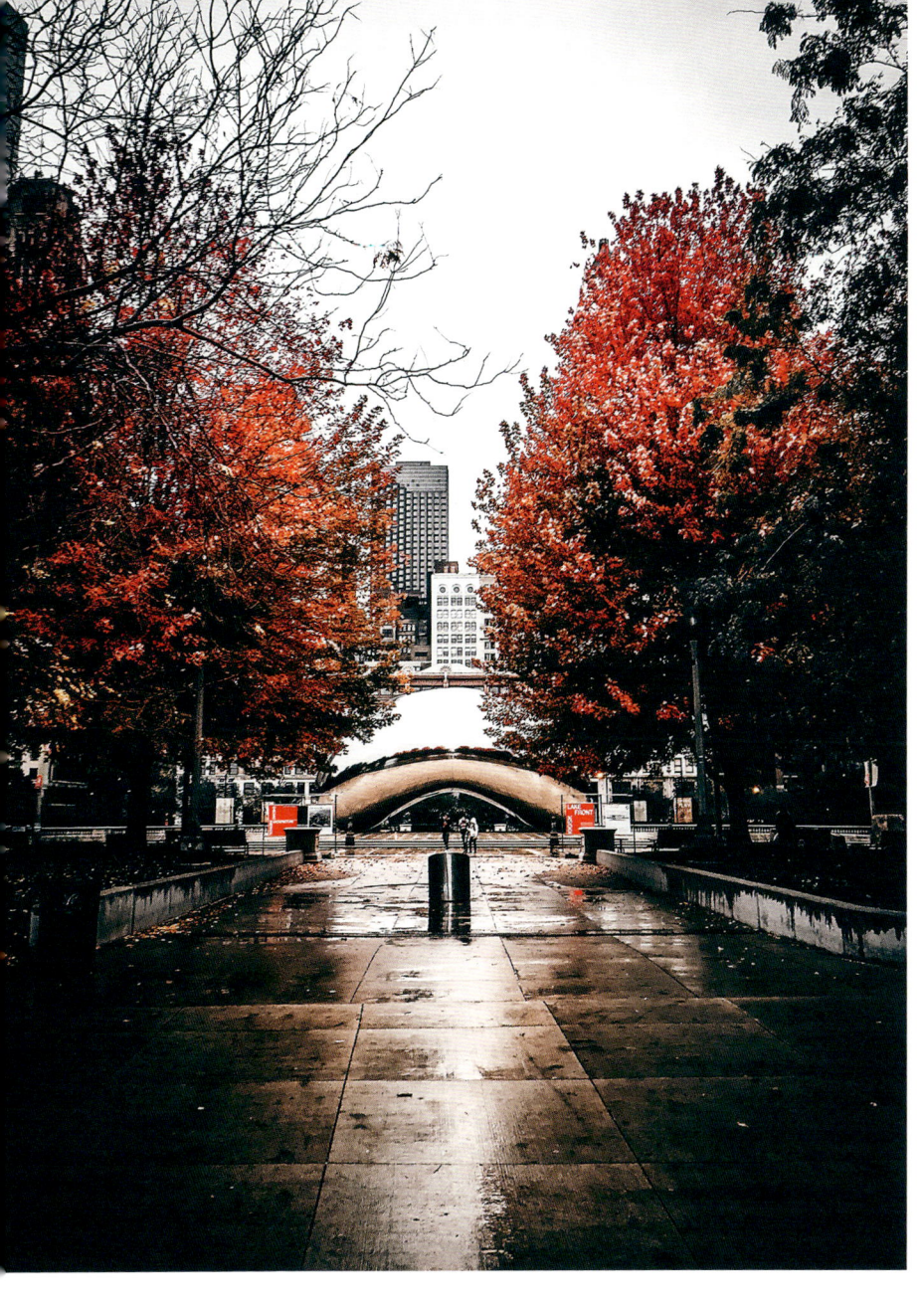

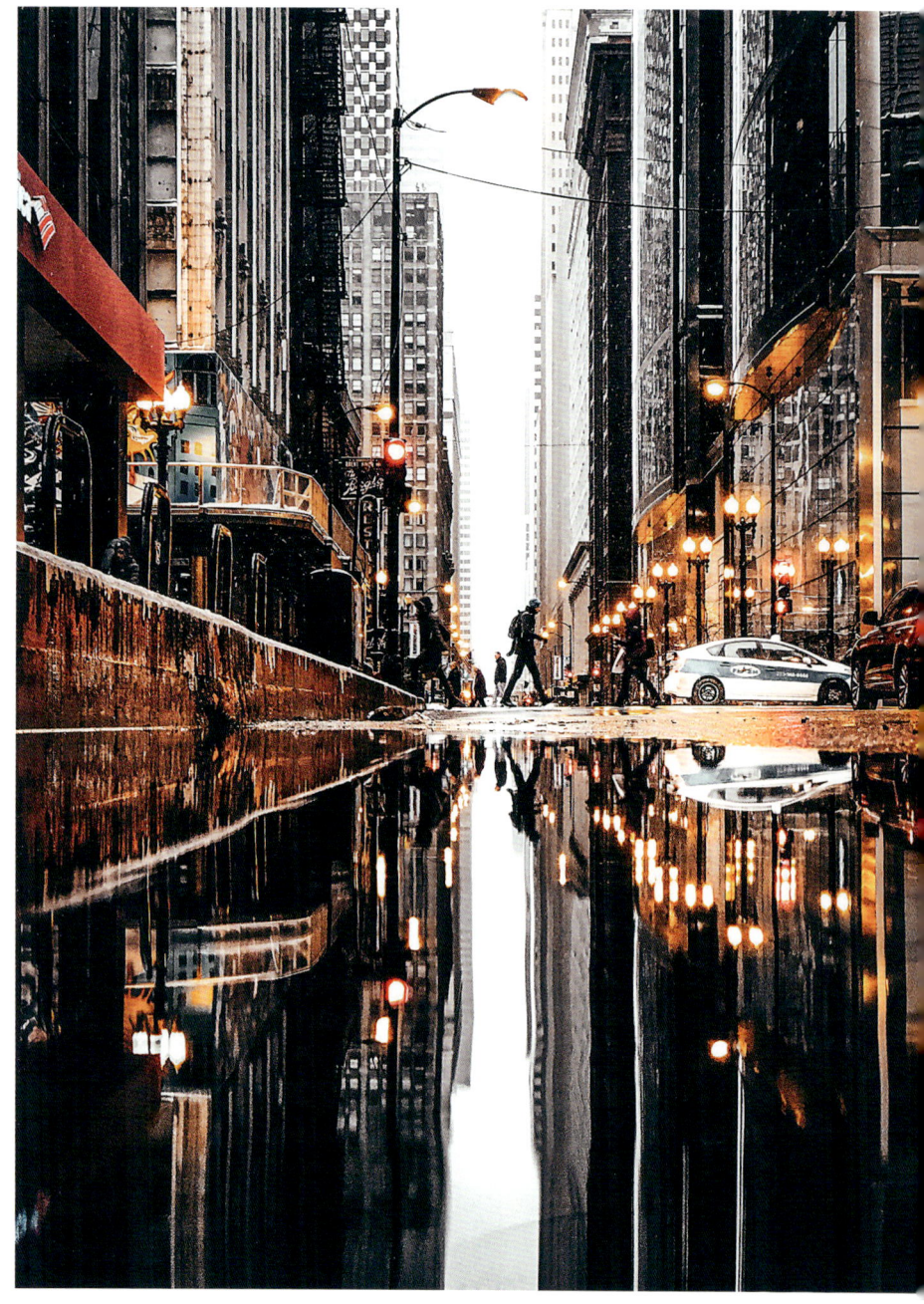

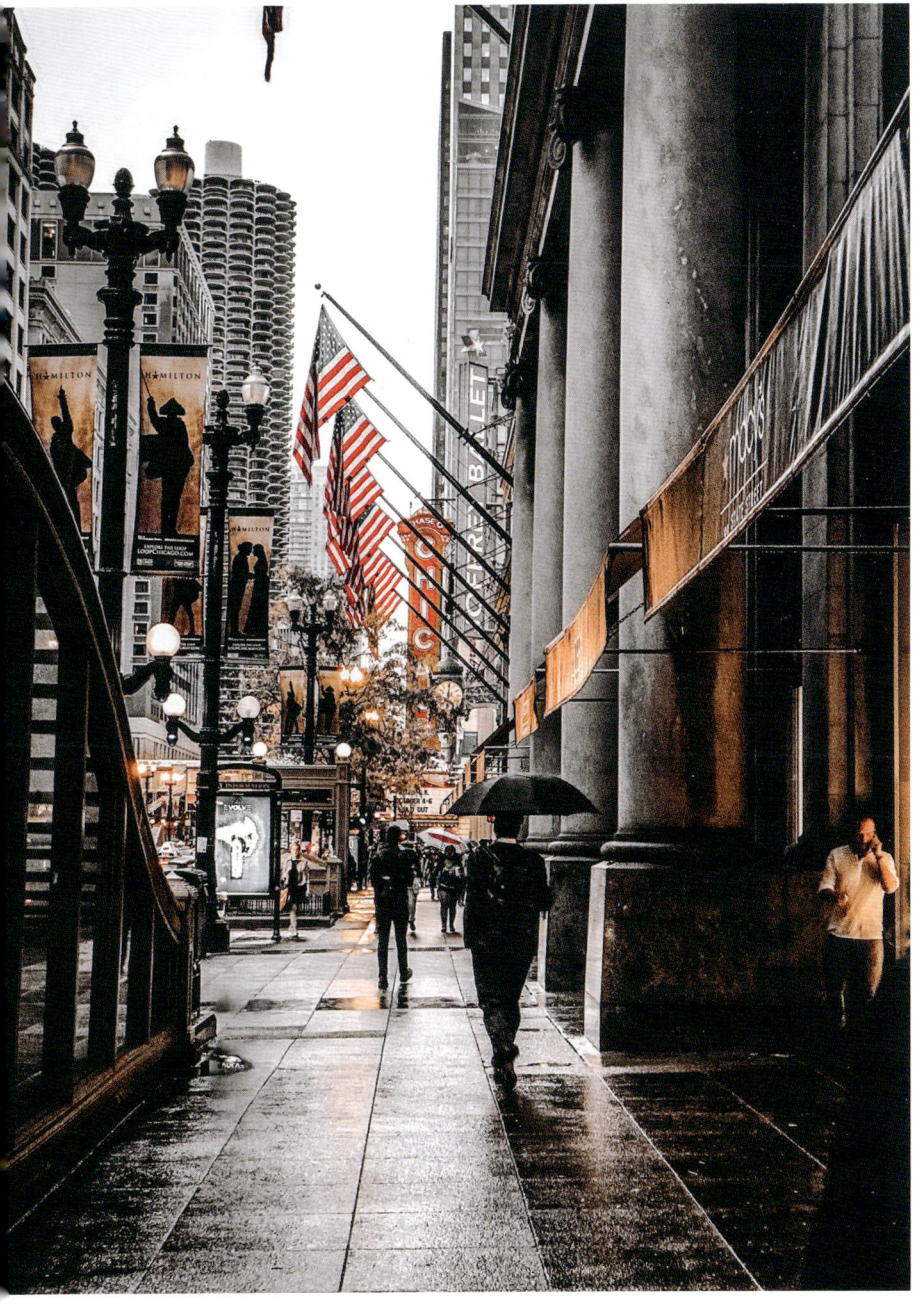

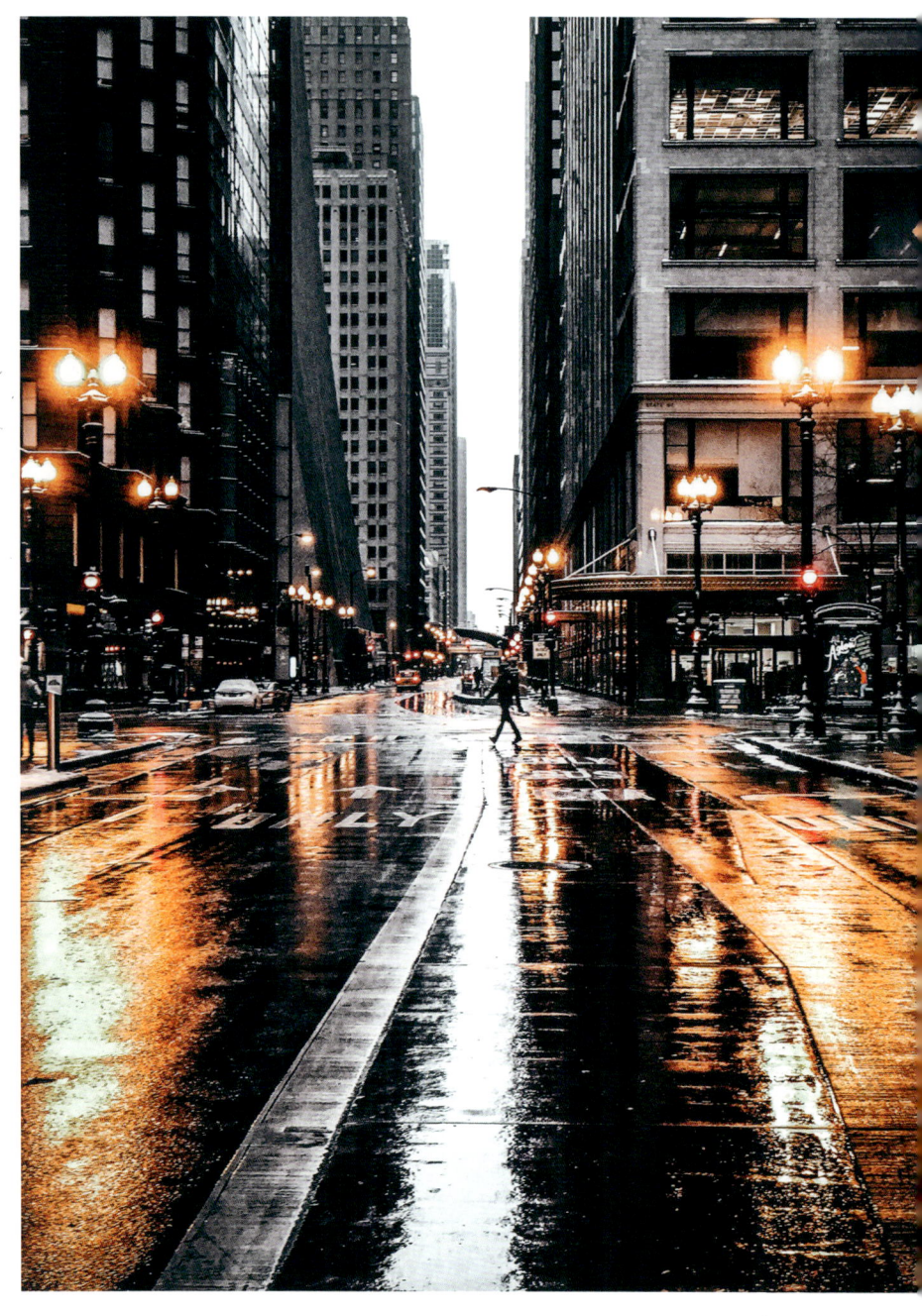

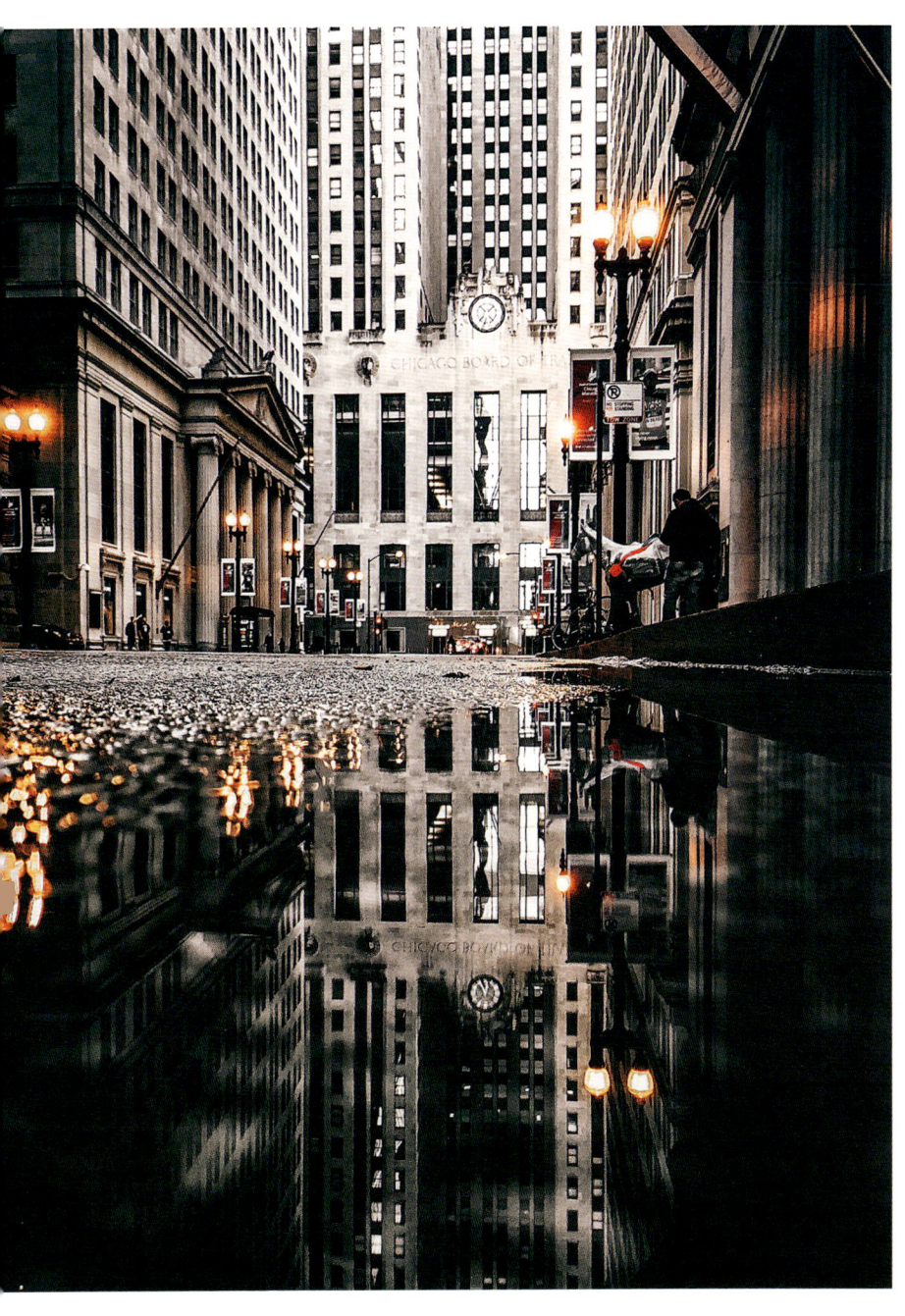

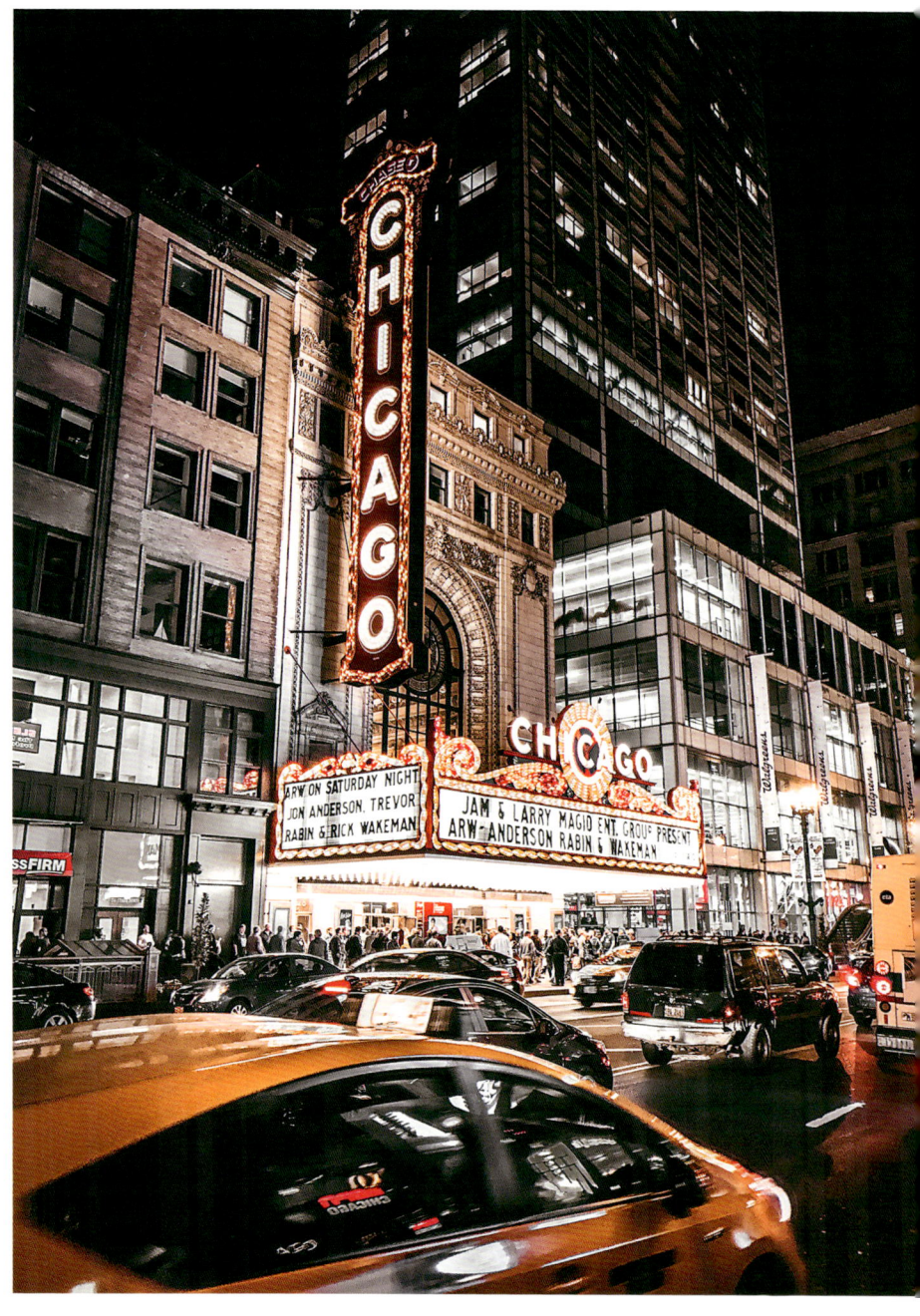

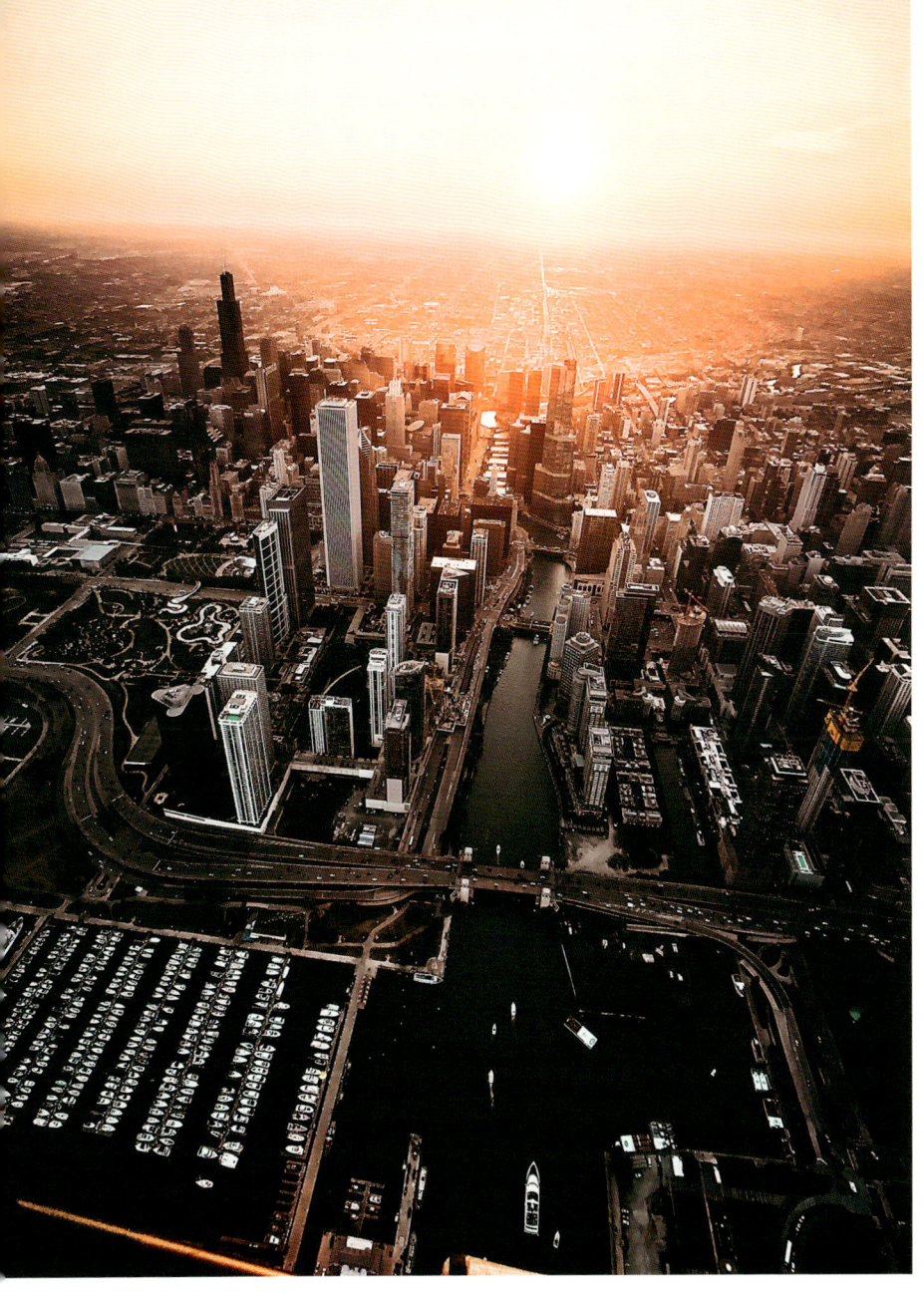

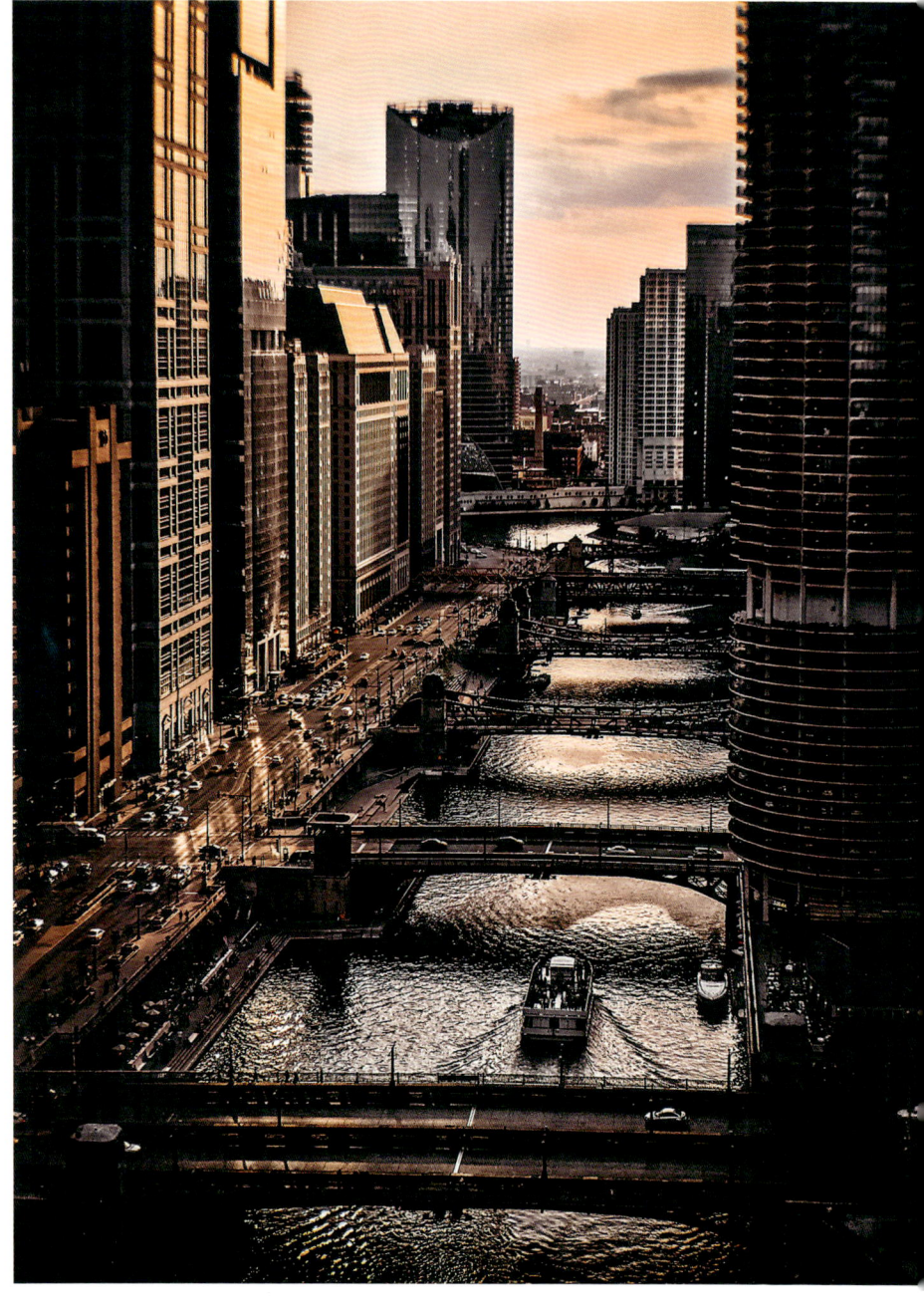

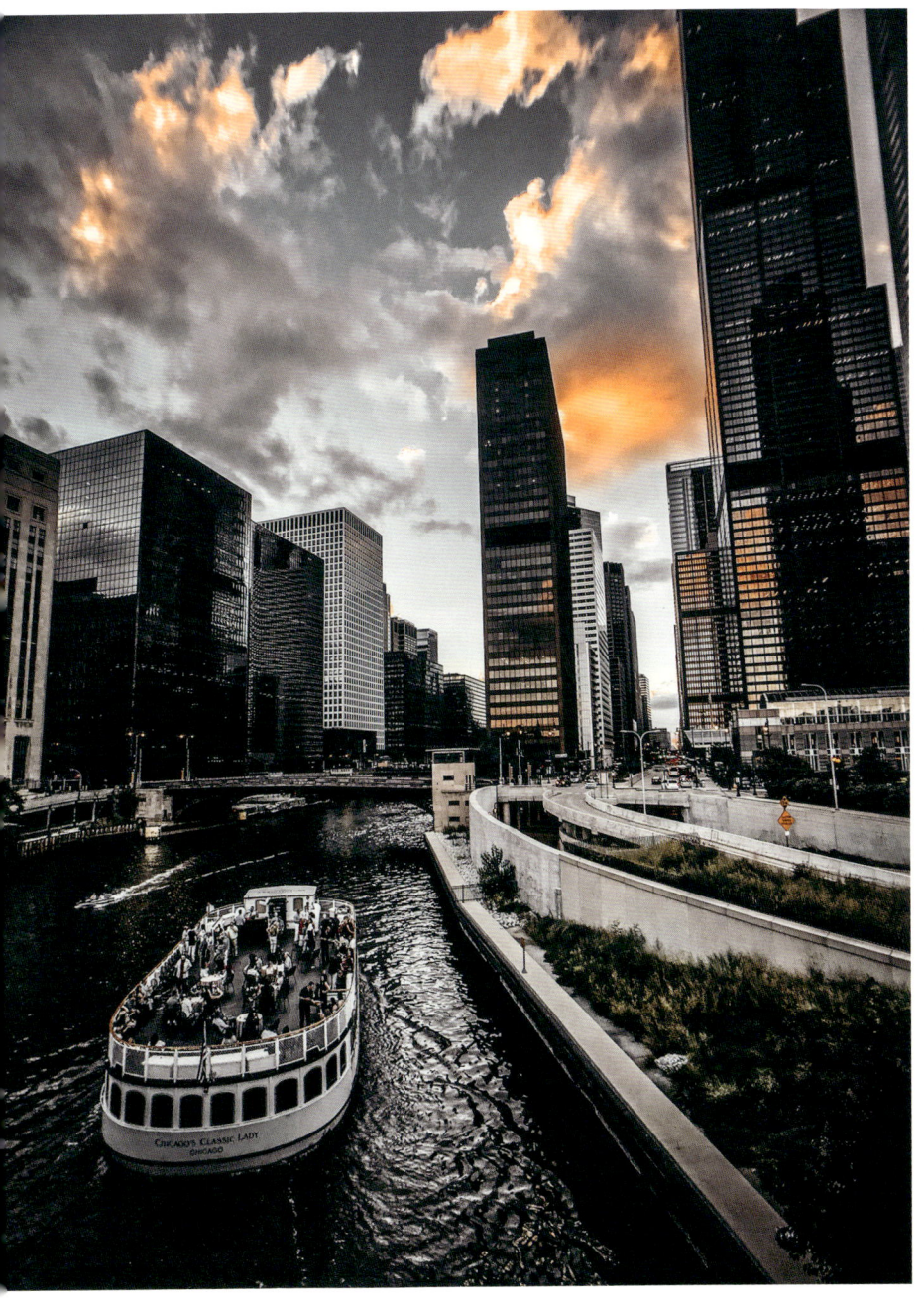

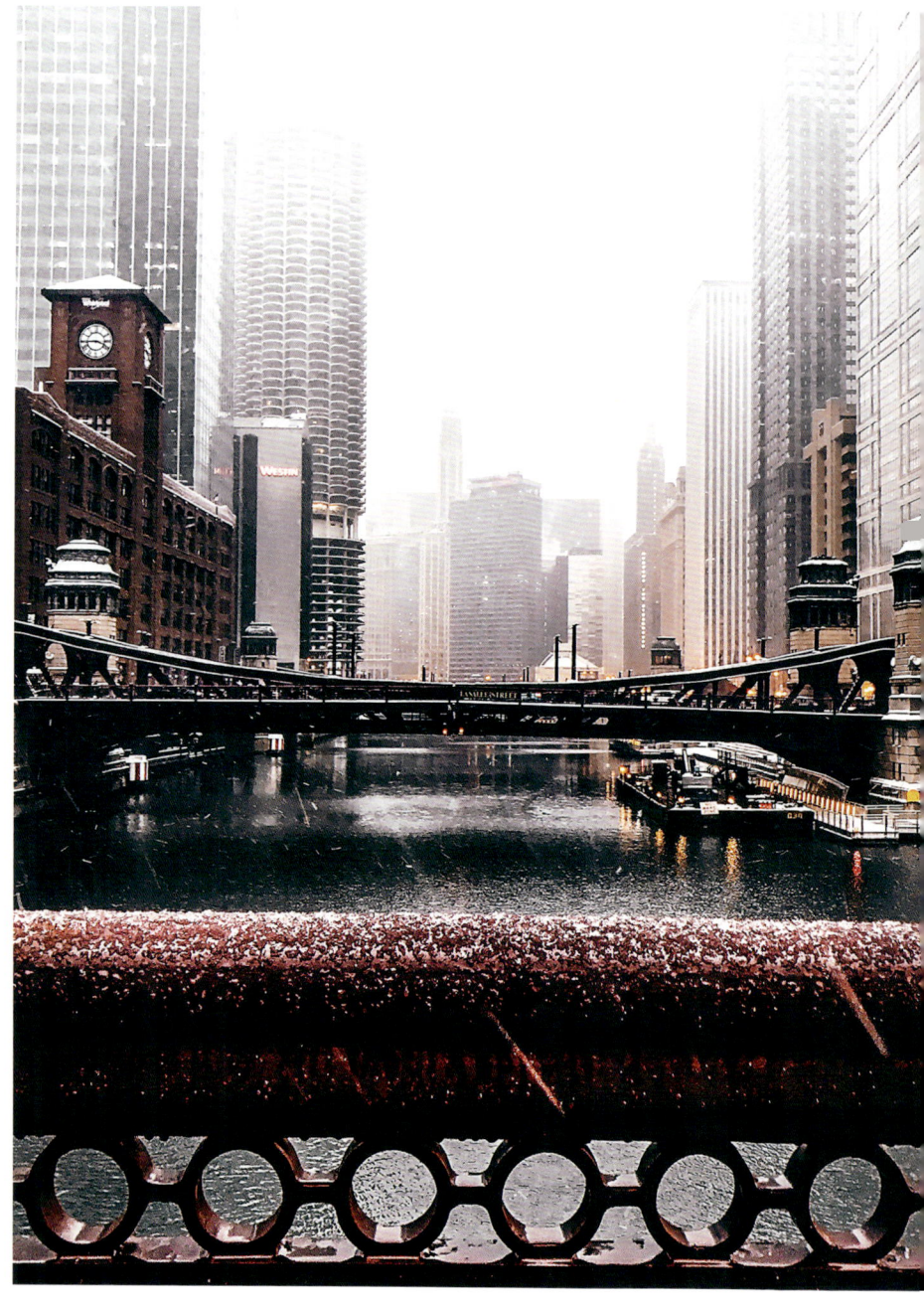

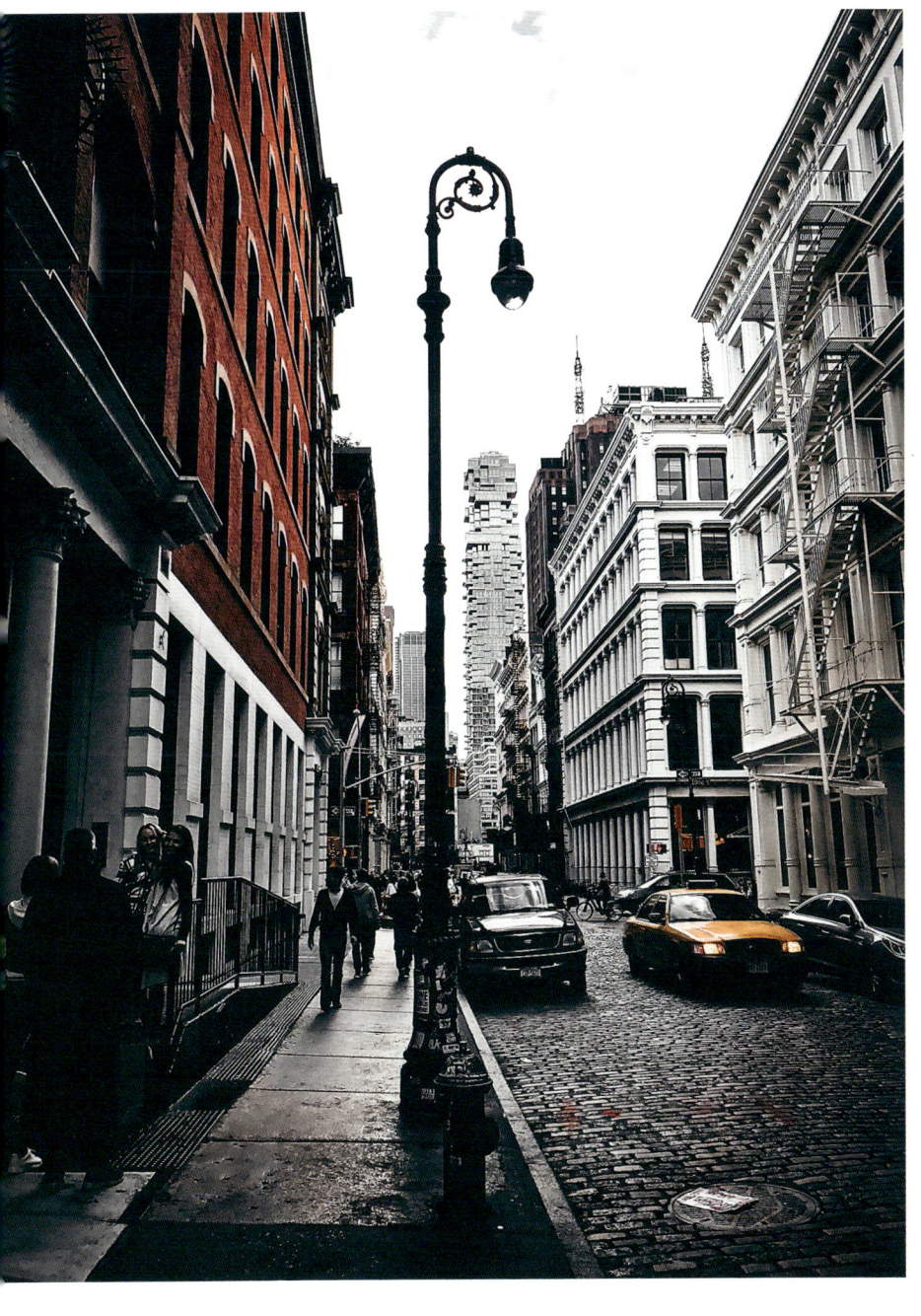

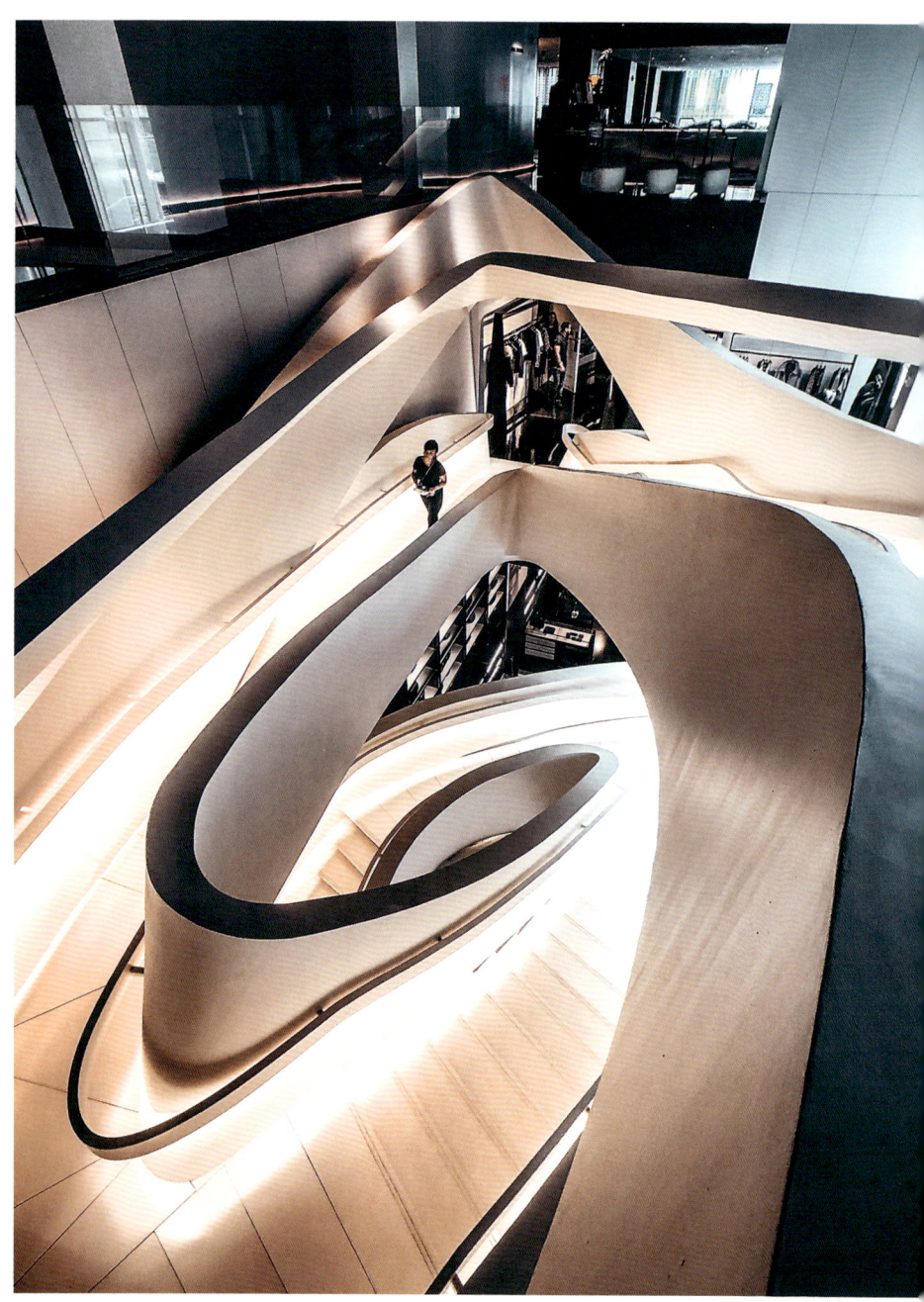

Around the time the iPhone X came out, I was finishing my residency and moving to Boston to join my wife, who had moved there the year before. Boston is a very different backdrop than Chicago; I had traded in canyons of skyscrapers for more contrast in scale and style, drama for history.

Dim light and night photos were leagues better than before. Less noise in the shadows especially meant I could bring out details that were lost before, like behind a light flare. The image files were much sturdier when I went to edit them; there was just more data there to work with, extending my editing possibilities.

I had more time and opportunity to travel; these years saw me go to New York, San Francisco, and abroad to Istanbul, Santorini, Italy and Japan. Whether it was Times Square at dusk, or a San Francisco sunrise, I had a lot more latitude with scenes that would have been impossible to take earlier without the foreground dissolving into shadow.

I get up very early when I travel; I'm up and ready to shoot at 5 or 6 in the morning, too excited to explore in that unique early-morning light. In Santorini I chased the sun across the island, planning different perspectives for sunrise versus sunset. I searched for new vantage points for the familiar, colorful beach towns crawling their way up the Amalfi Coast and chased the birds along the waterfront under overcast skies.

Tokyo, on the other hand, comes alive at night, and I put the phone's night-shot capabilities to the test. I used apps to vary the shutter speed for light trails and experiment with double-zooming. I couldn't exactly set up a tripod in the narrow, dark yokocho alleys, but the shots were as crisp as if I had, not blurry or grainy. I could capture and edit a variety of natural light like never before.

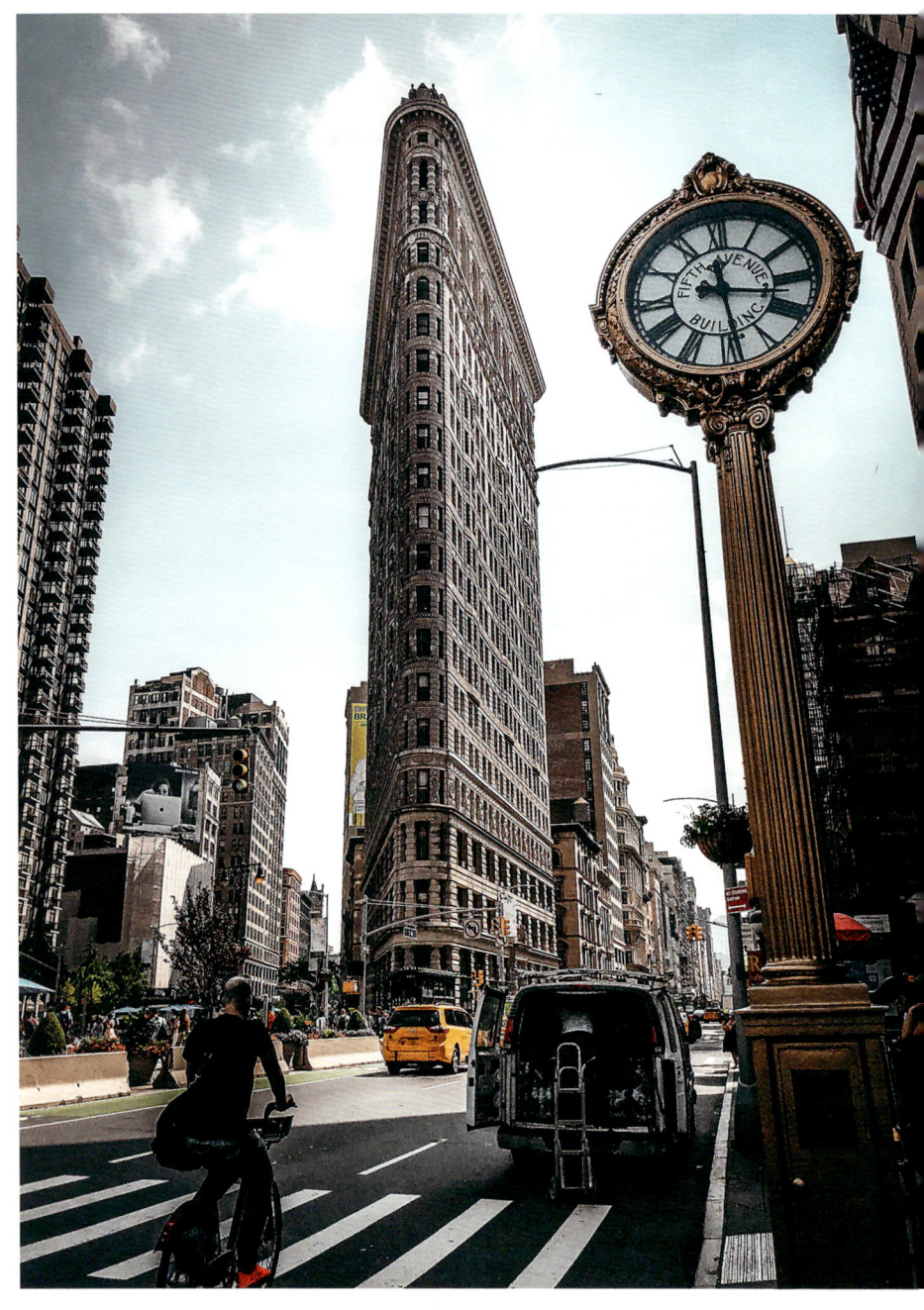

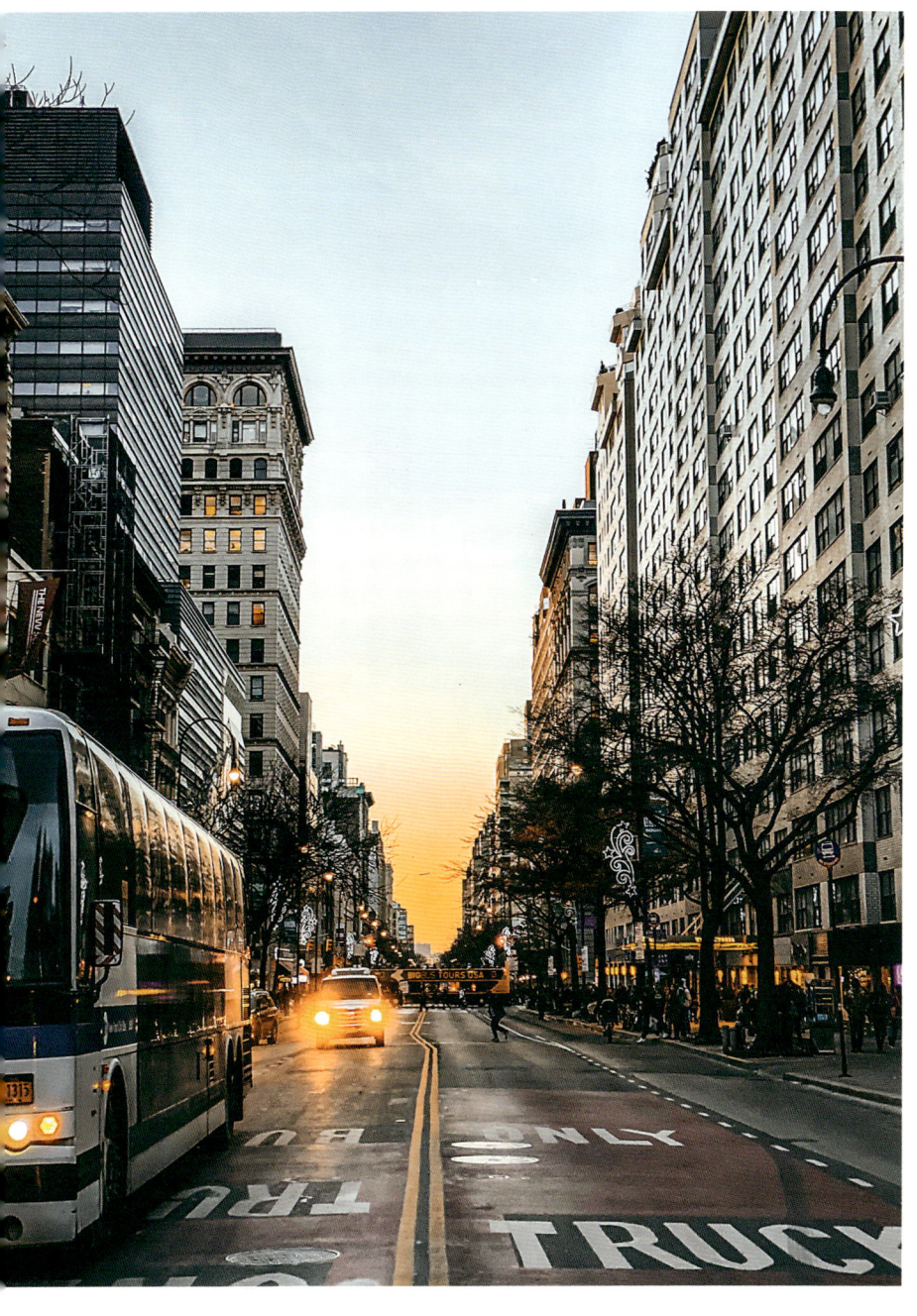

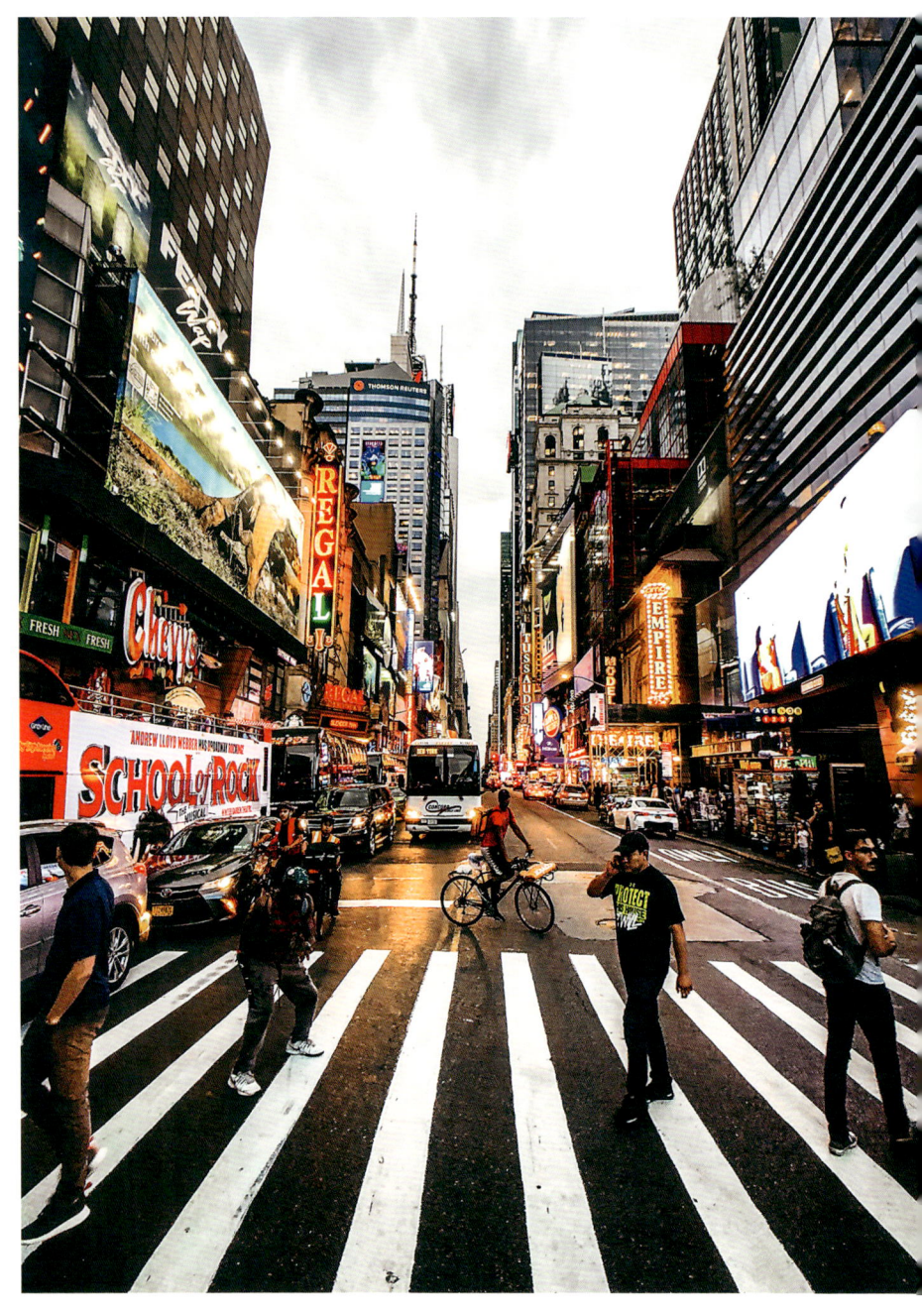

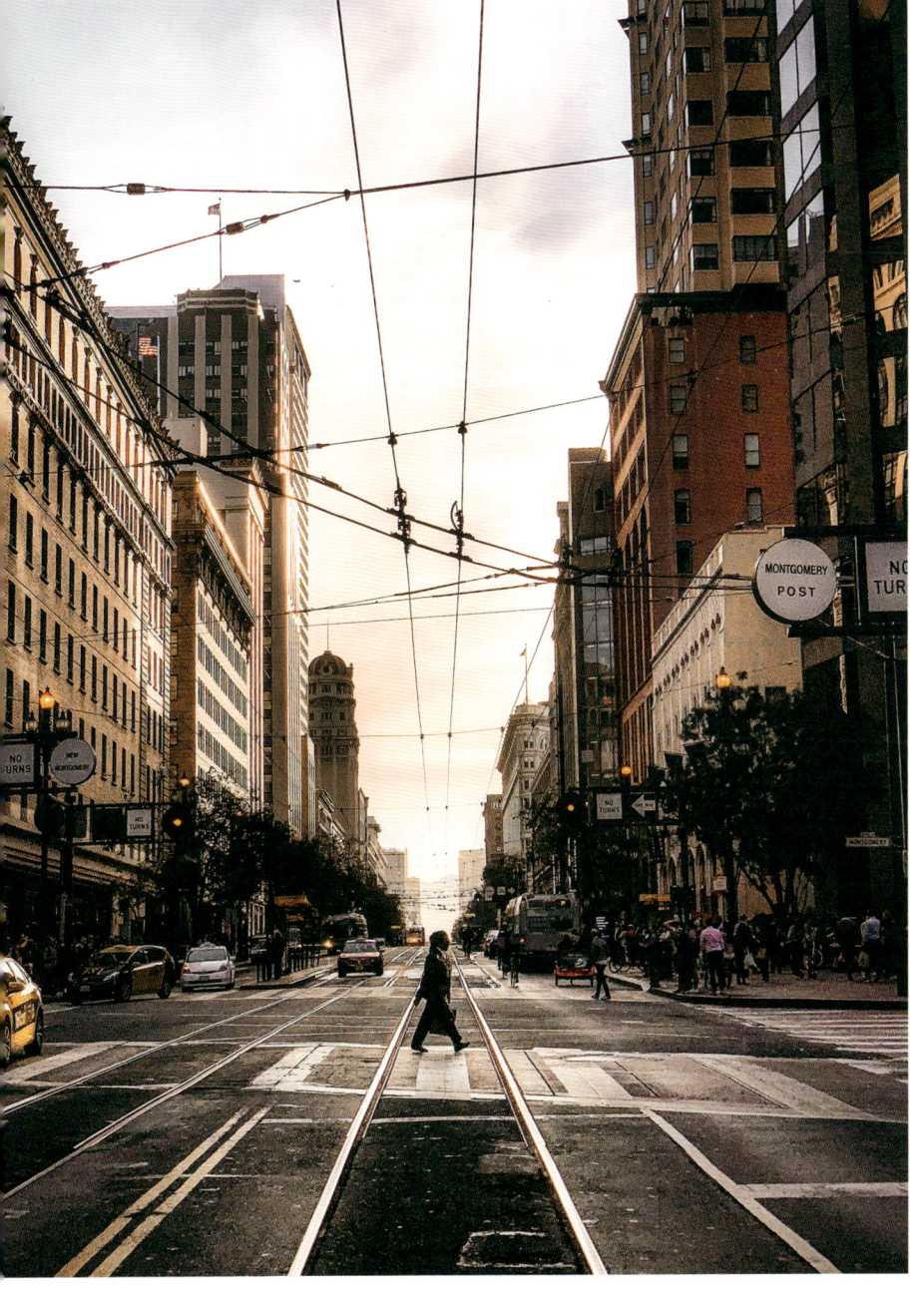

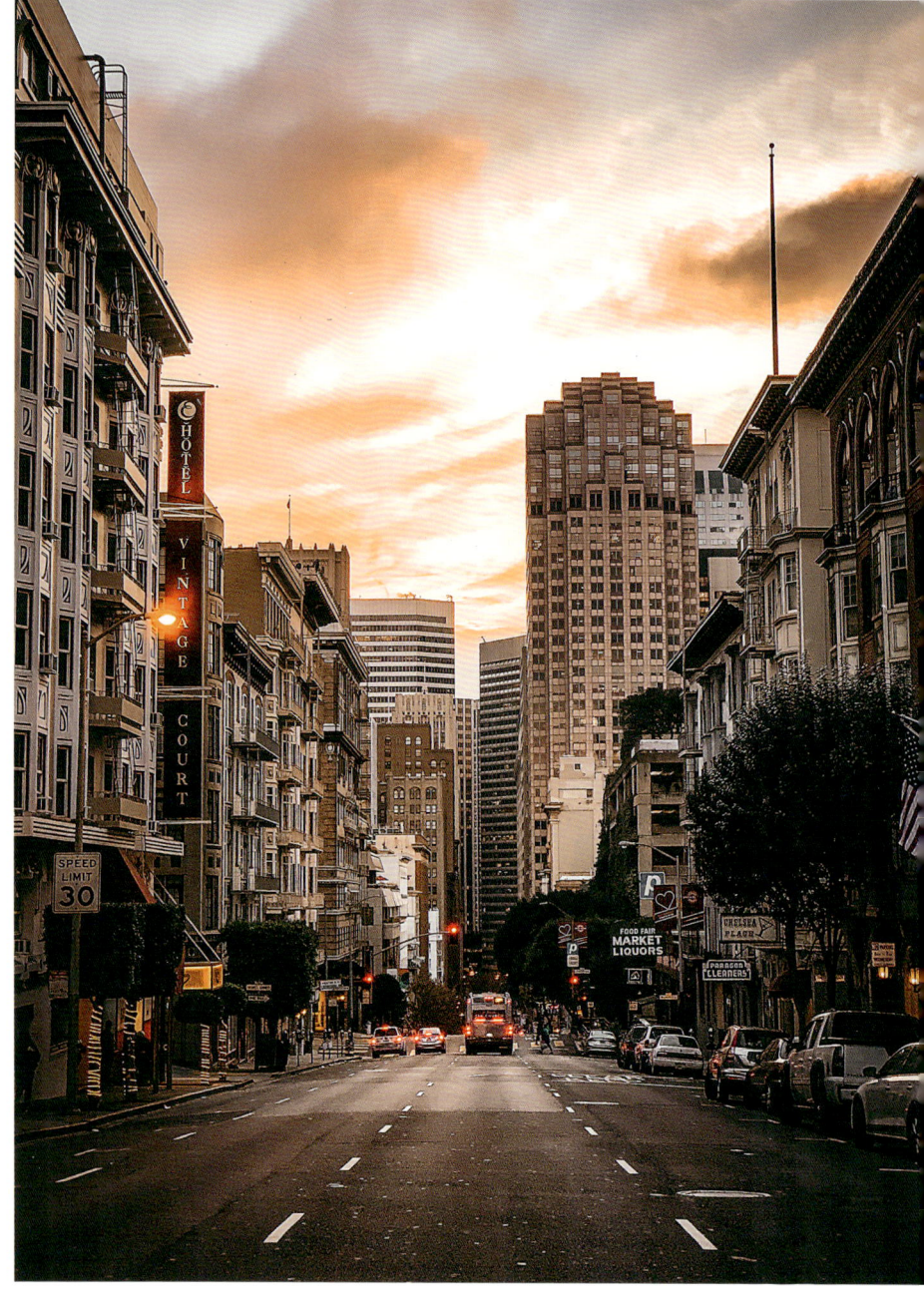

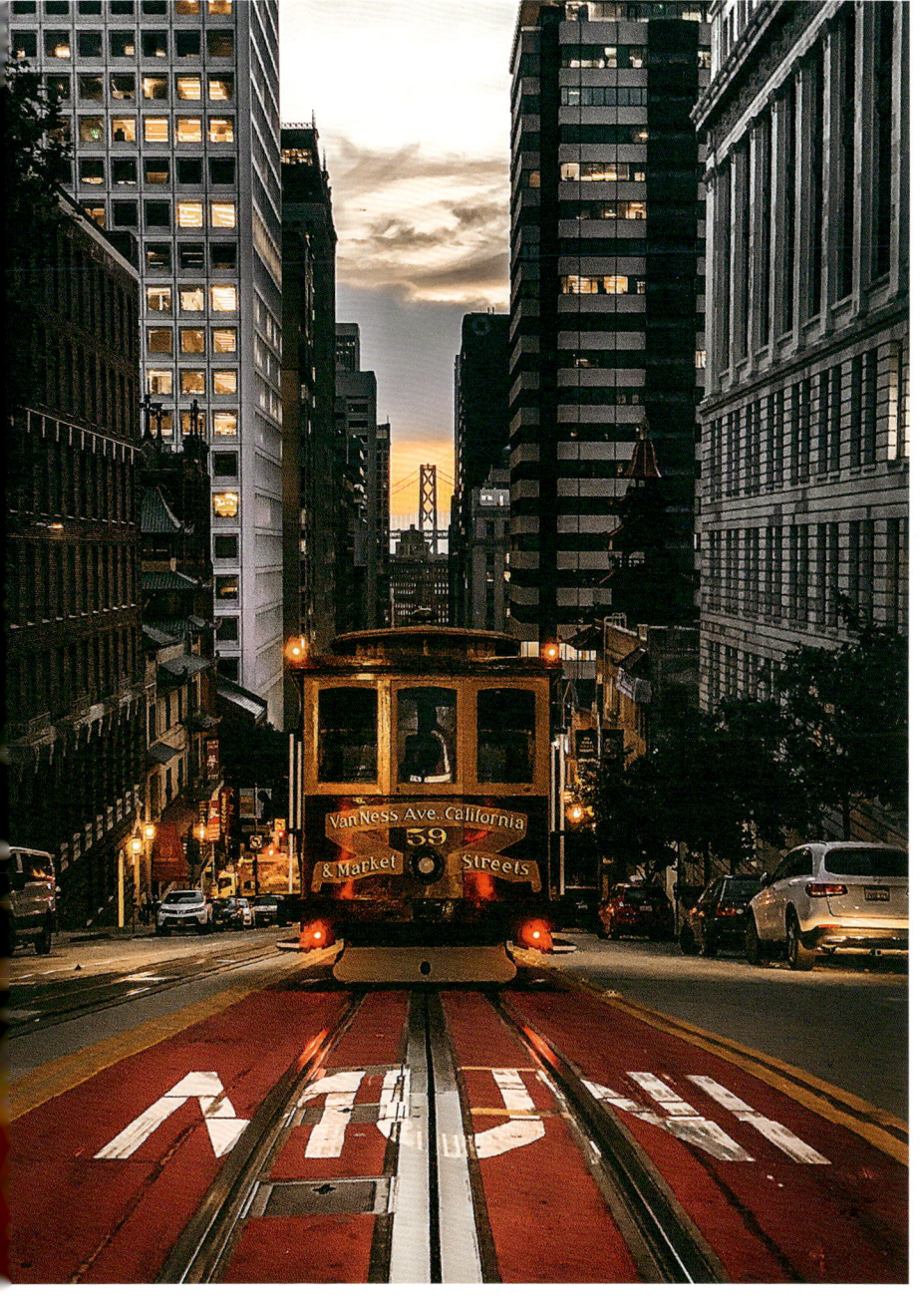

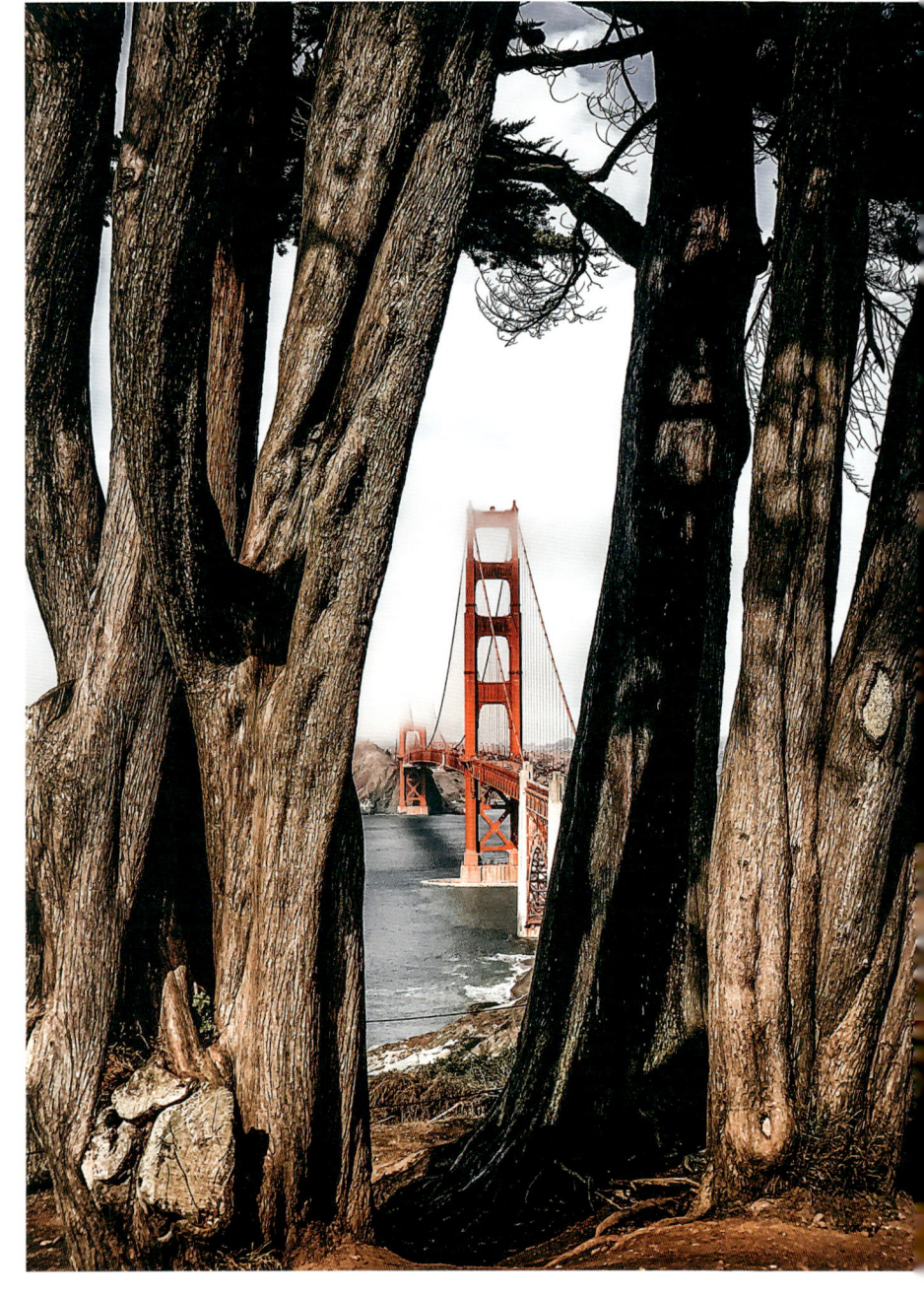

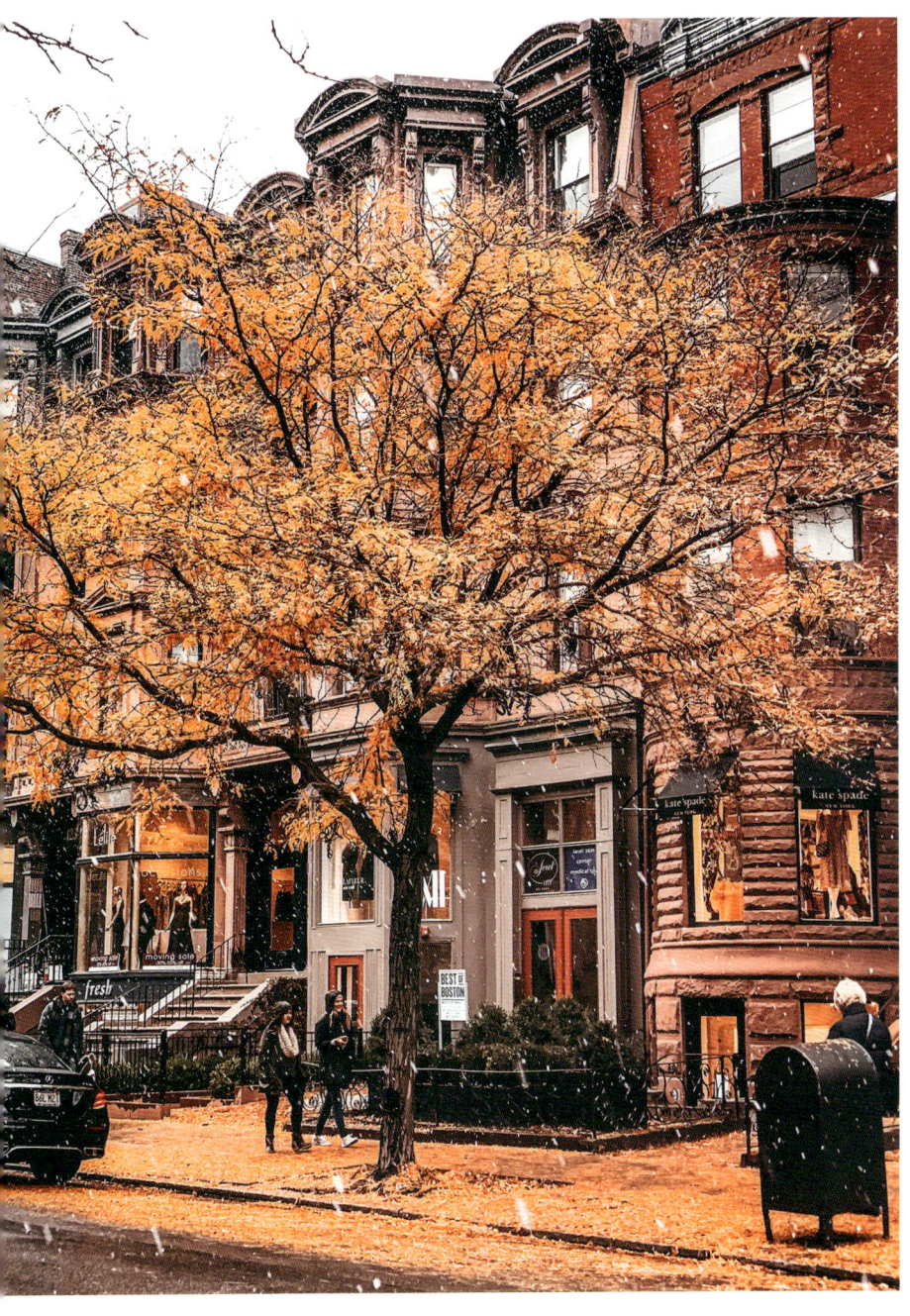

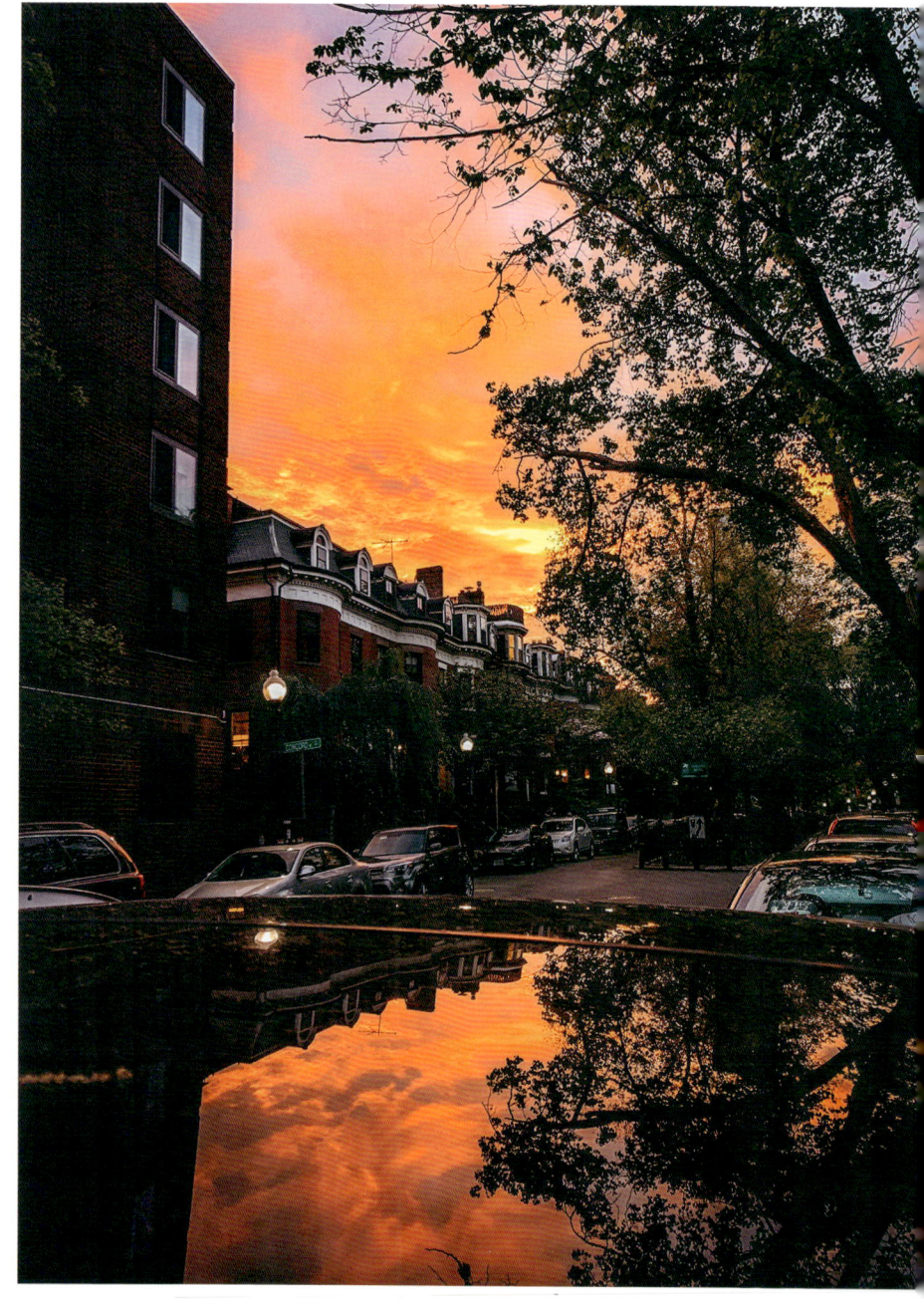

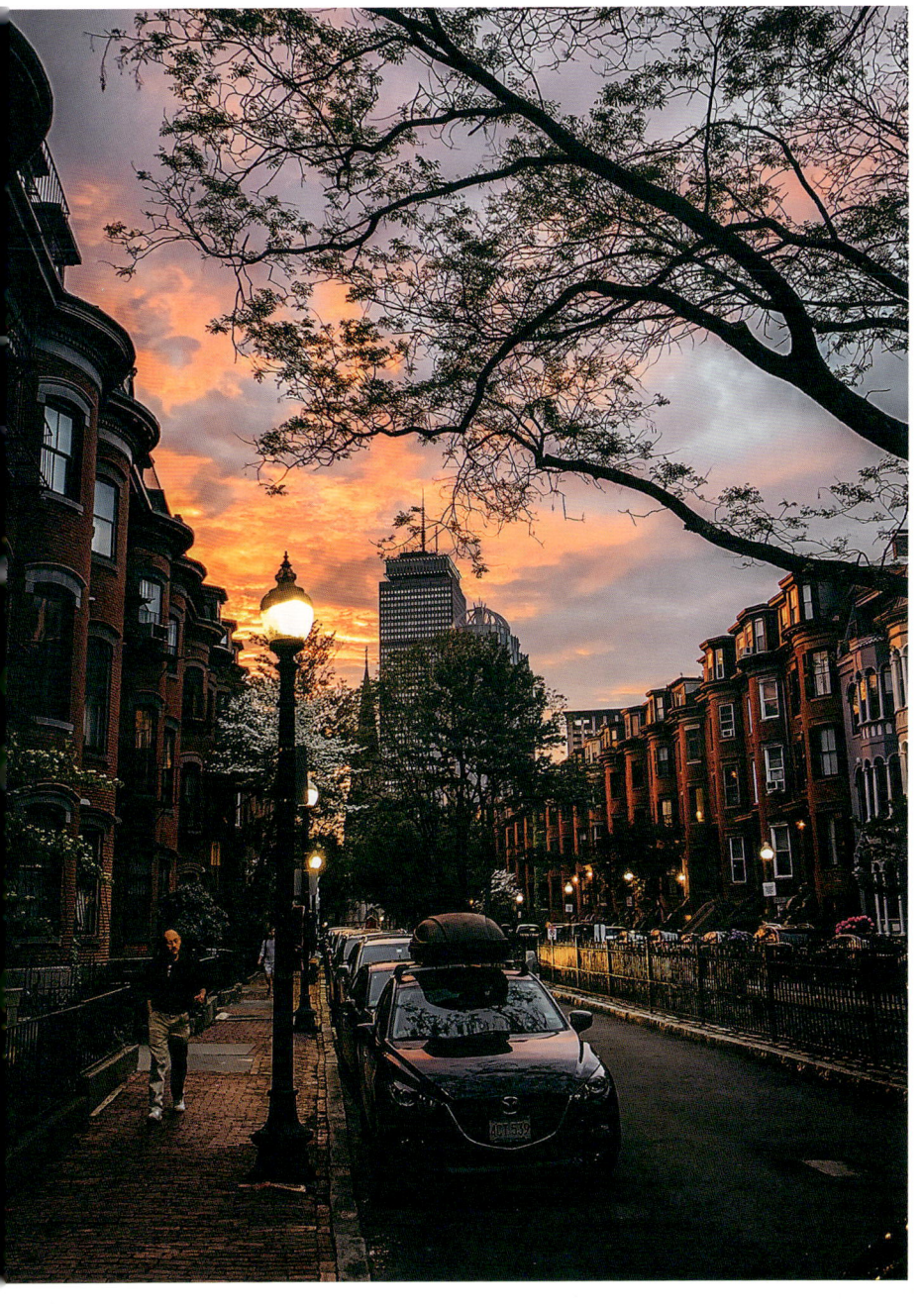

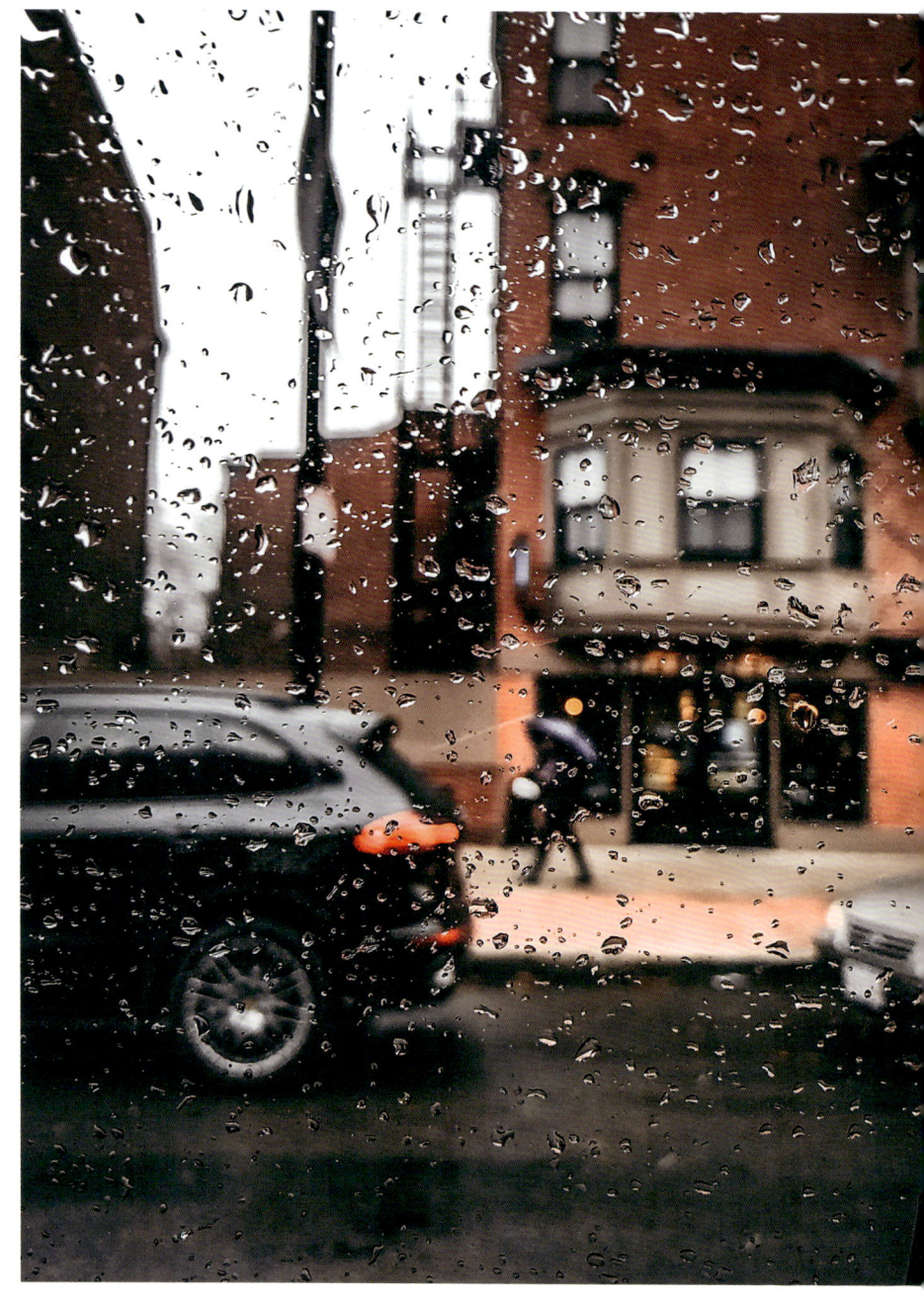

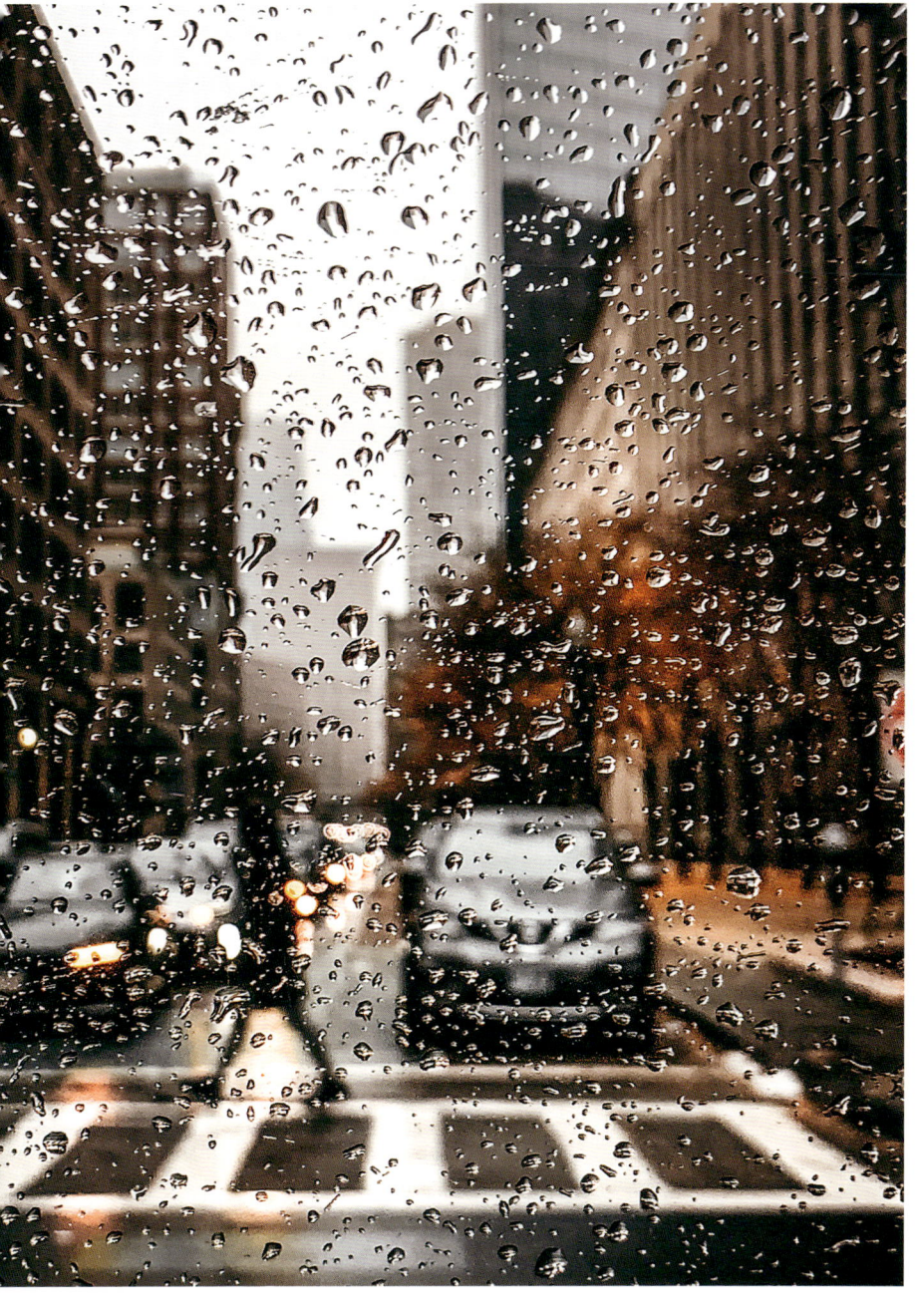

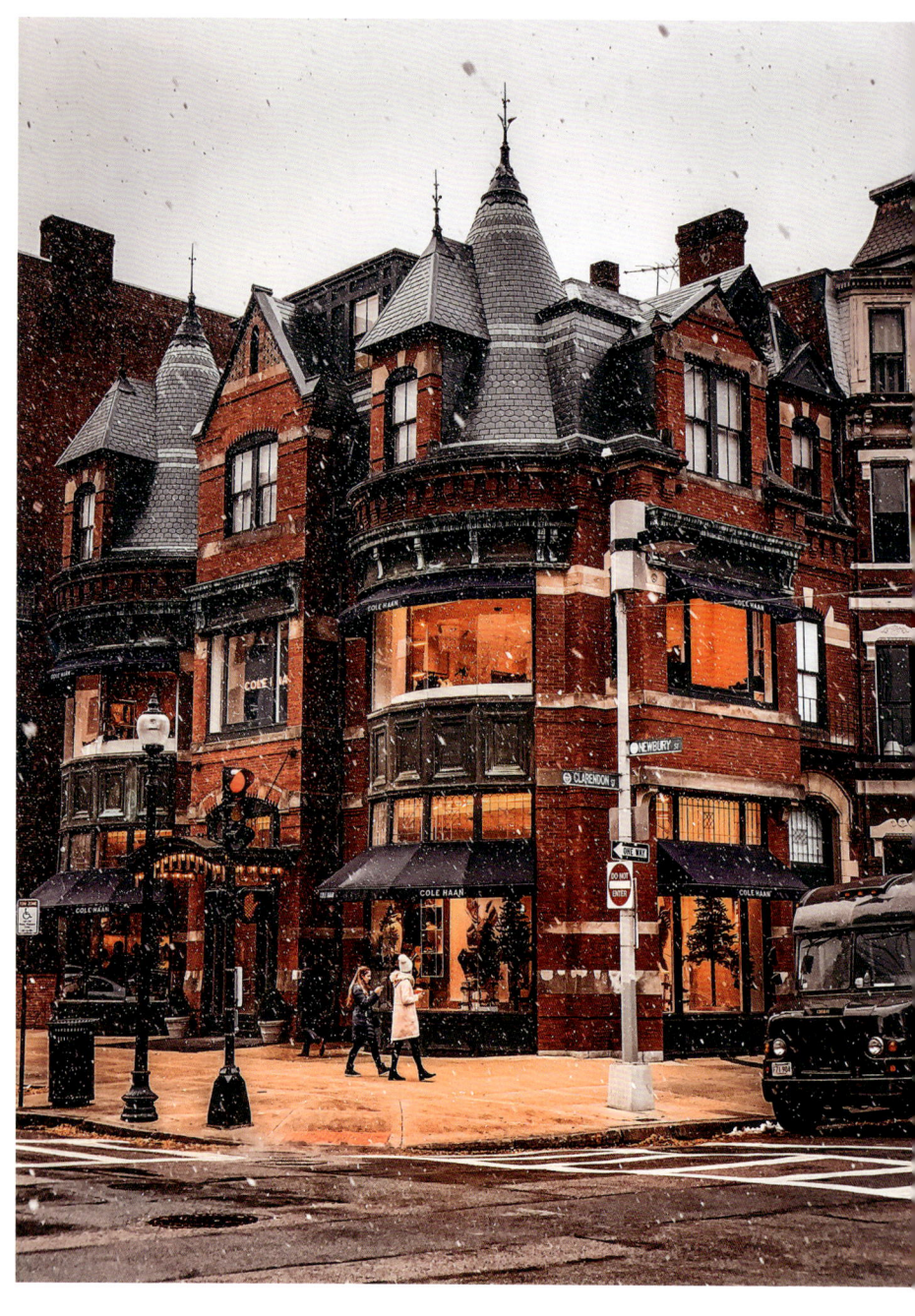

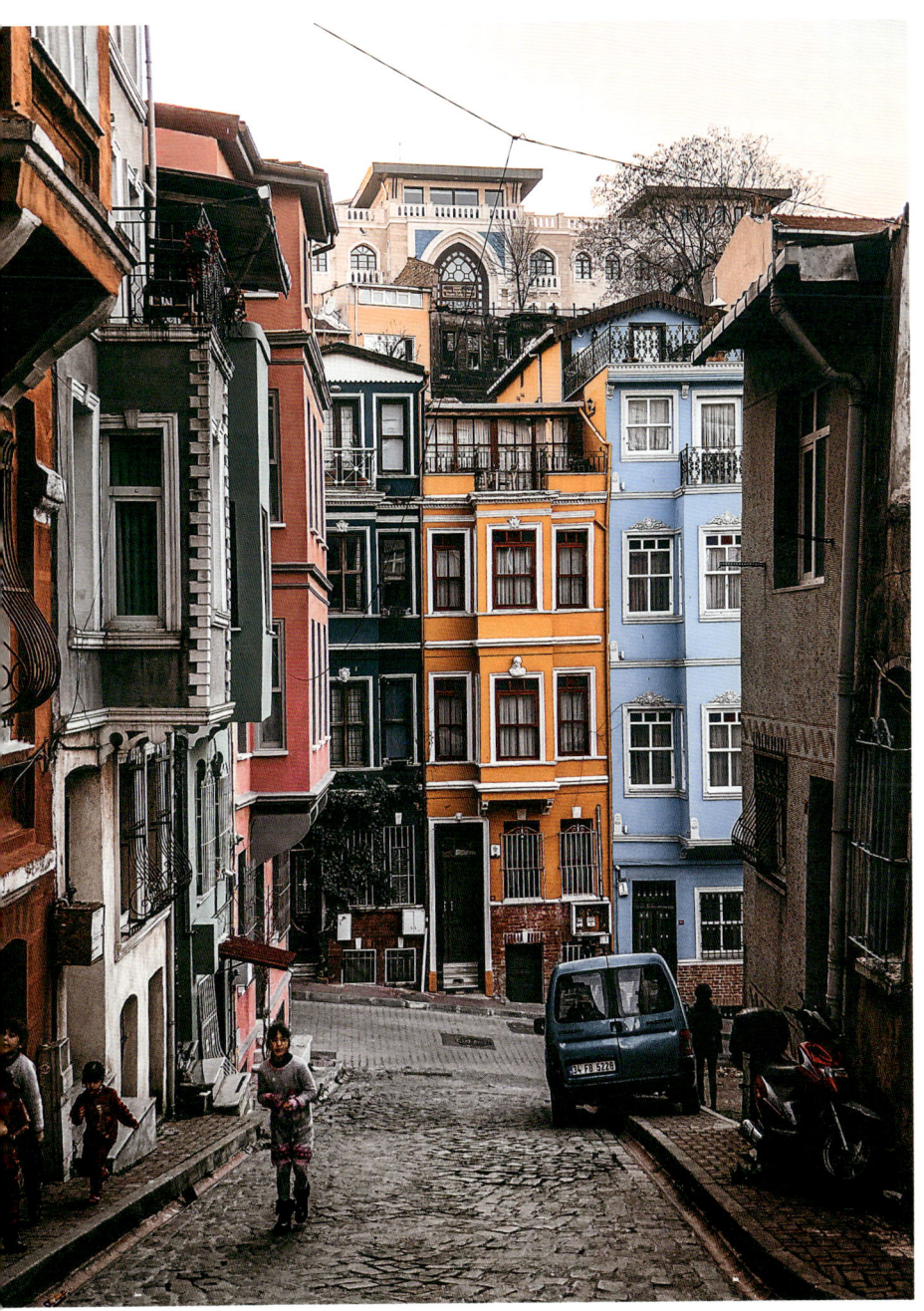

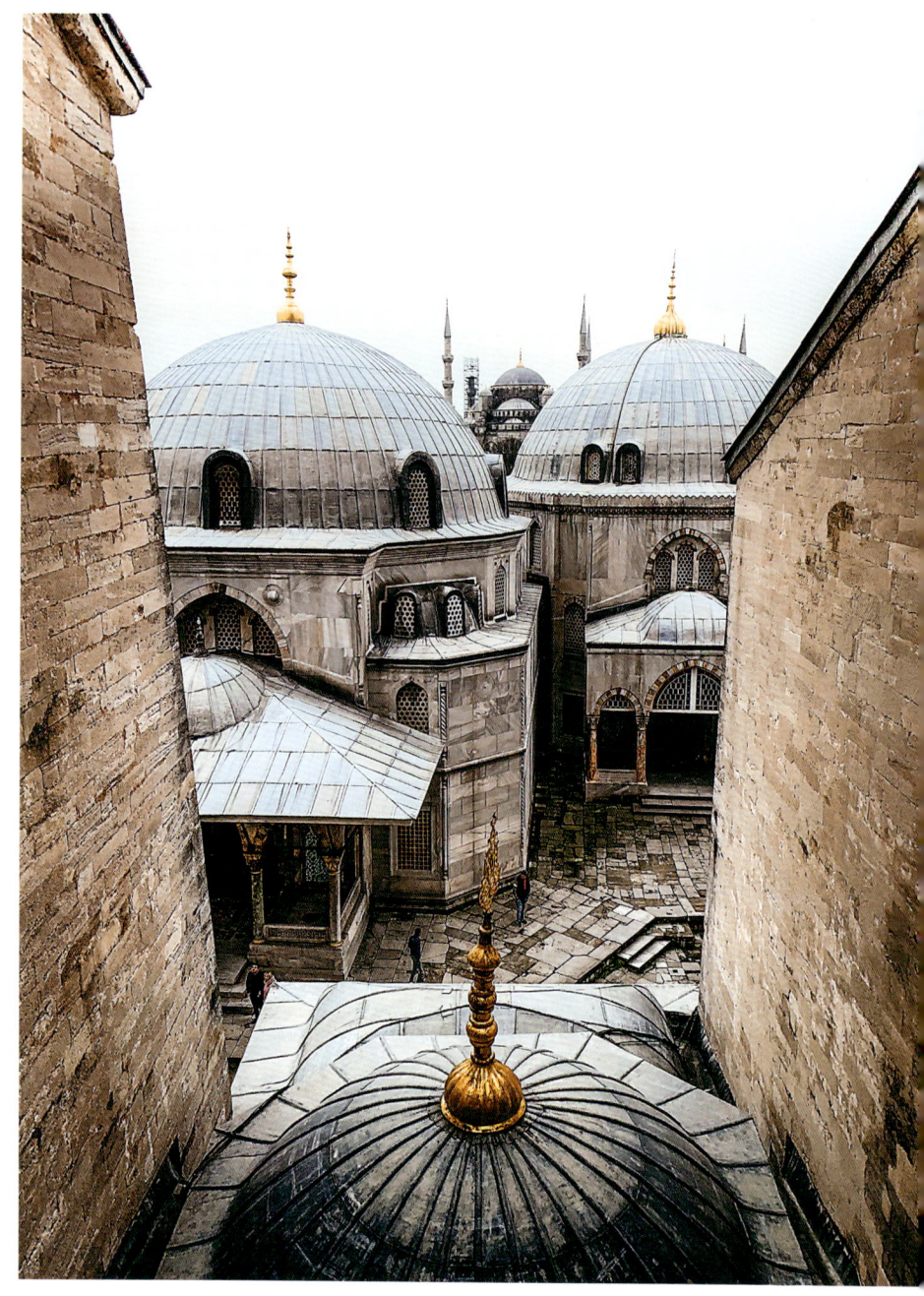

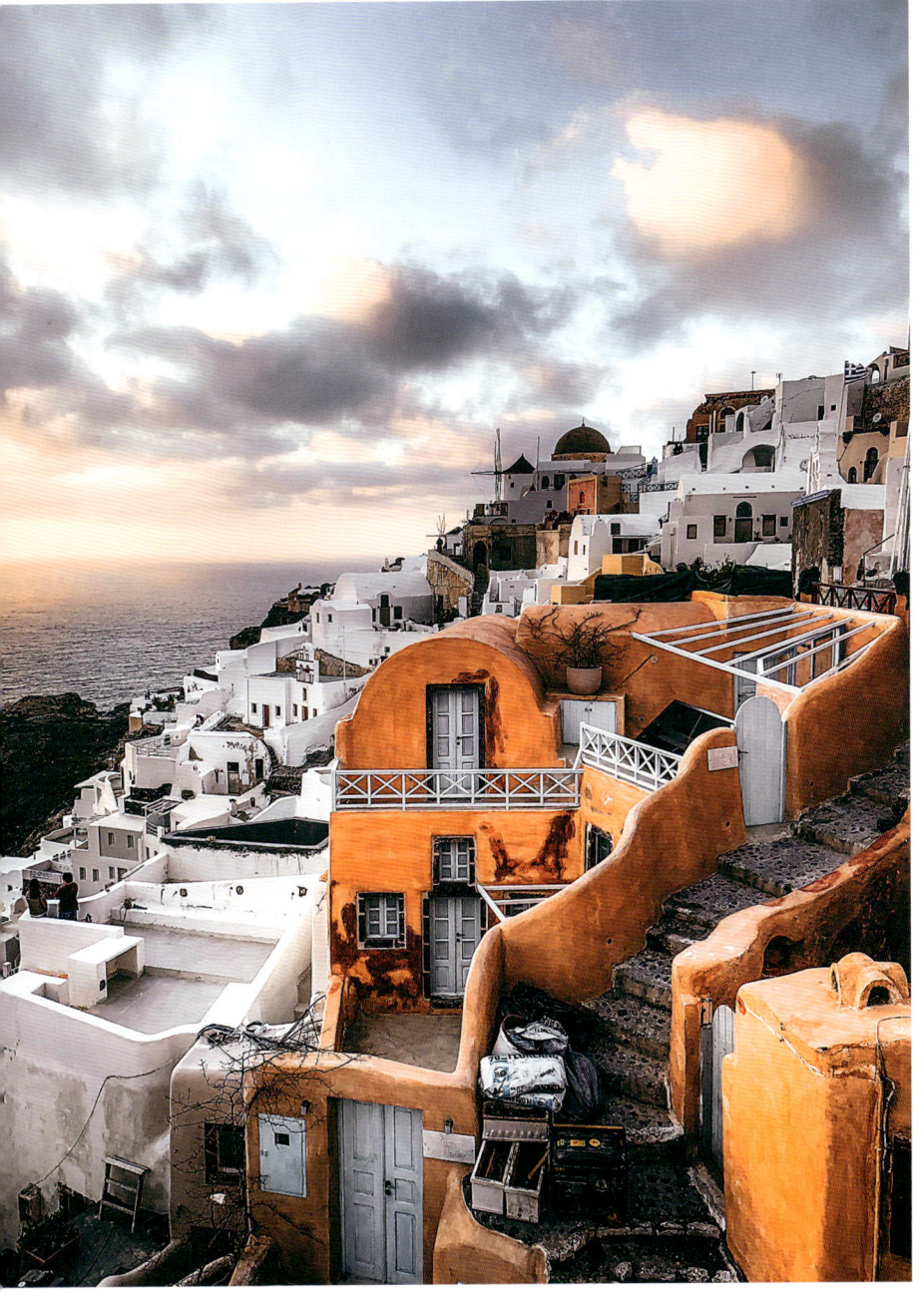

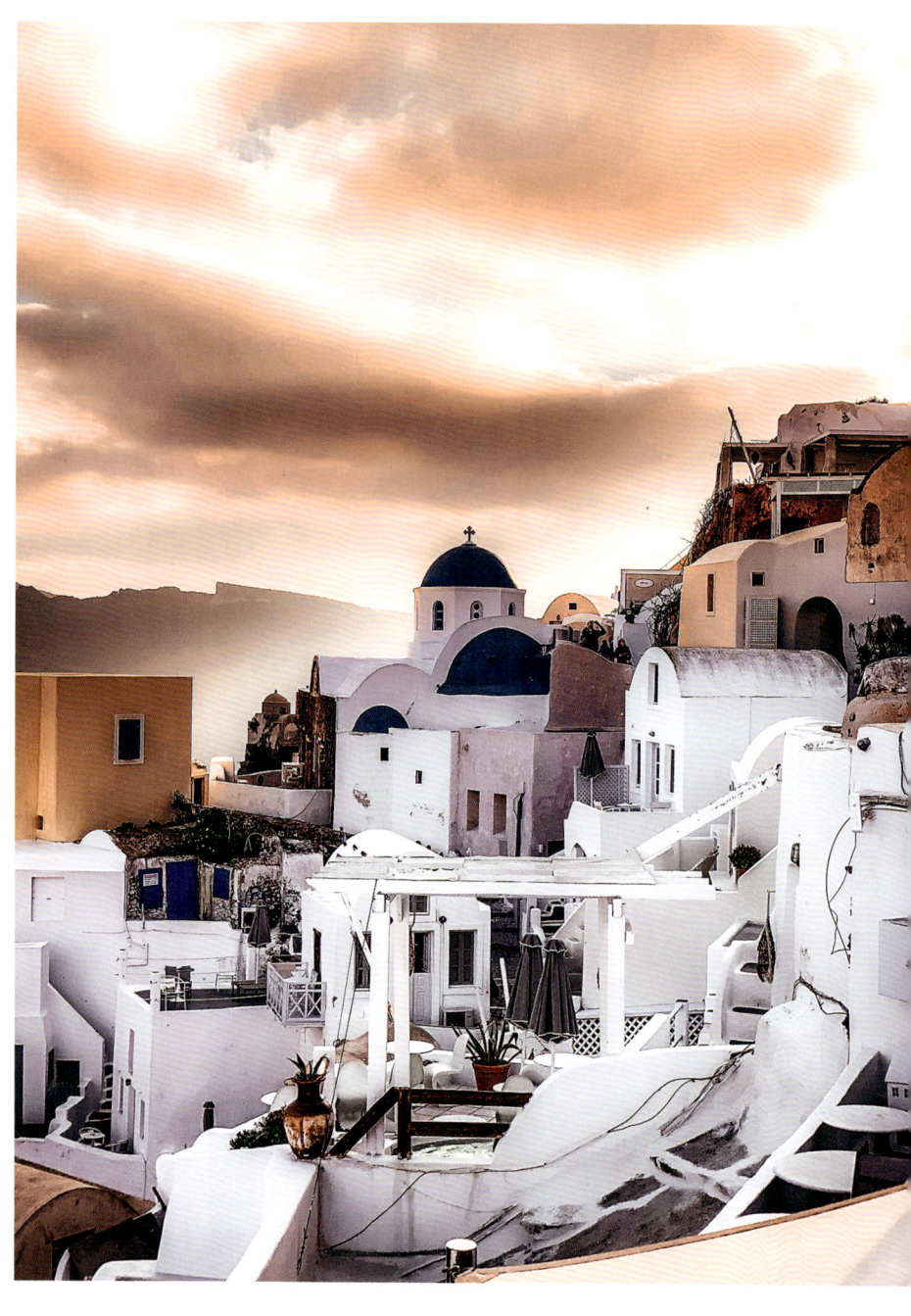

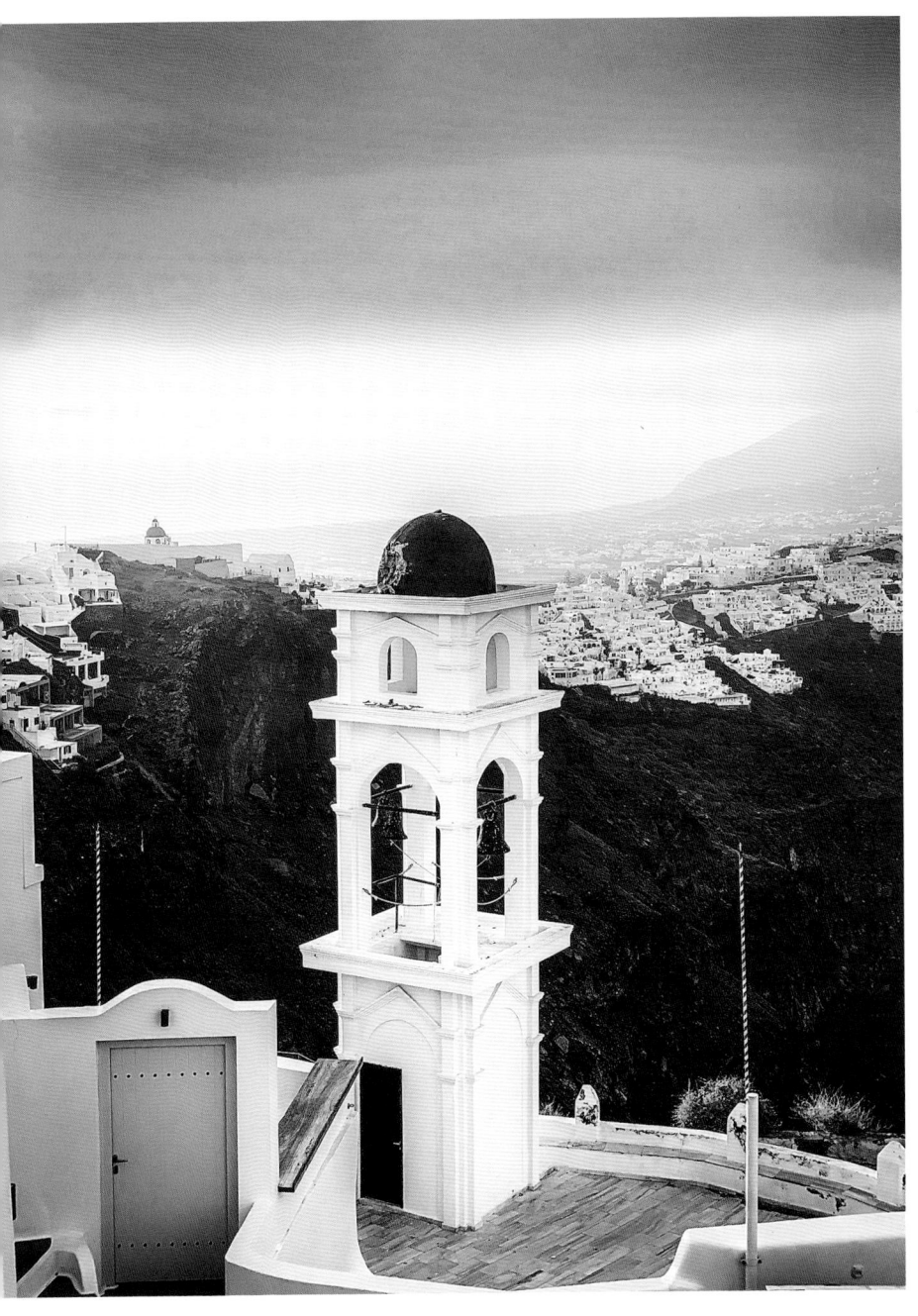

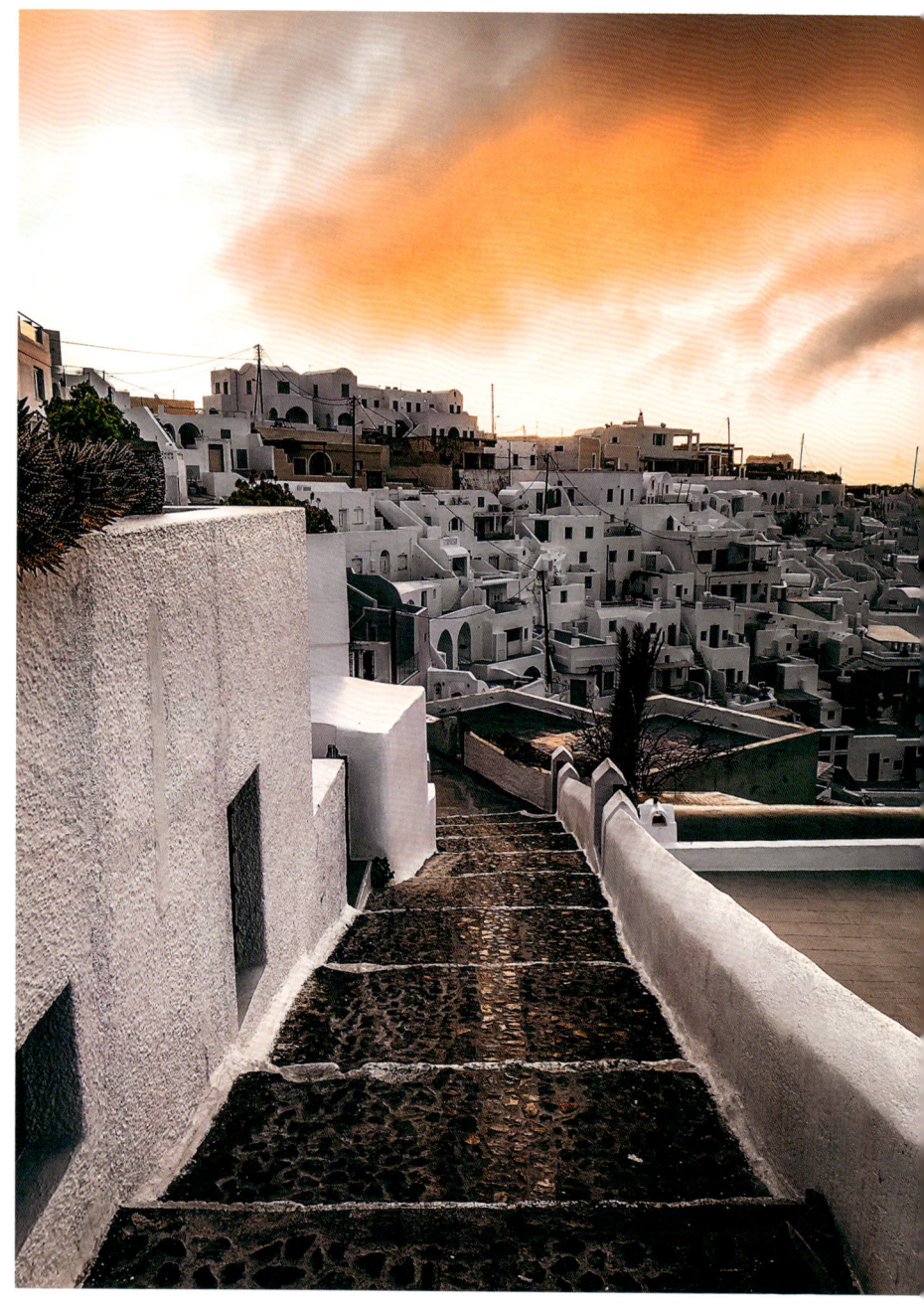

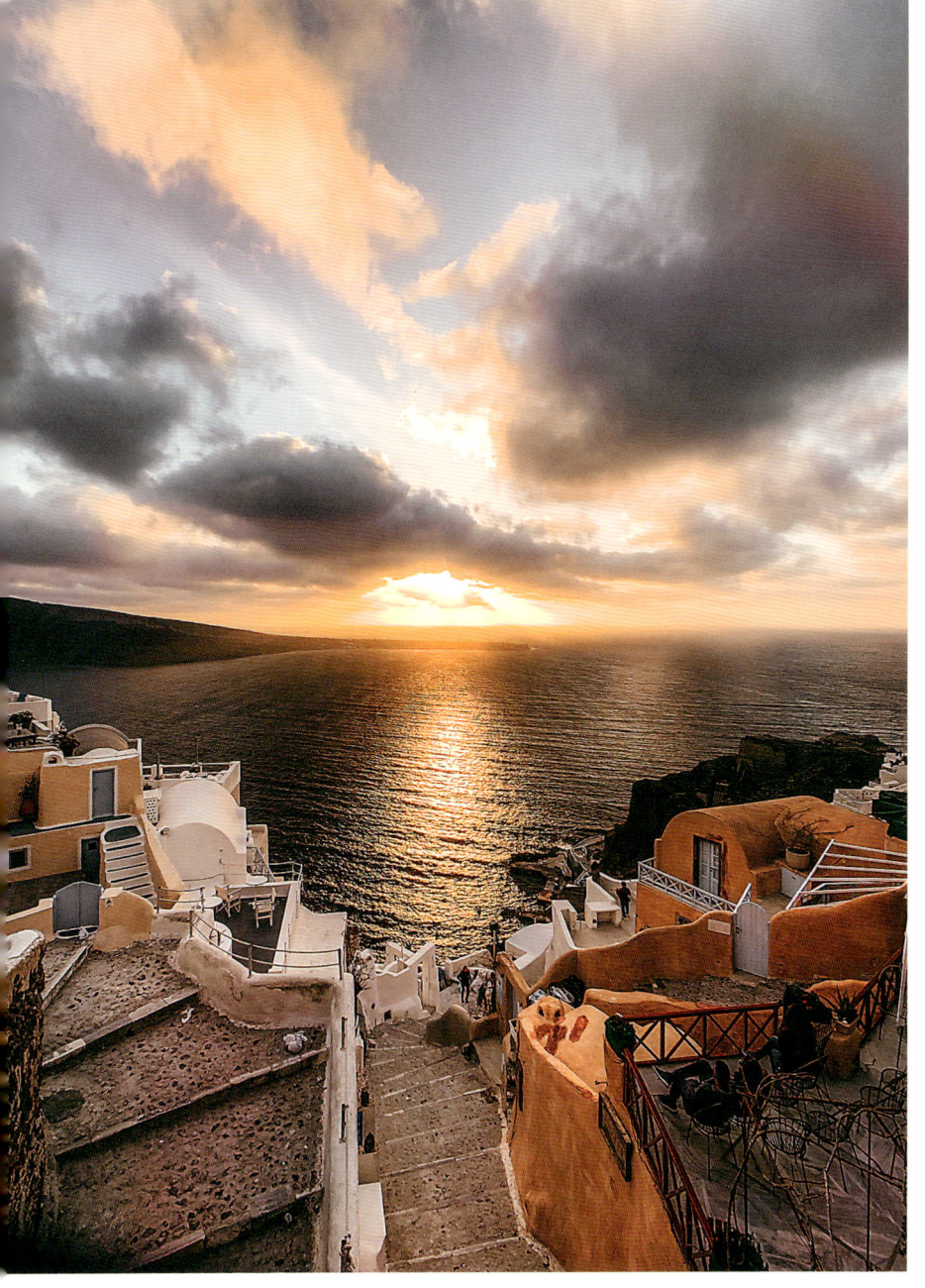

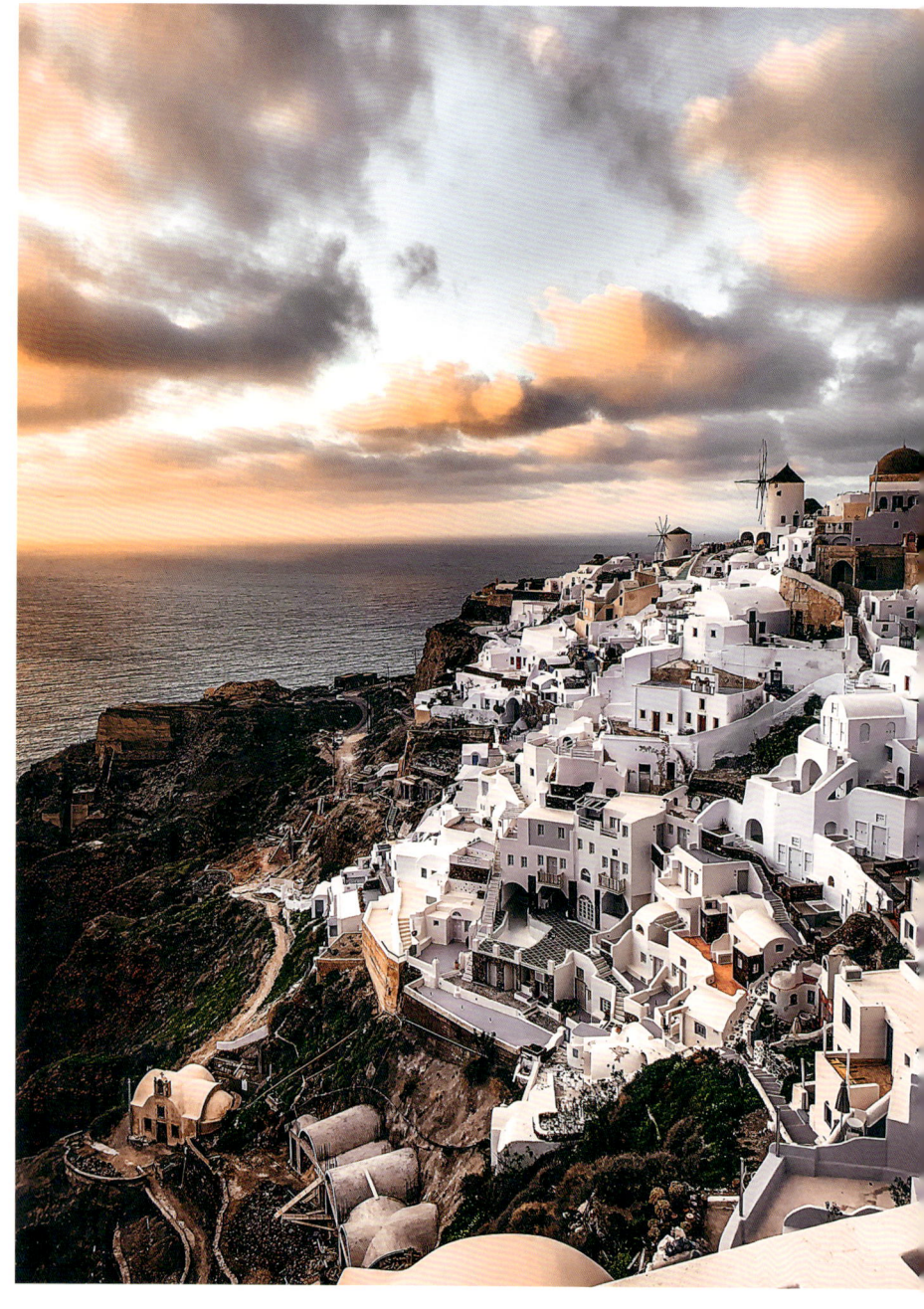

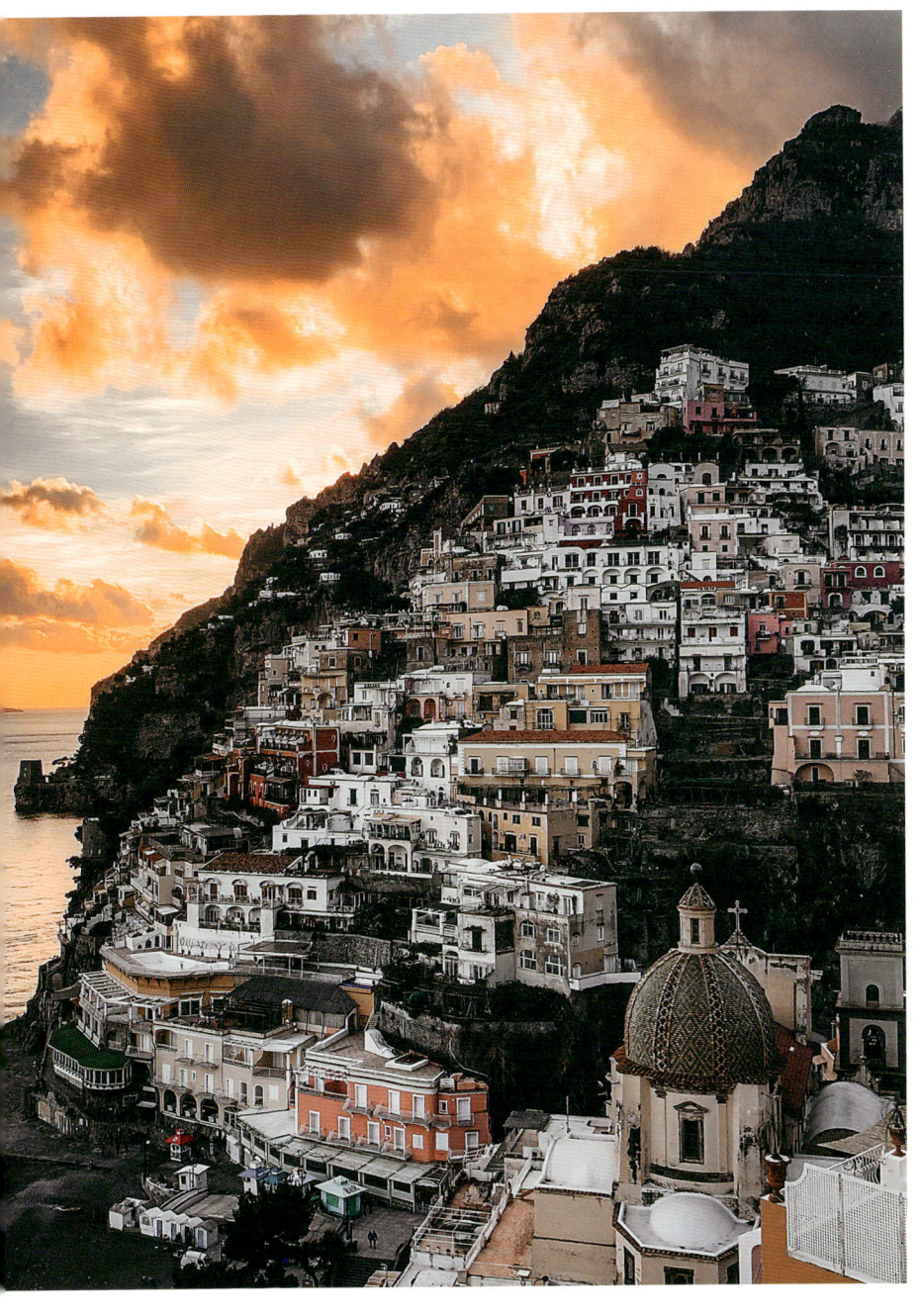

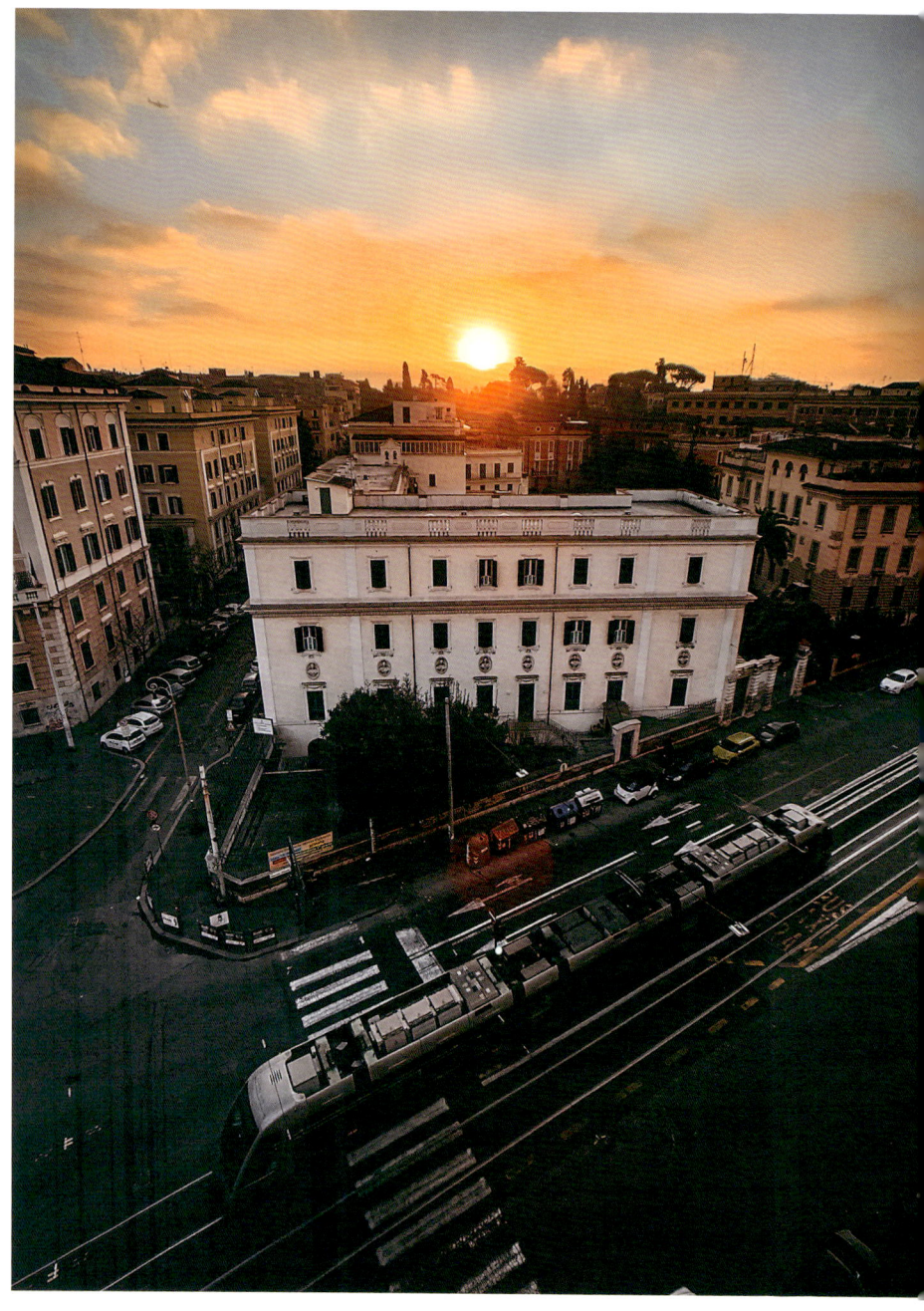

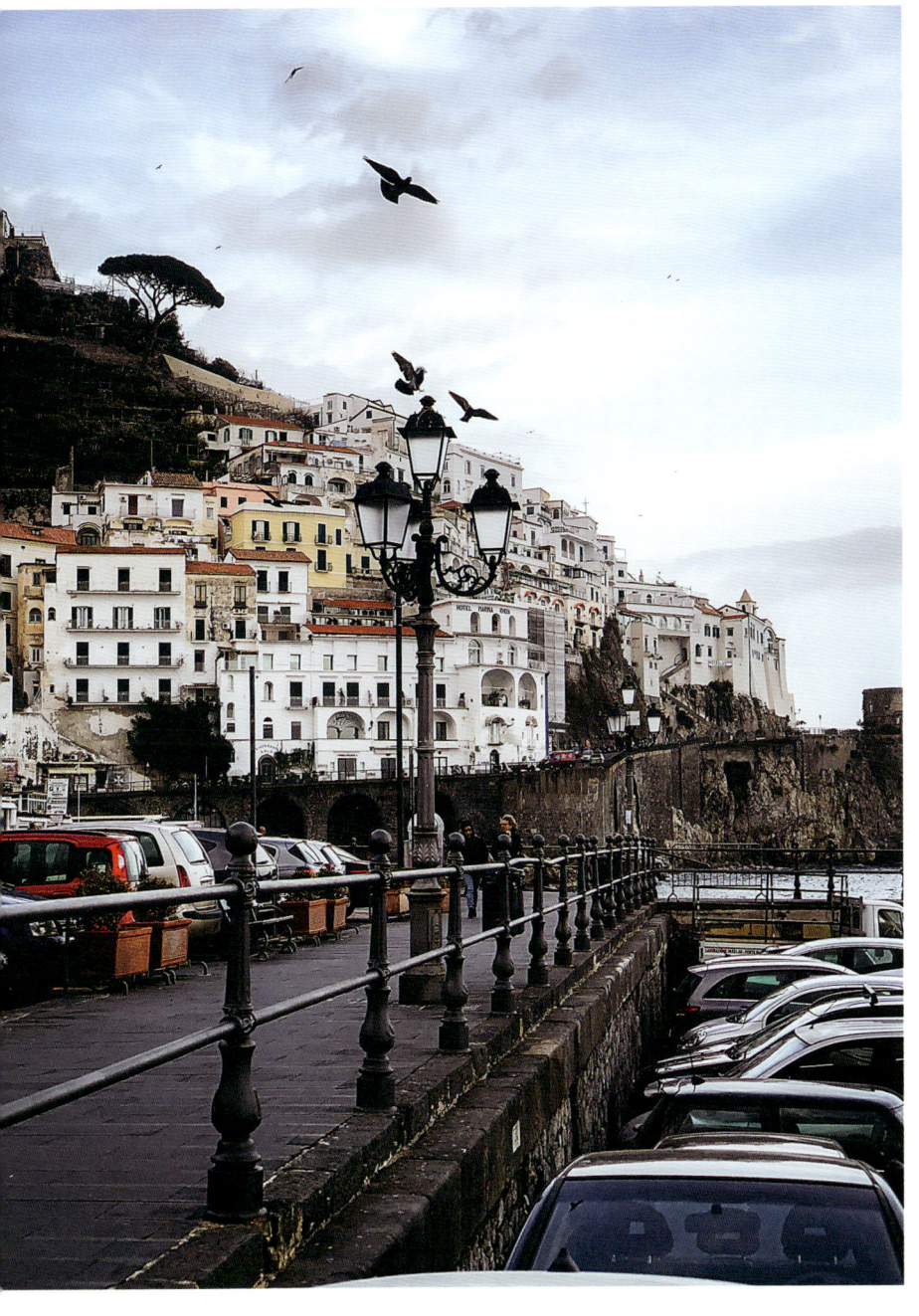

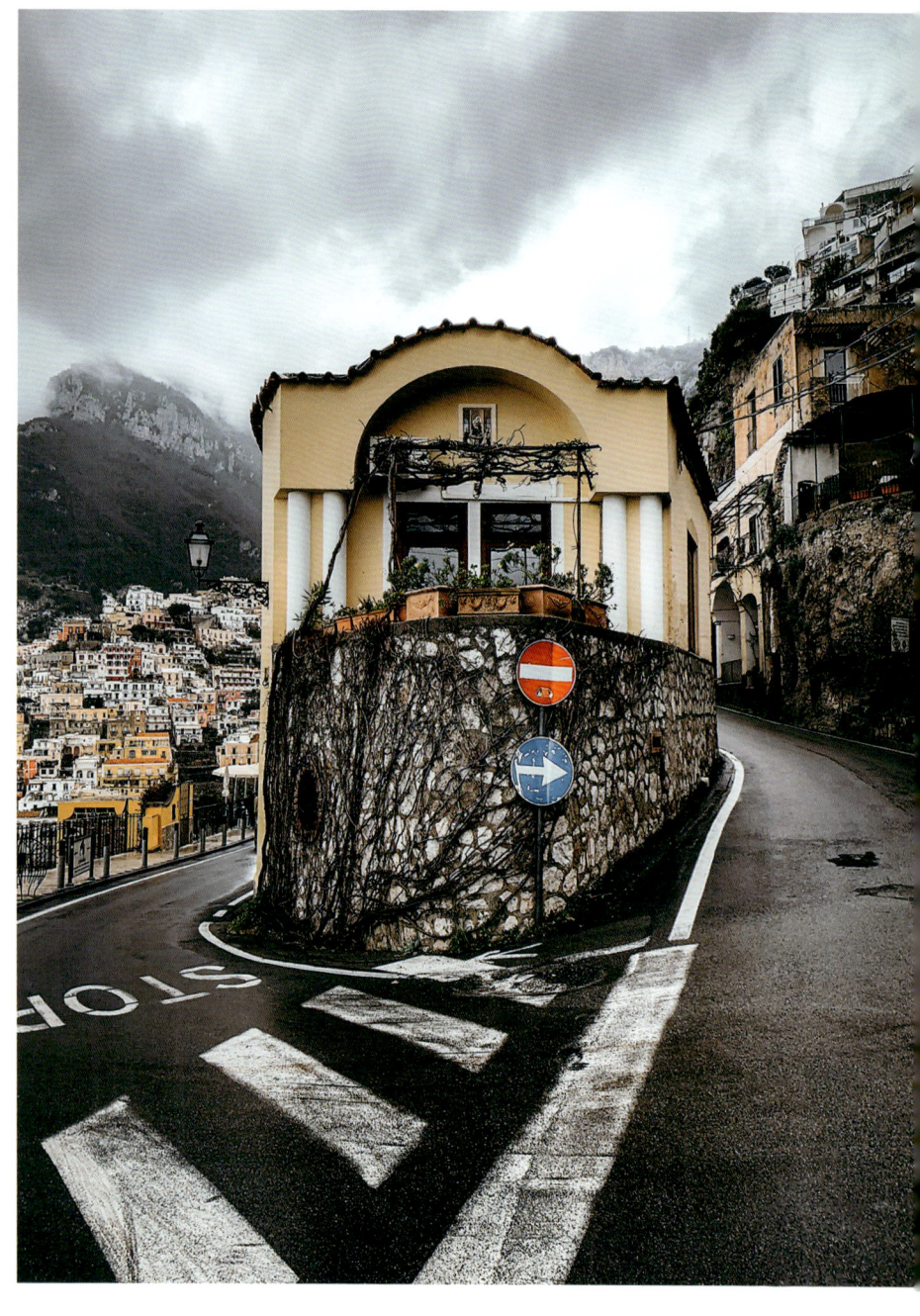

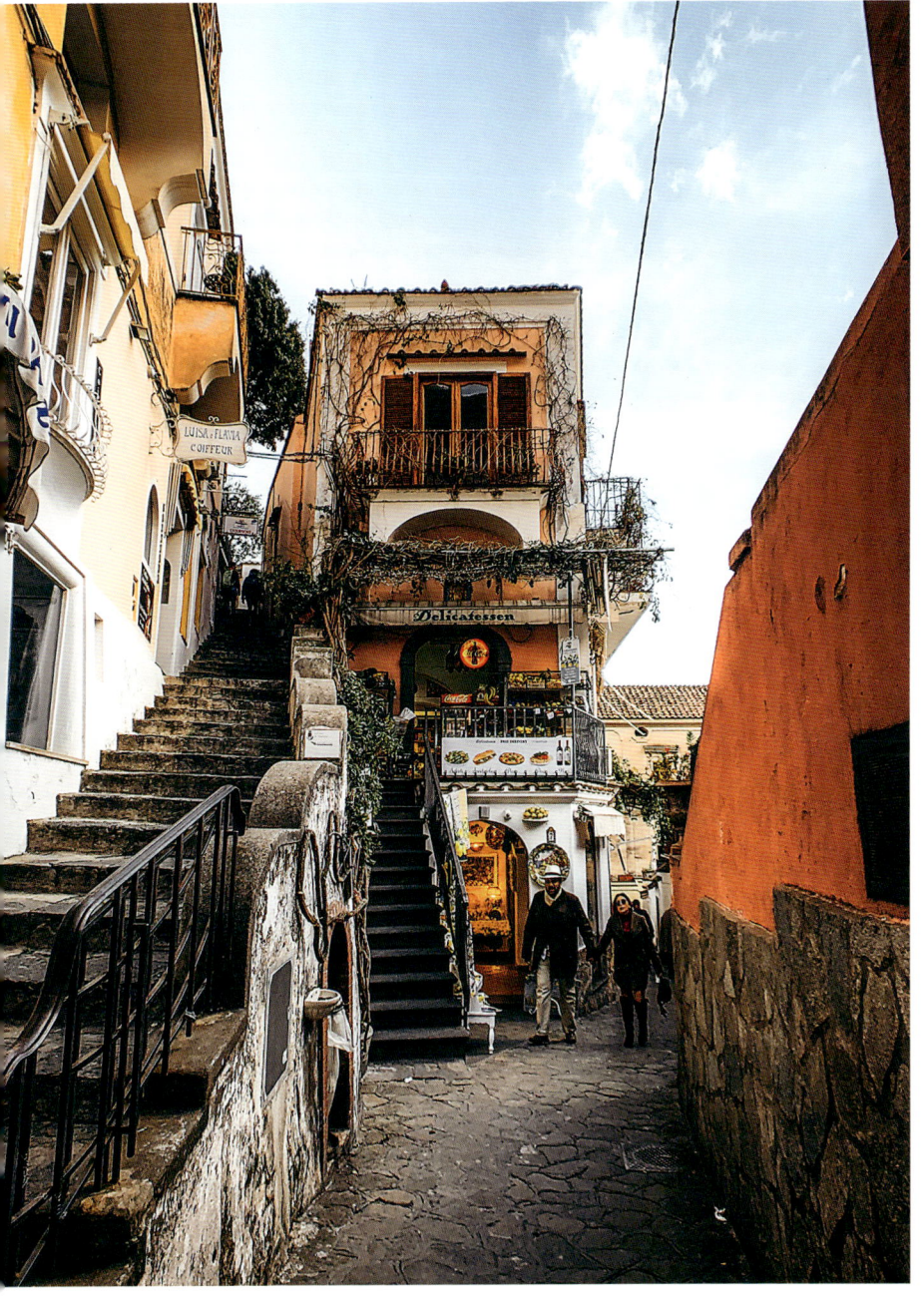

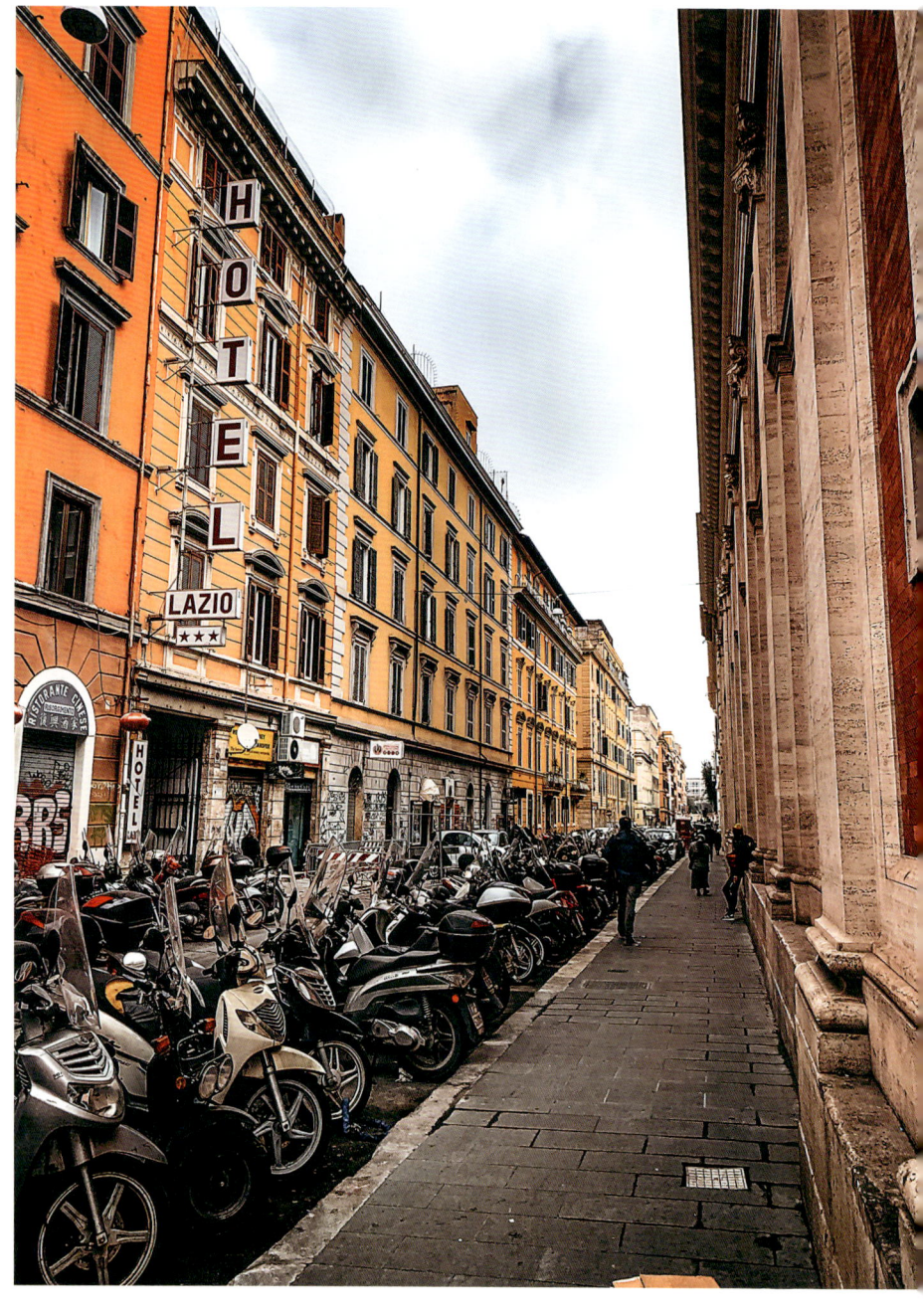

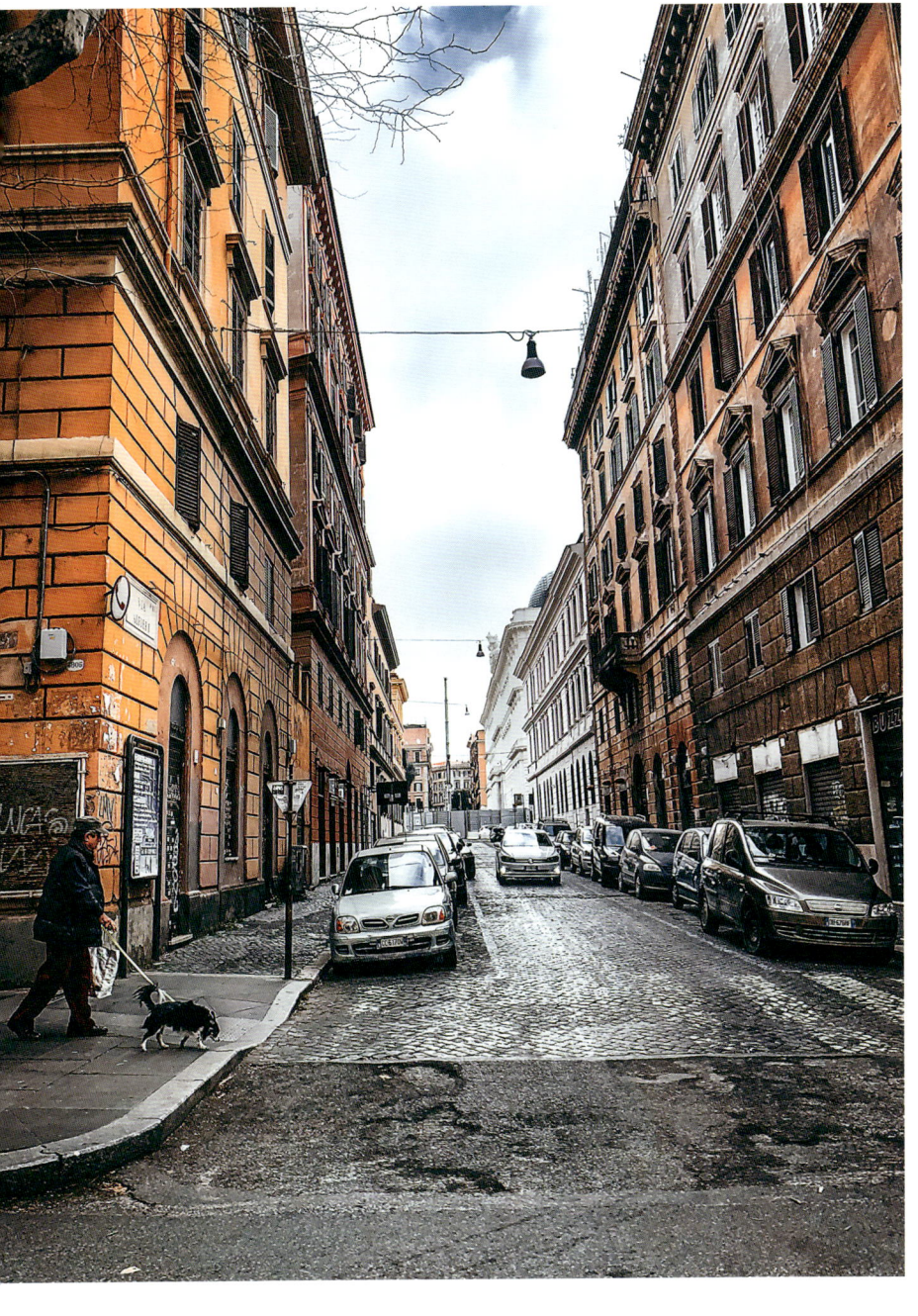

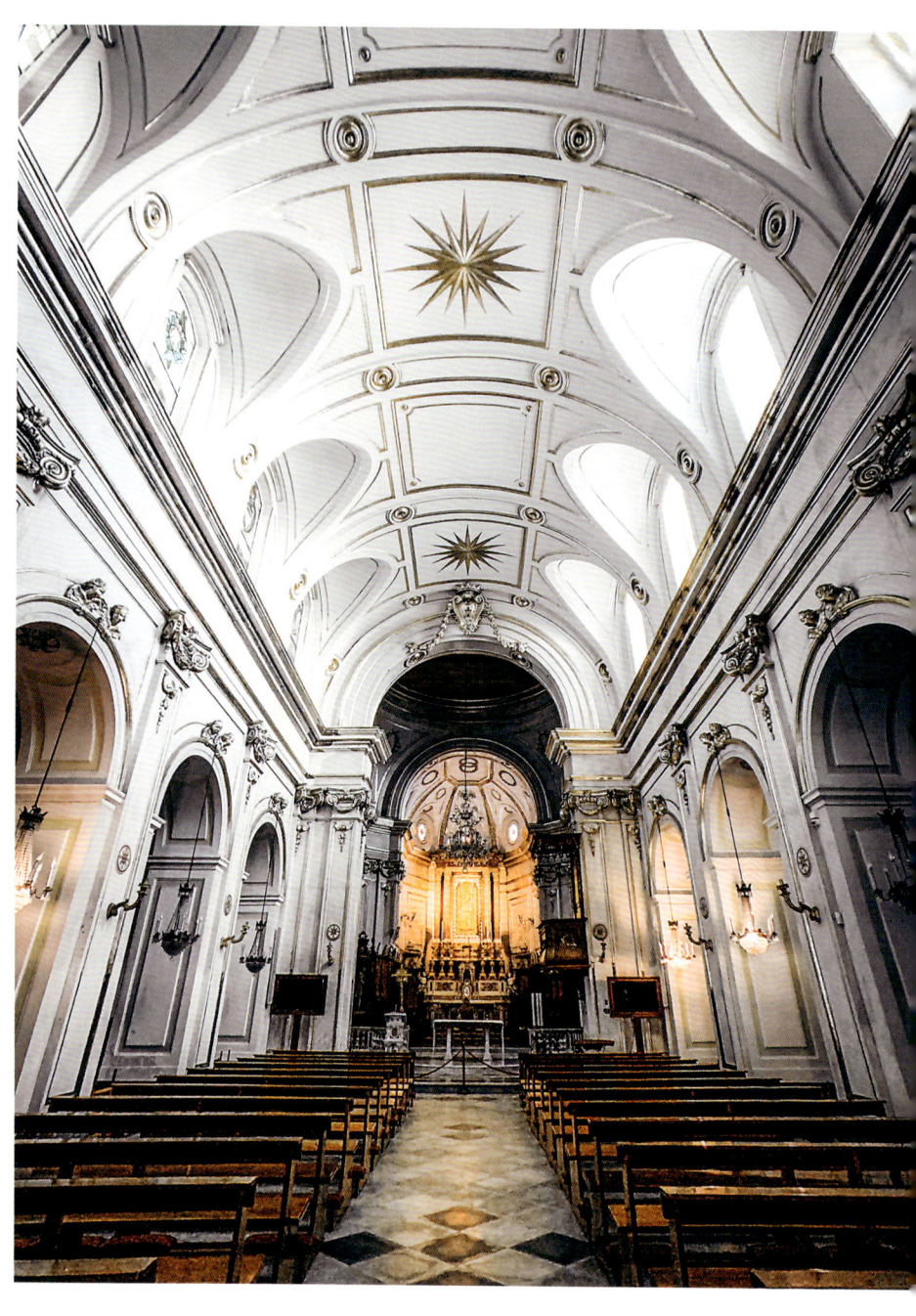

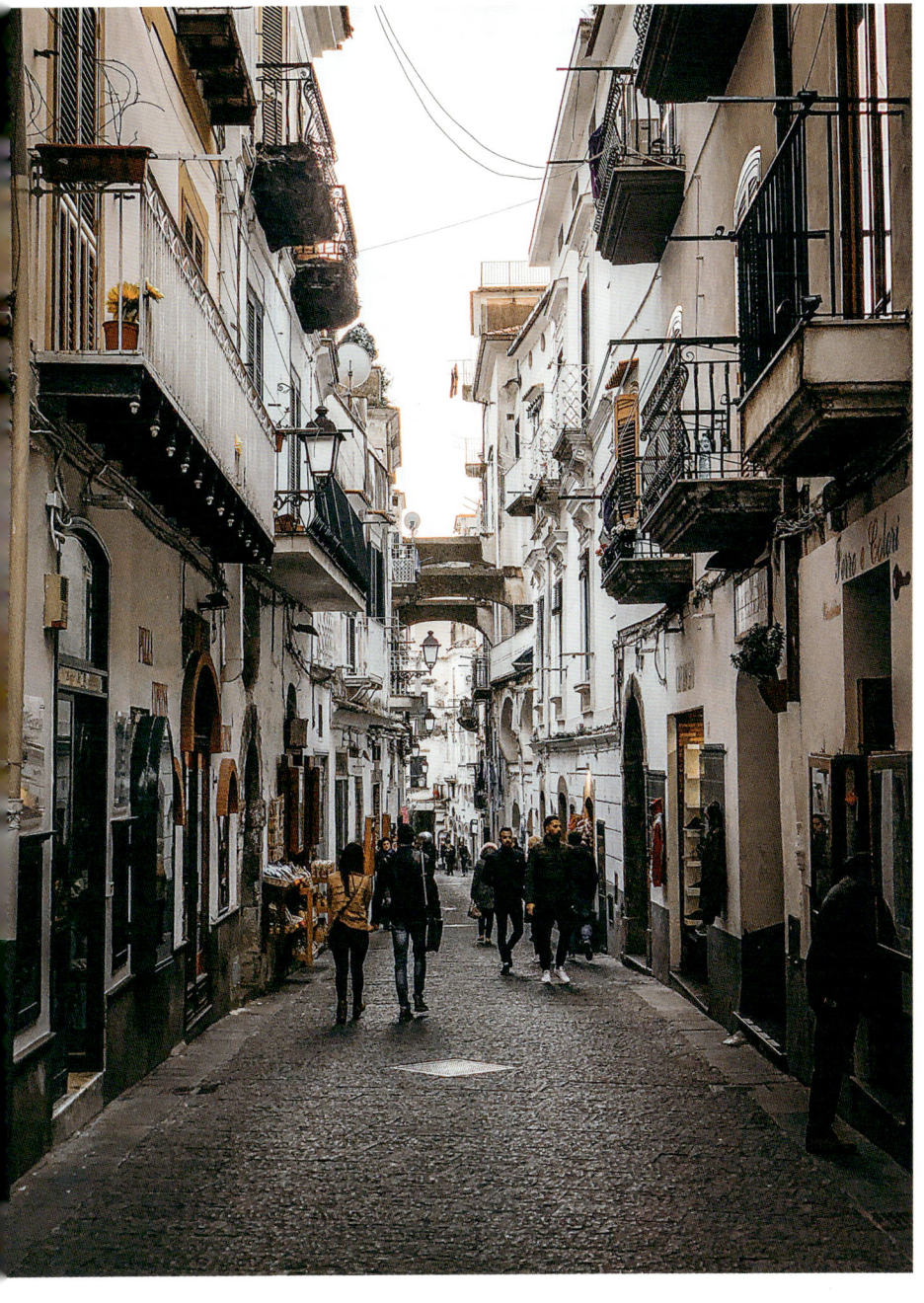

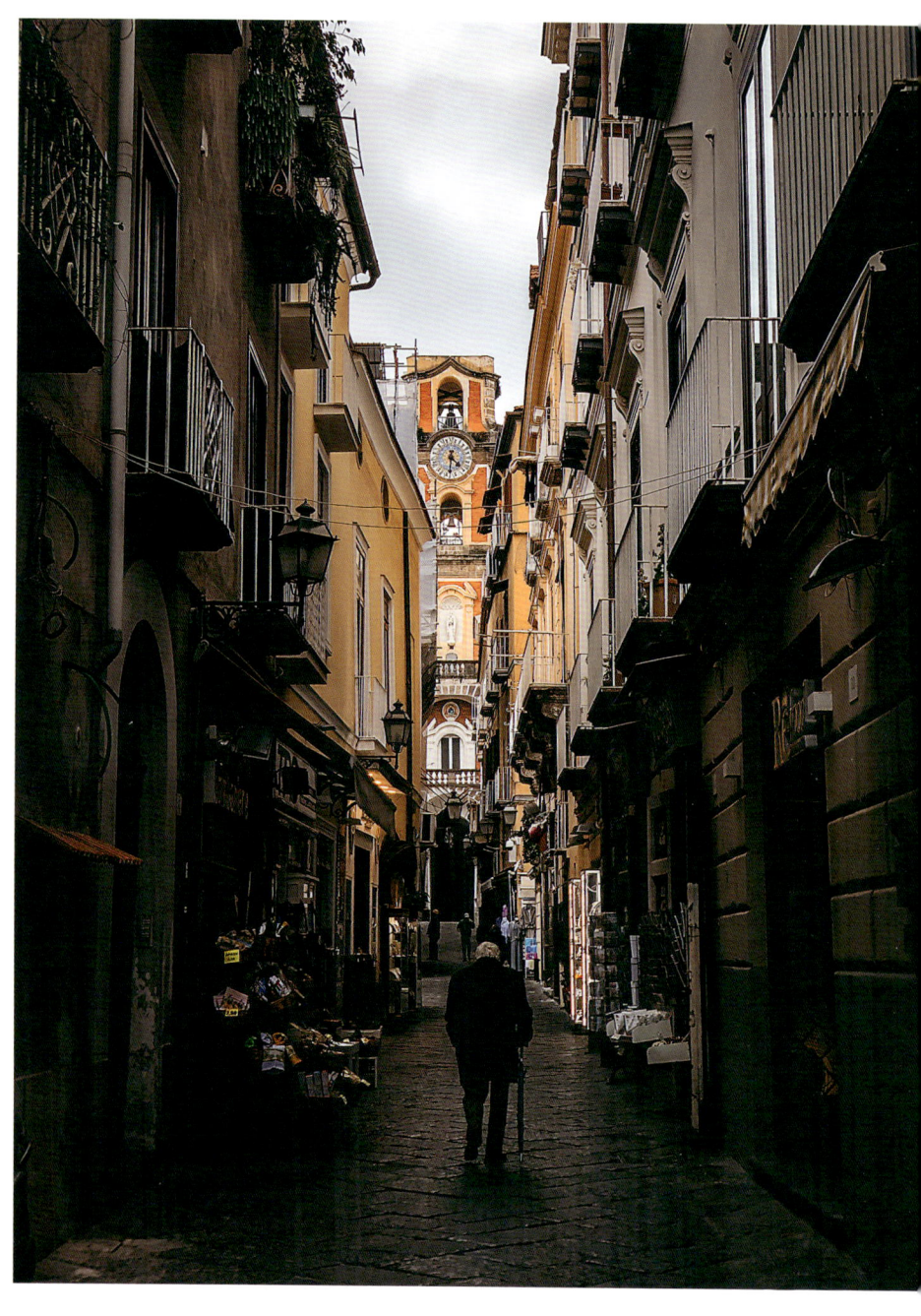

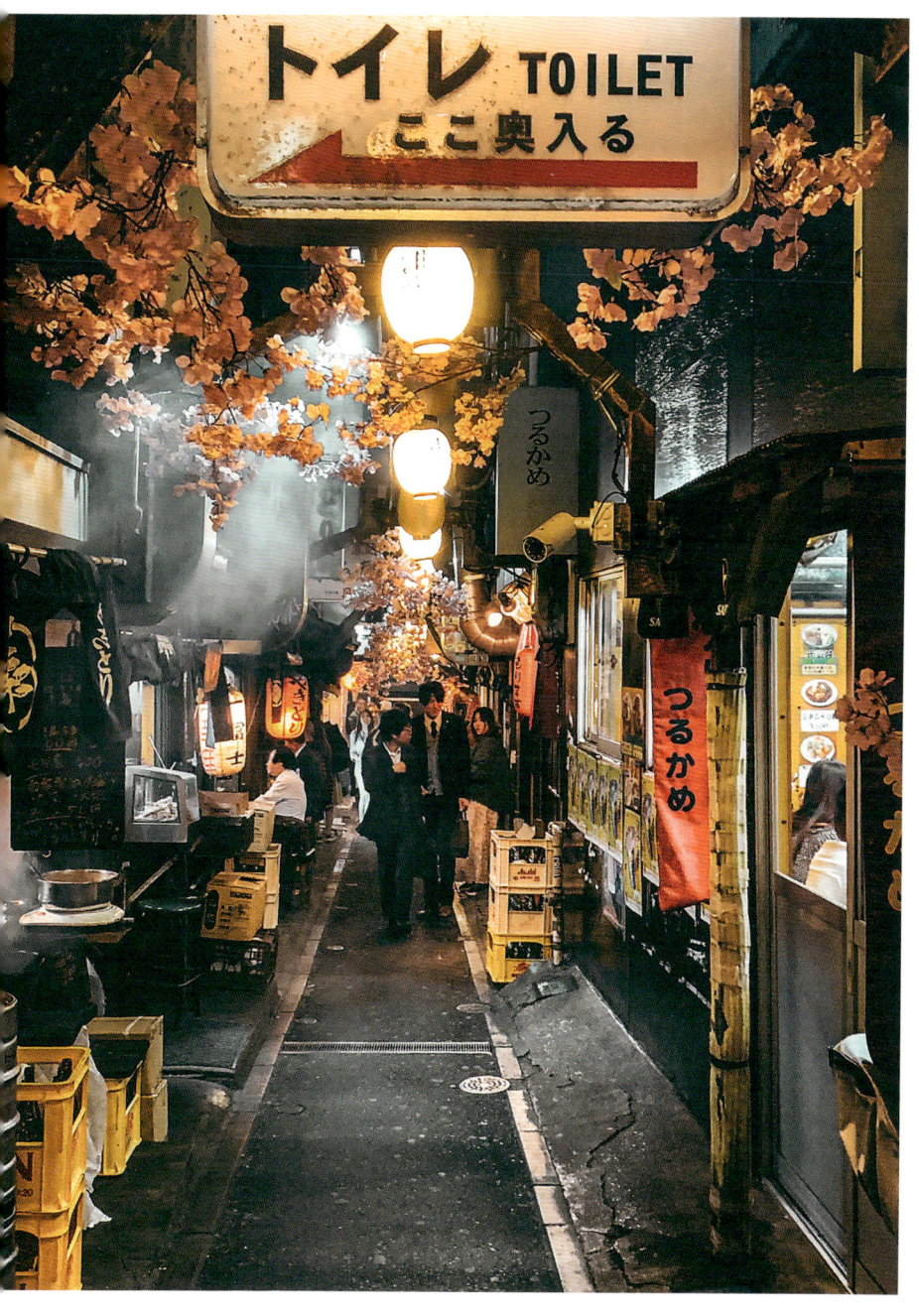

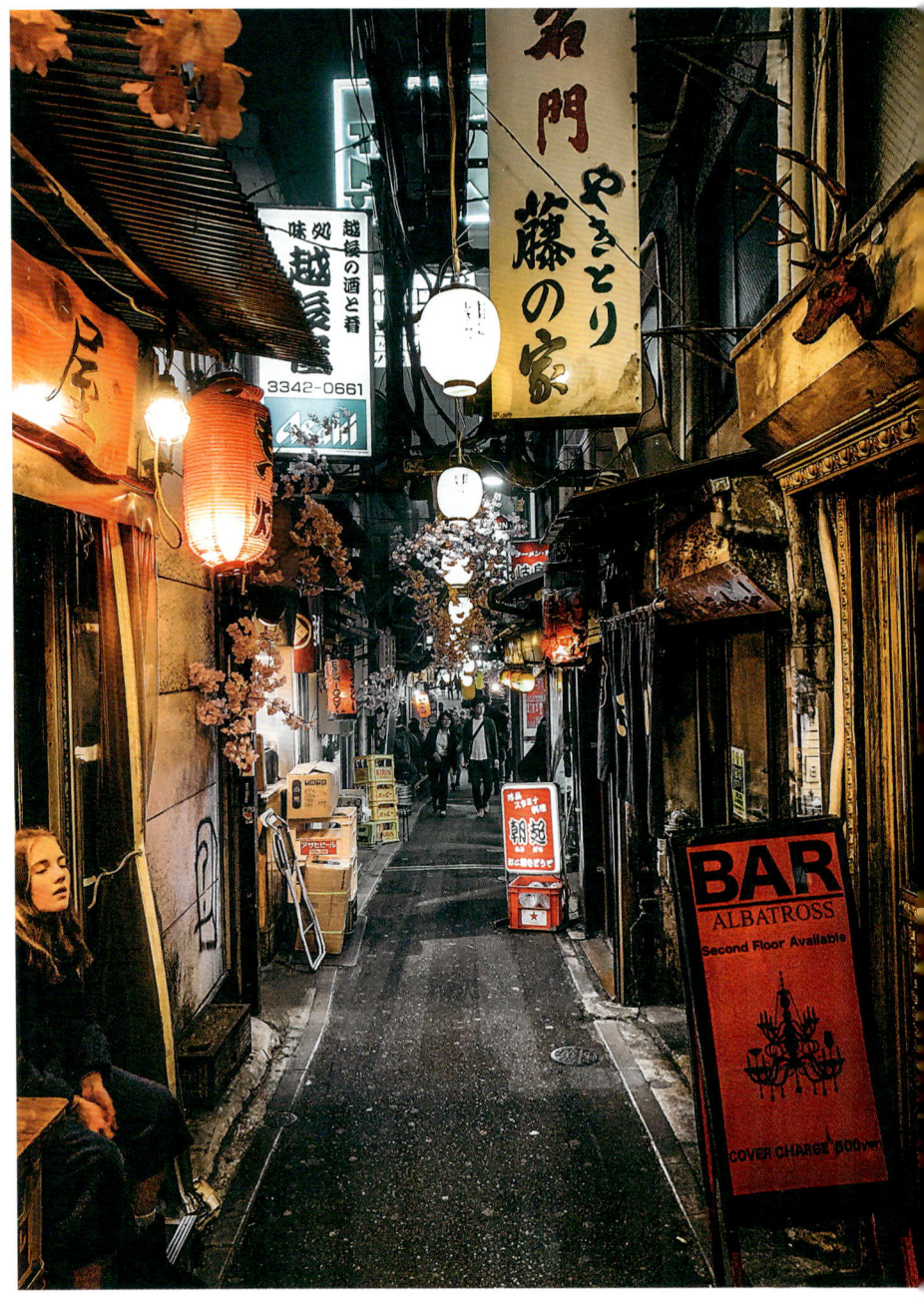

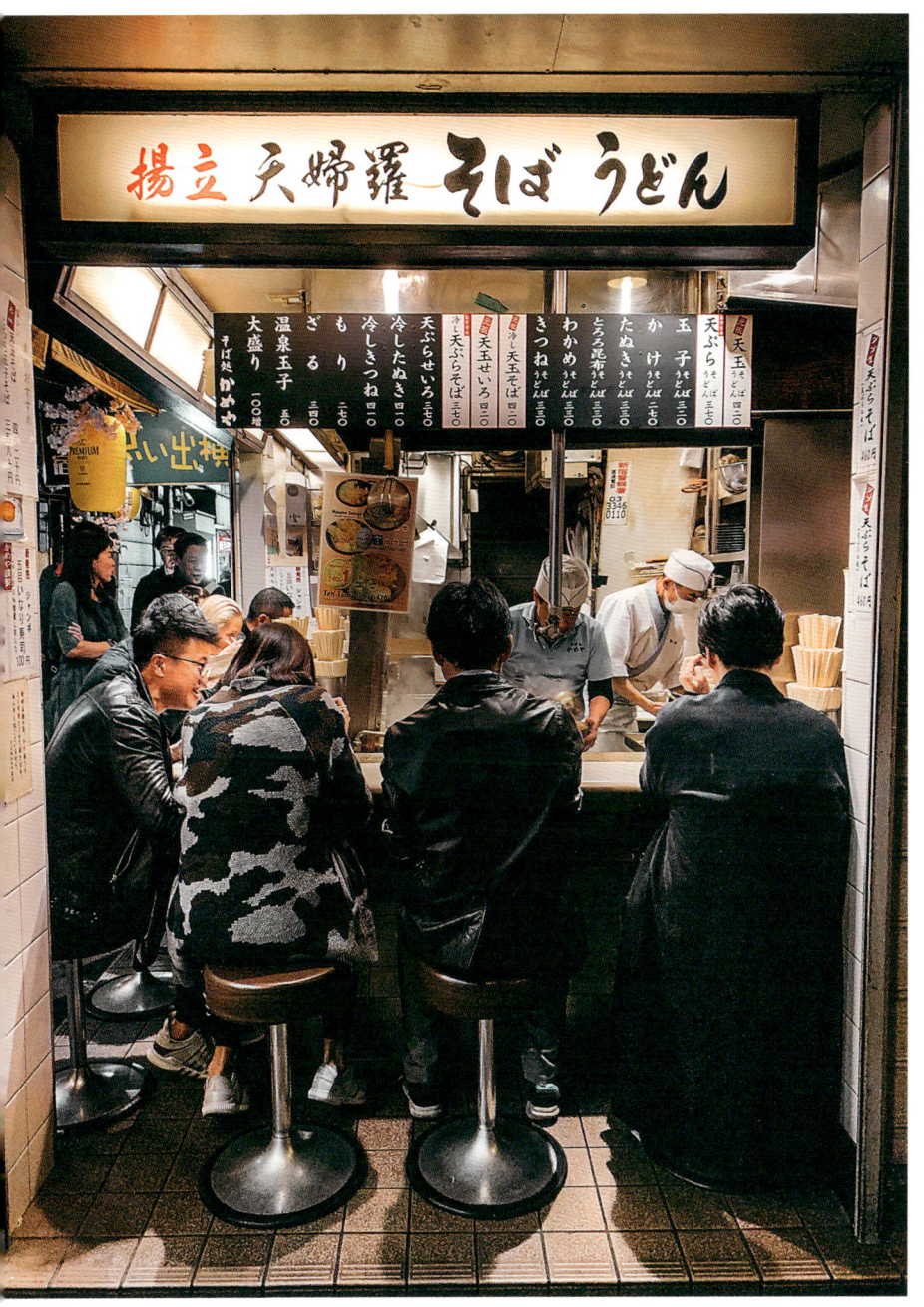

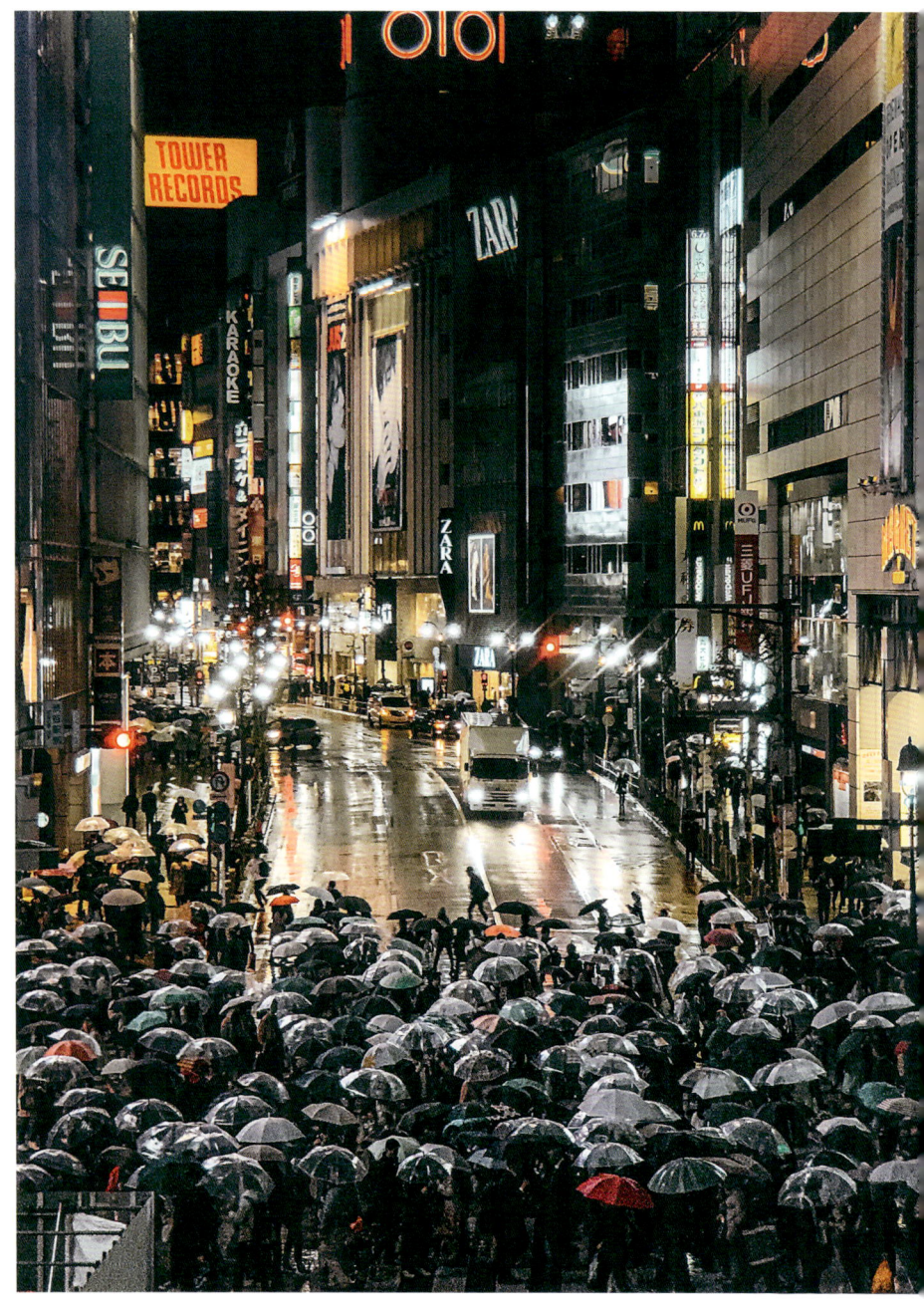

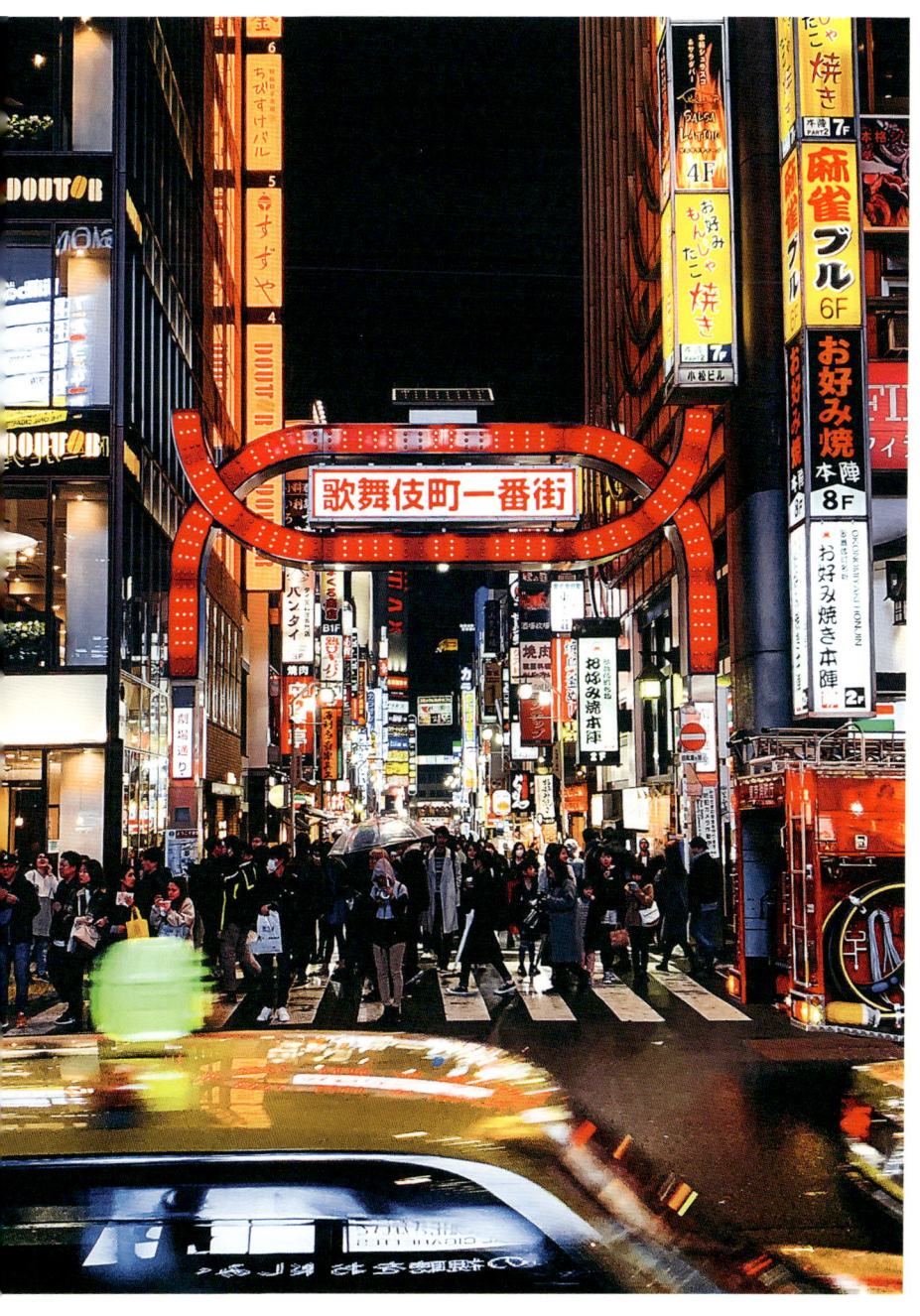

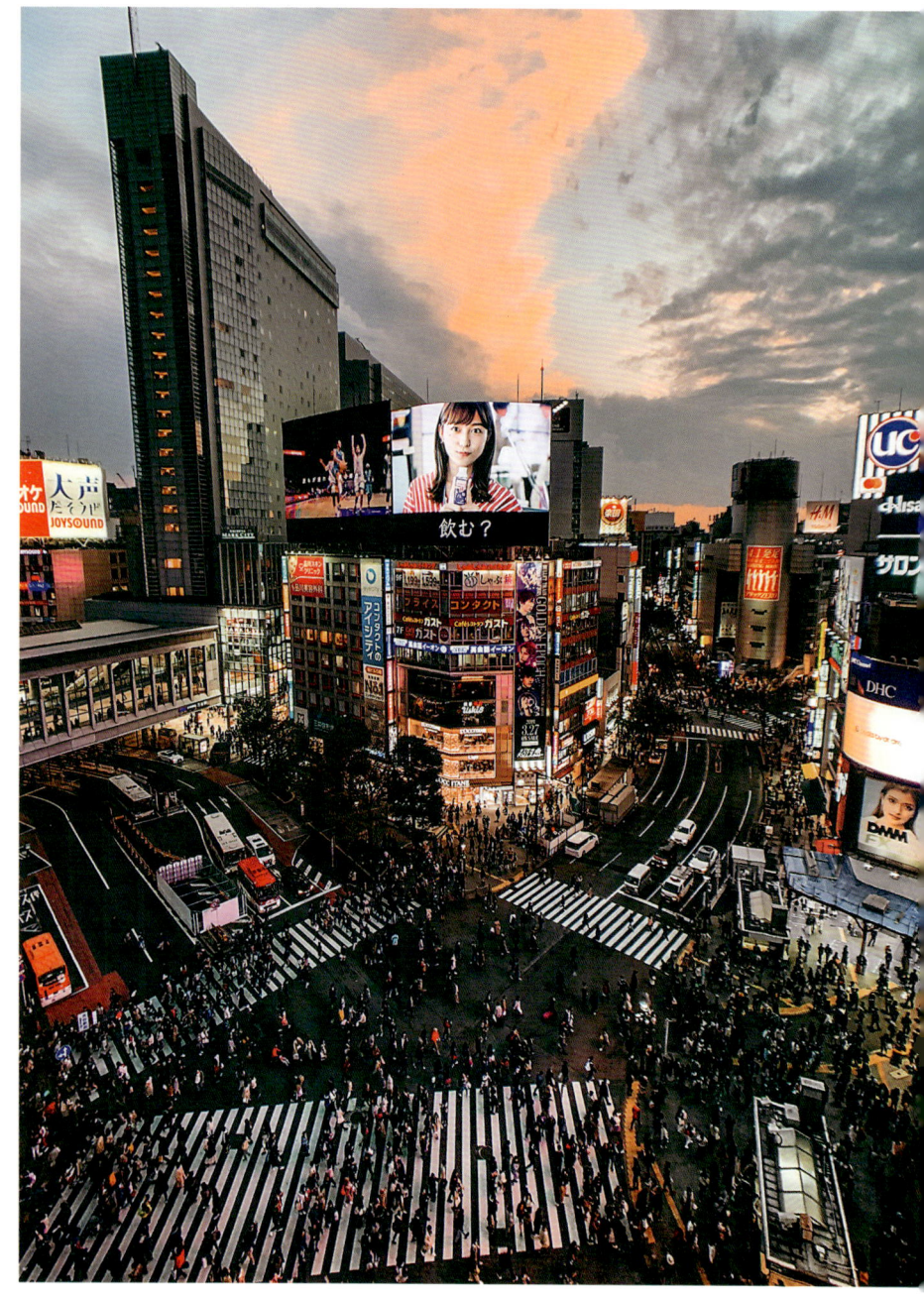

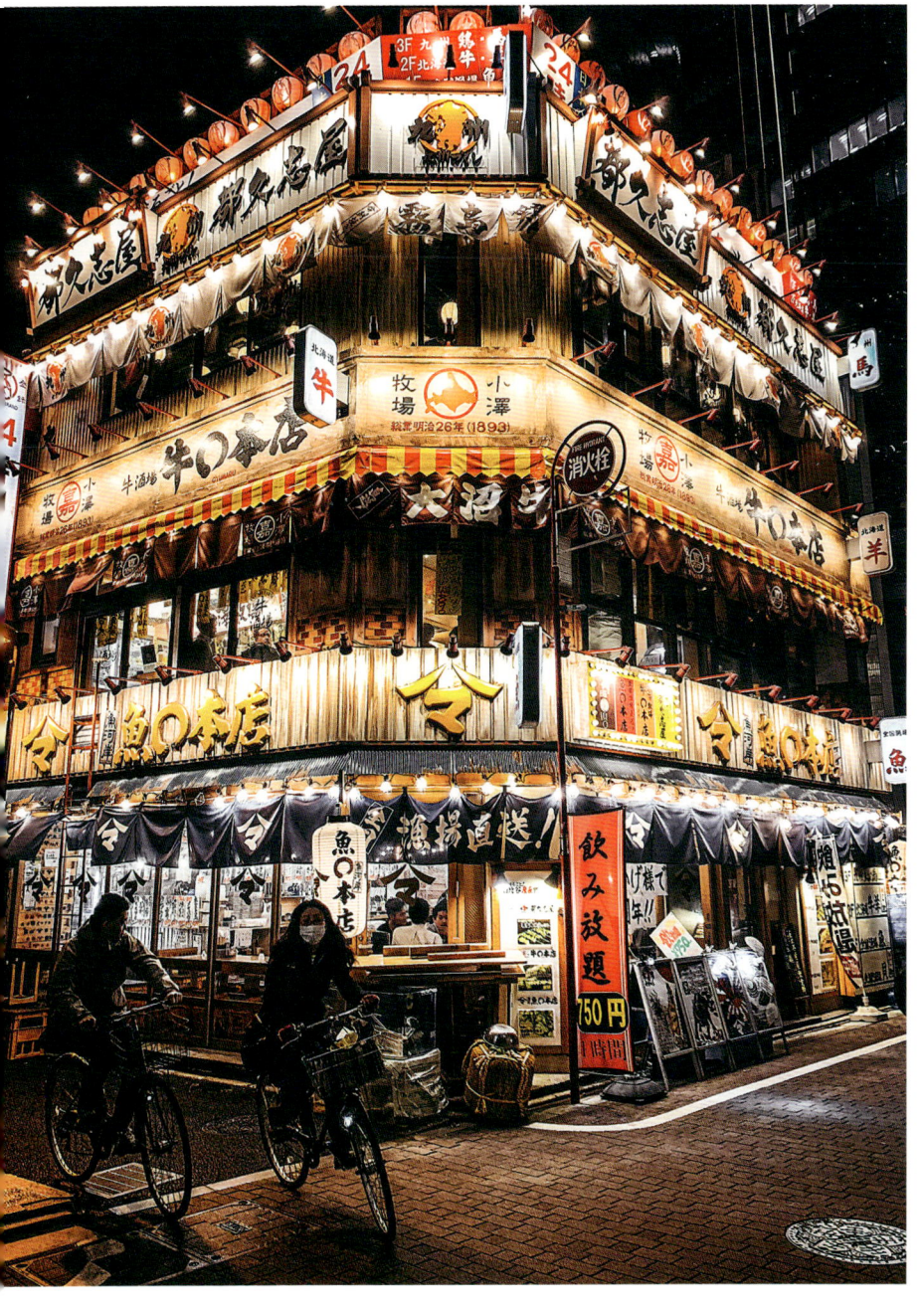

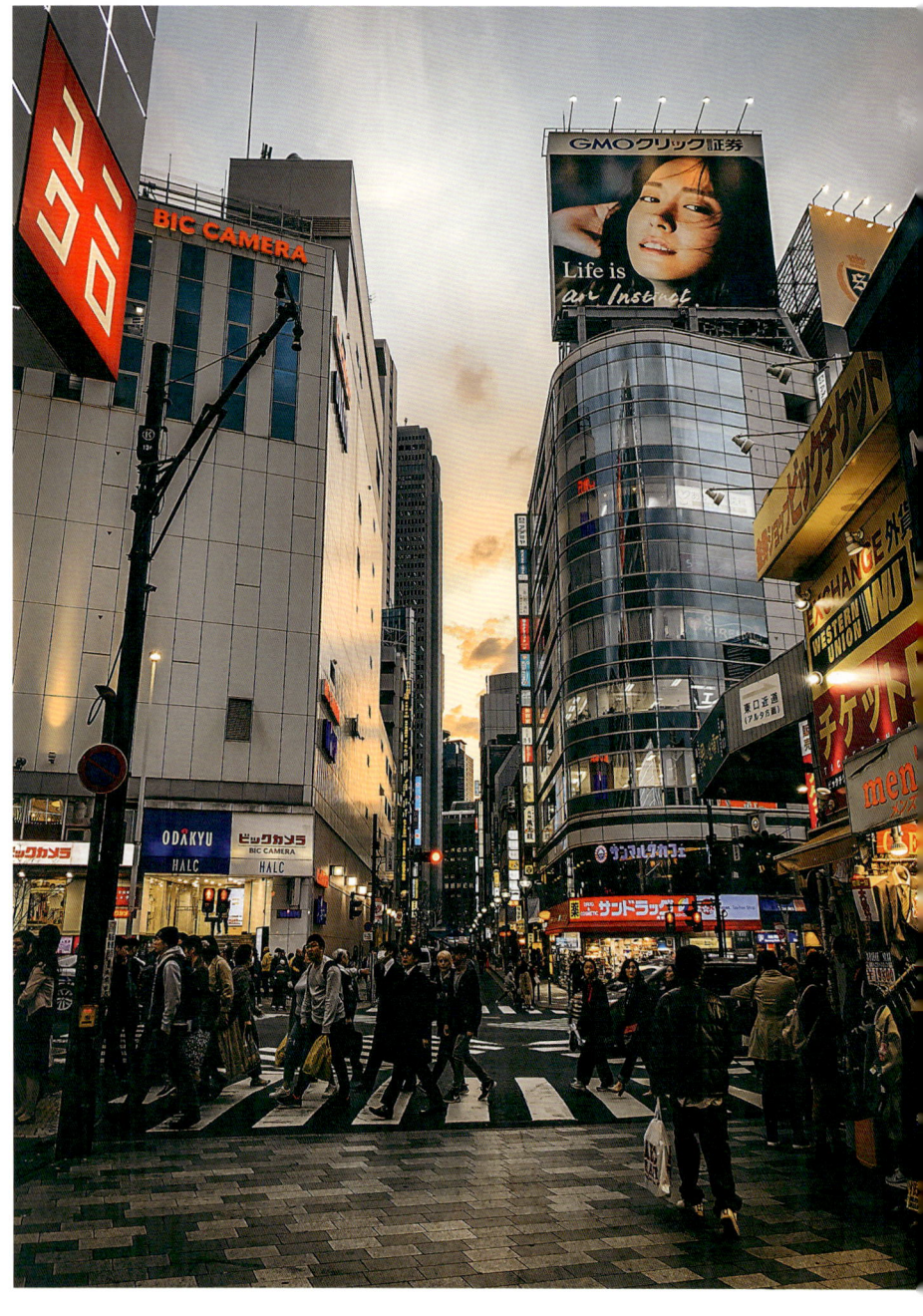

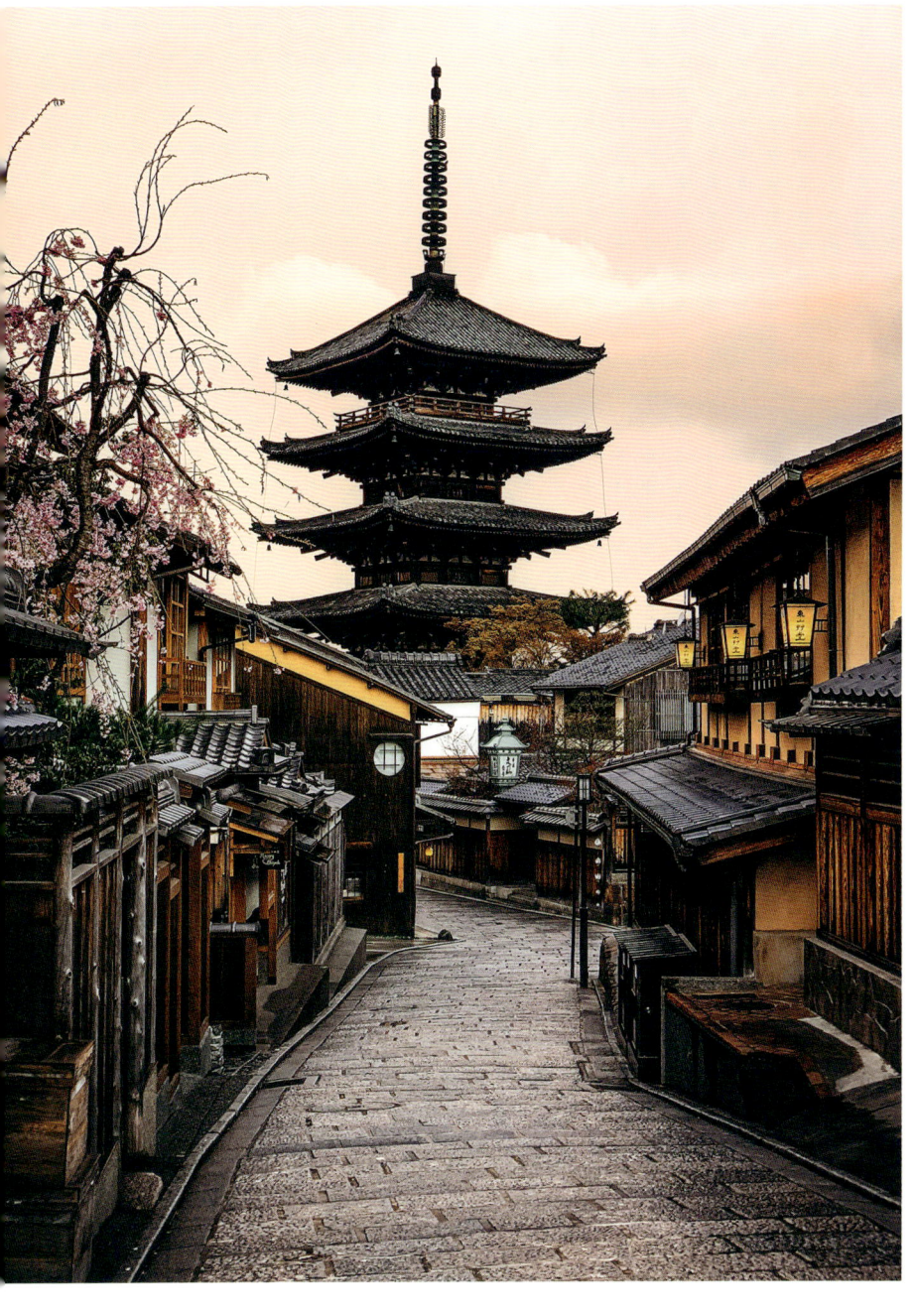

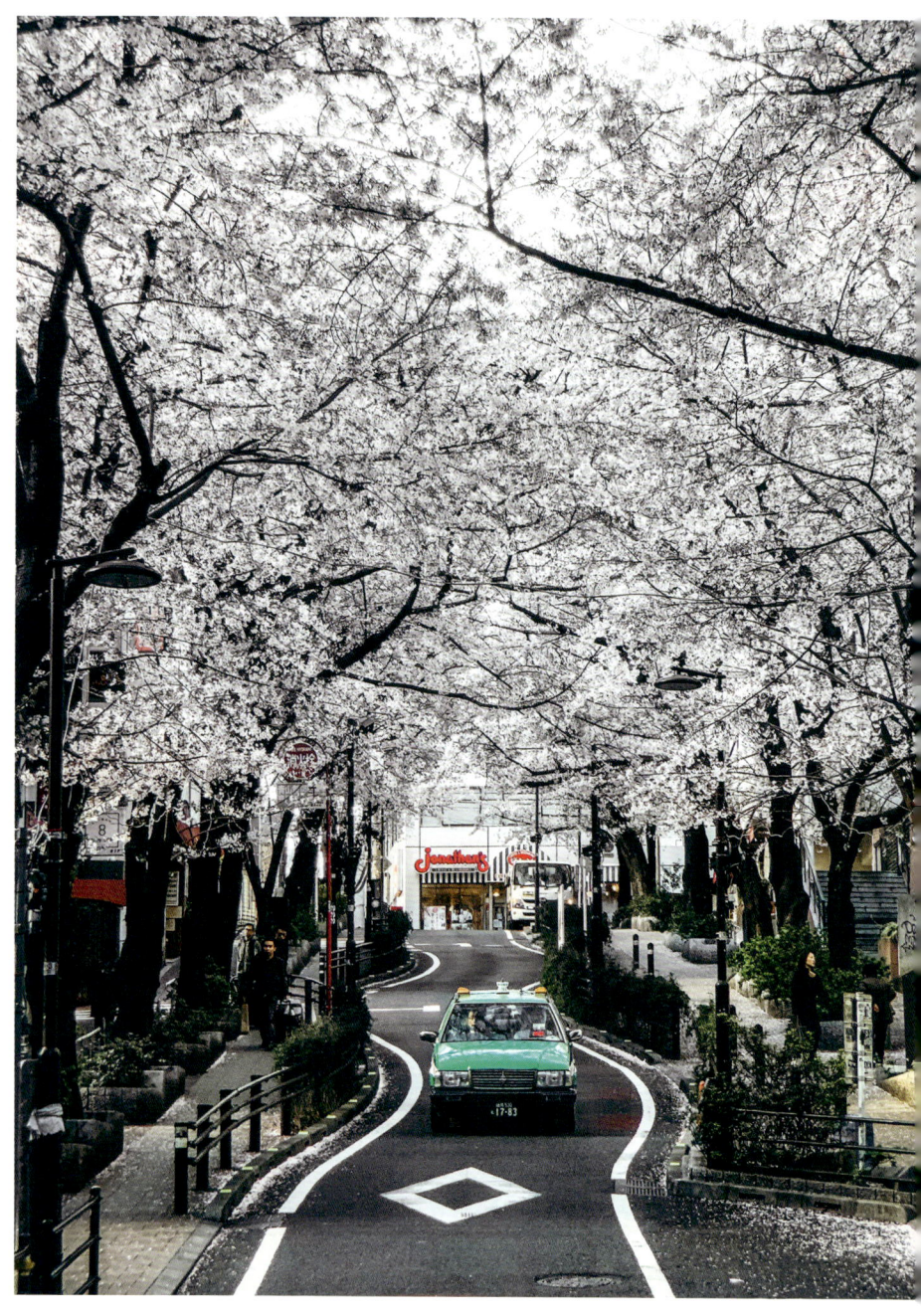

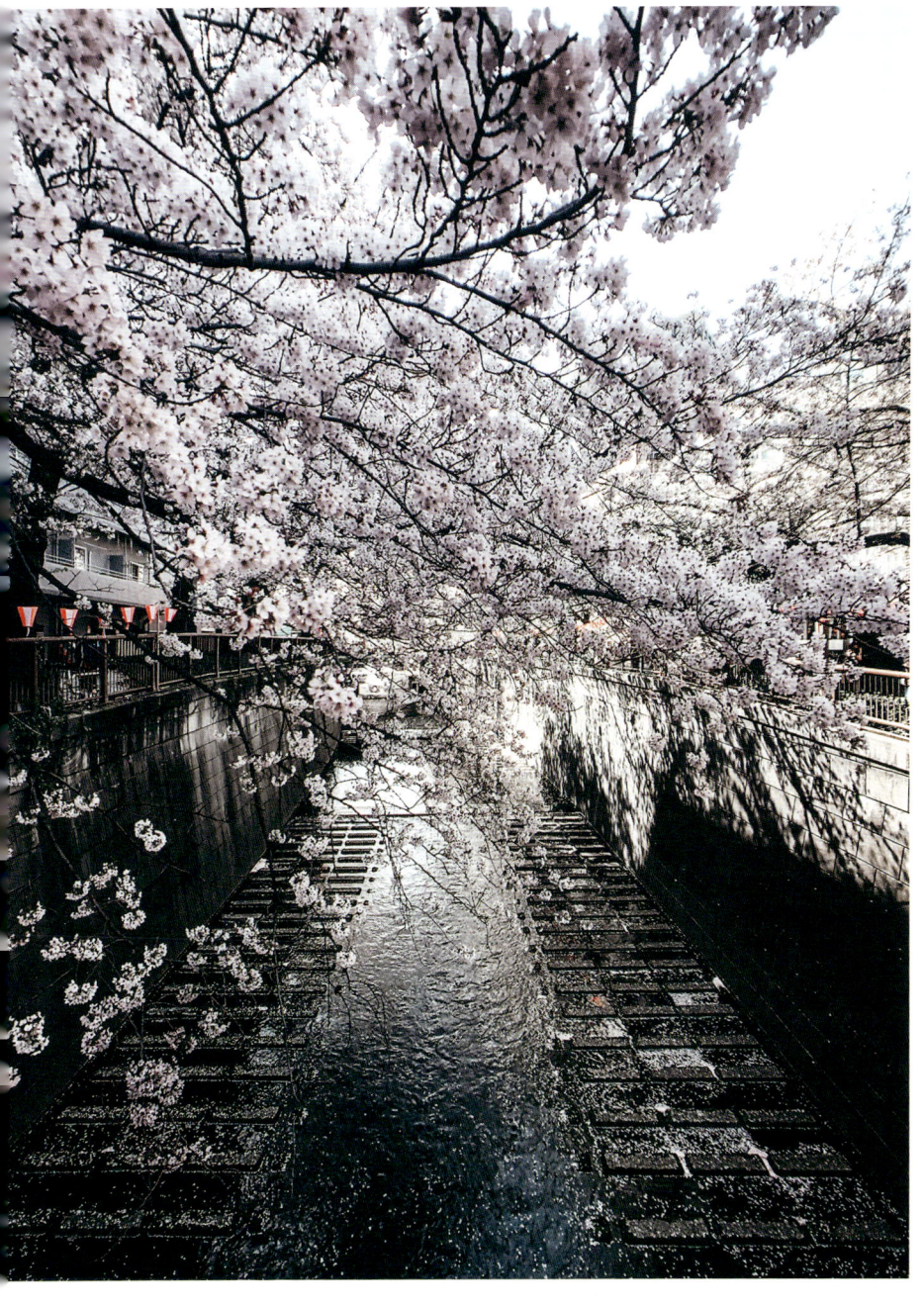

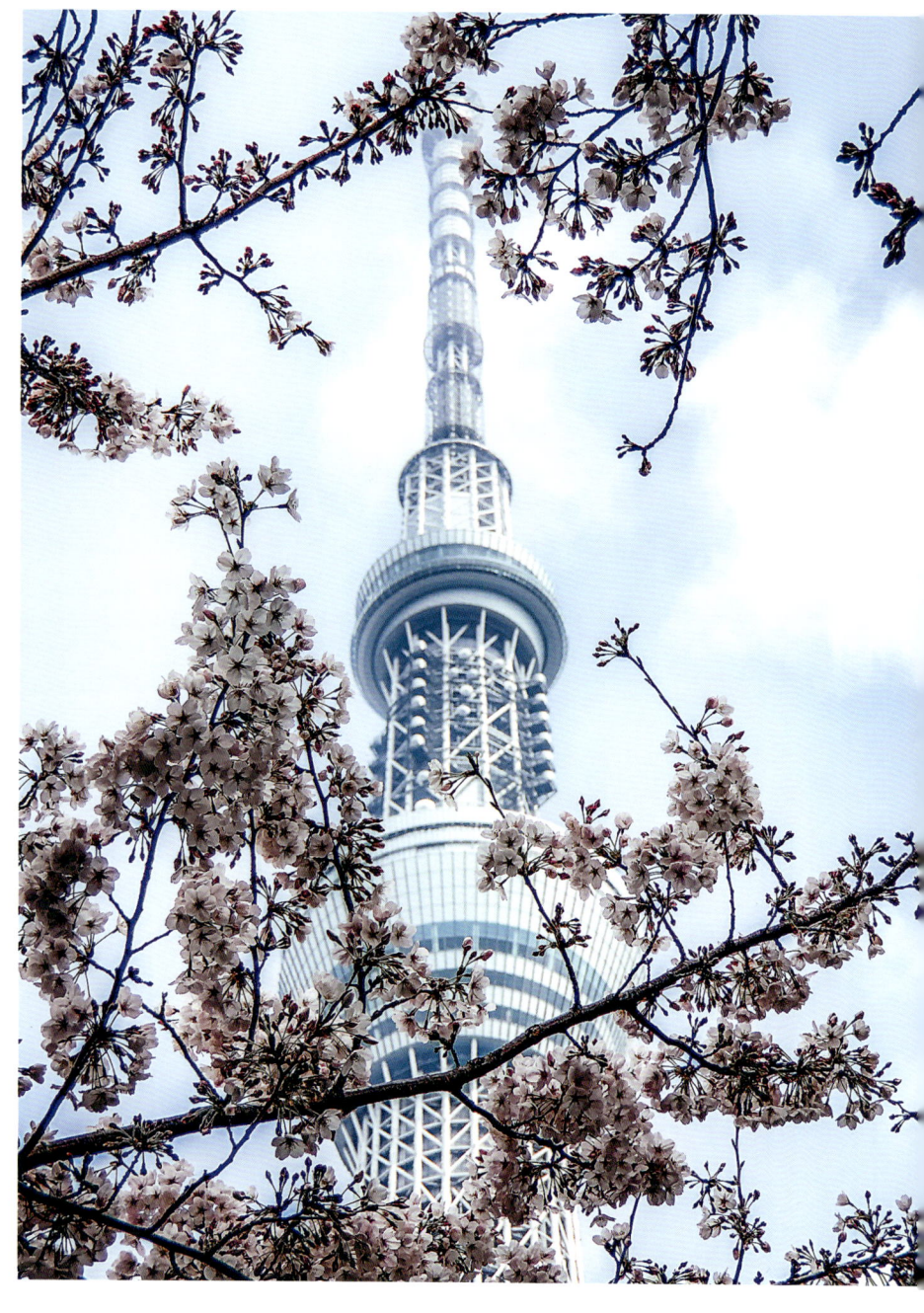

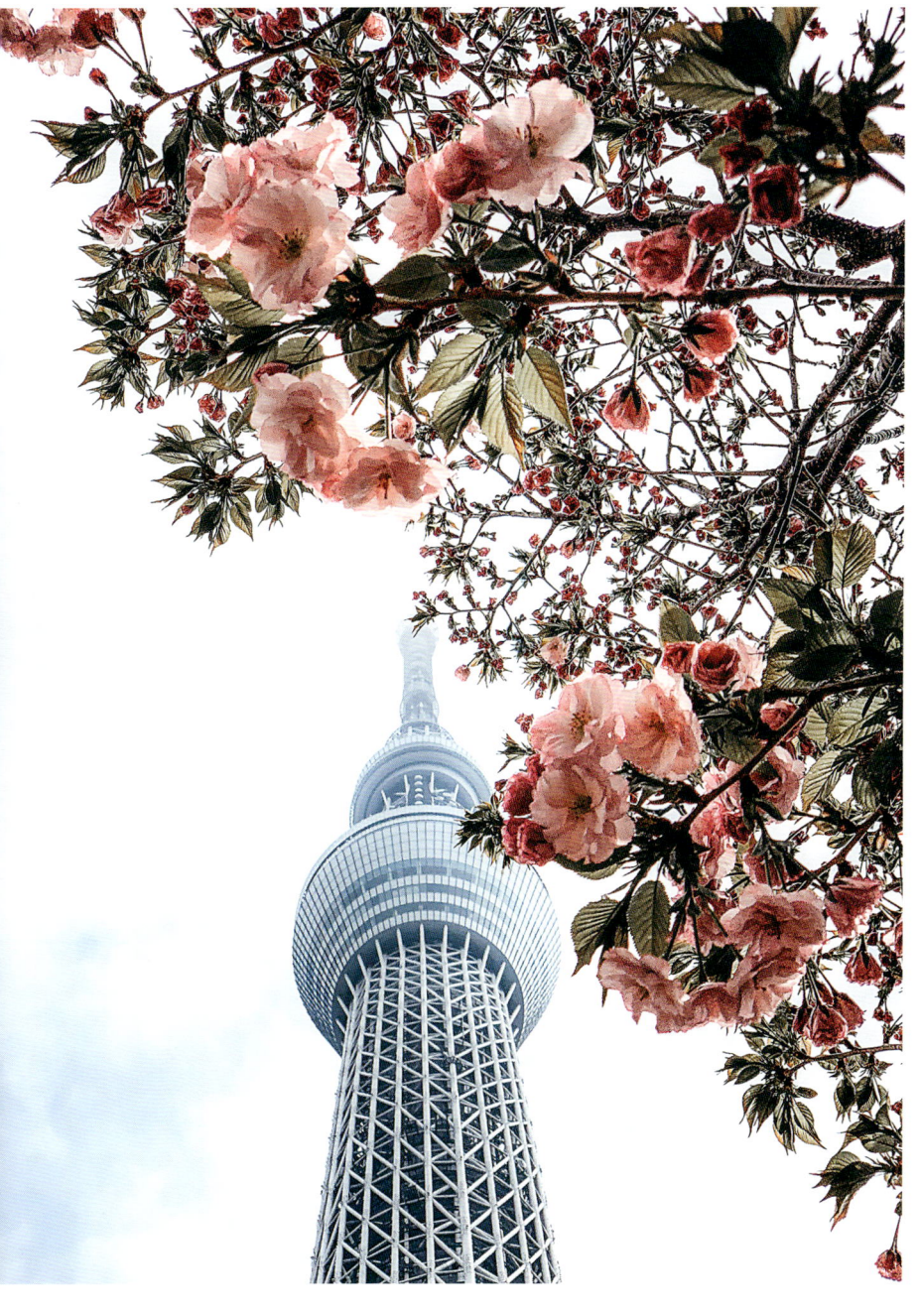

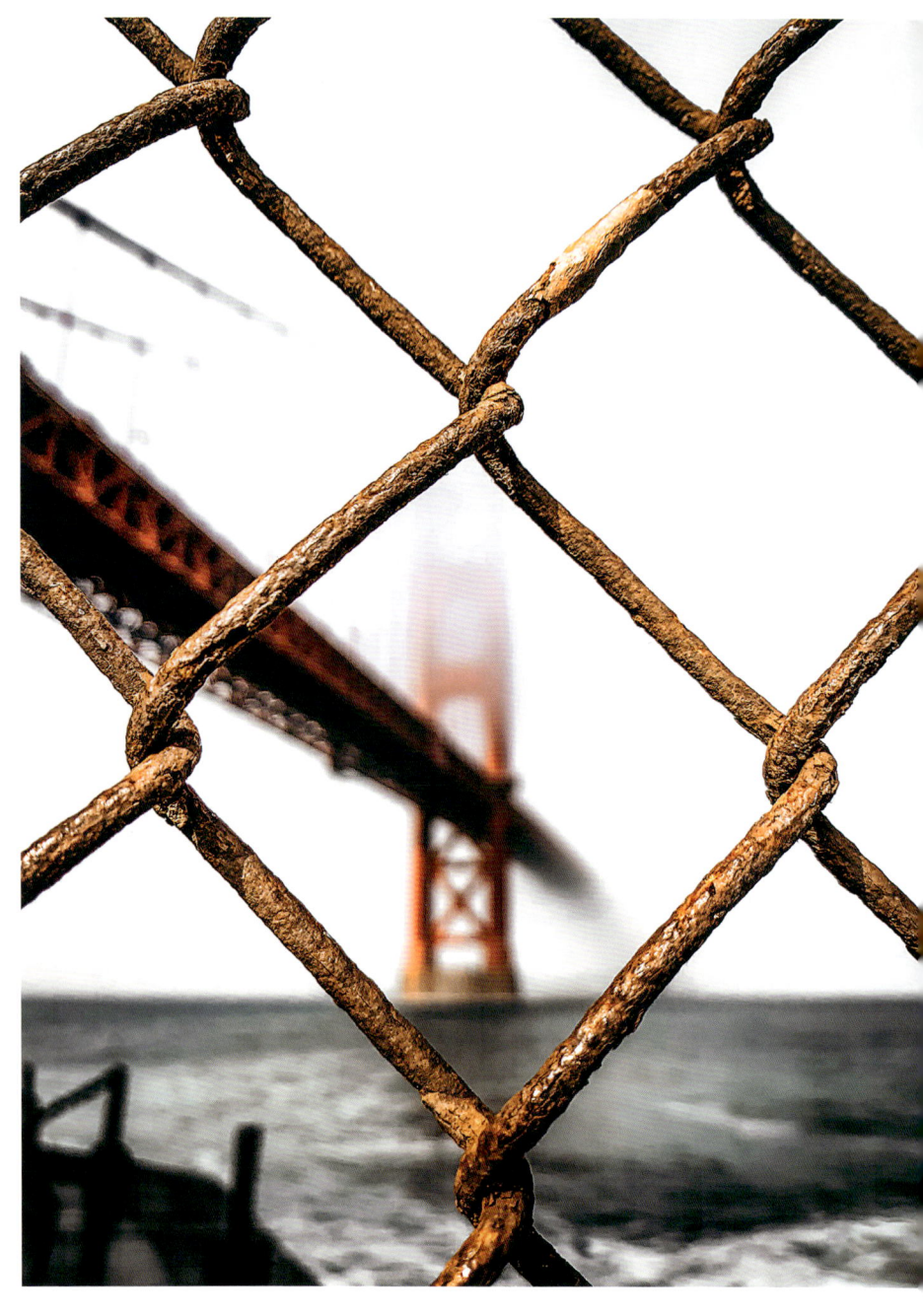

The iPhone 11 was all about more, better, faster. The two (or three, in the case of the Pro models) lenses had been redesigned to work together more smoothly, with radical improvements in image processing to match. The wide and telephoto lenses were more sensitive to light, with much faster minimum exposure speed.

Shadows were clean, not muddy, even at sunset. I could capture details on a rusty fence or perfect cloud trails with equal sharpness. Great optical stabilization means I can shoot on the fly, even while walking, without getting blurry shots, something I really appreciate when I'm on the hunt for new and unusual street scenes. Finally having a built-in ultrawide lens opened up new angles and perspectives. I have a particular fondness for finding spiral staircases when I travel; the wide angle finally let me do them justice with a mobile camera.

Admittedly, as mobile cameras continue to get better and better, the limitations that I enjoyed working around in the early days are falling away. It's no longer an "inferior" tool, just a different - and no less fascinating - one.

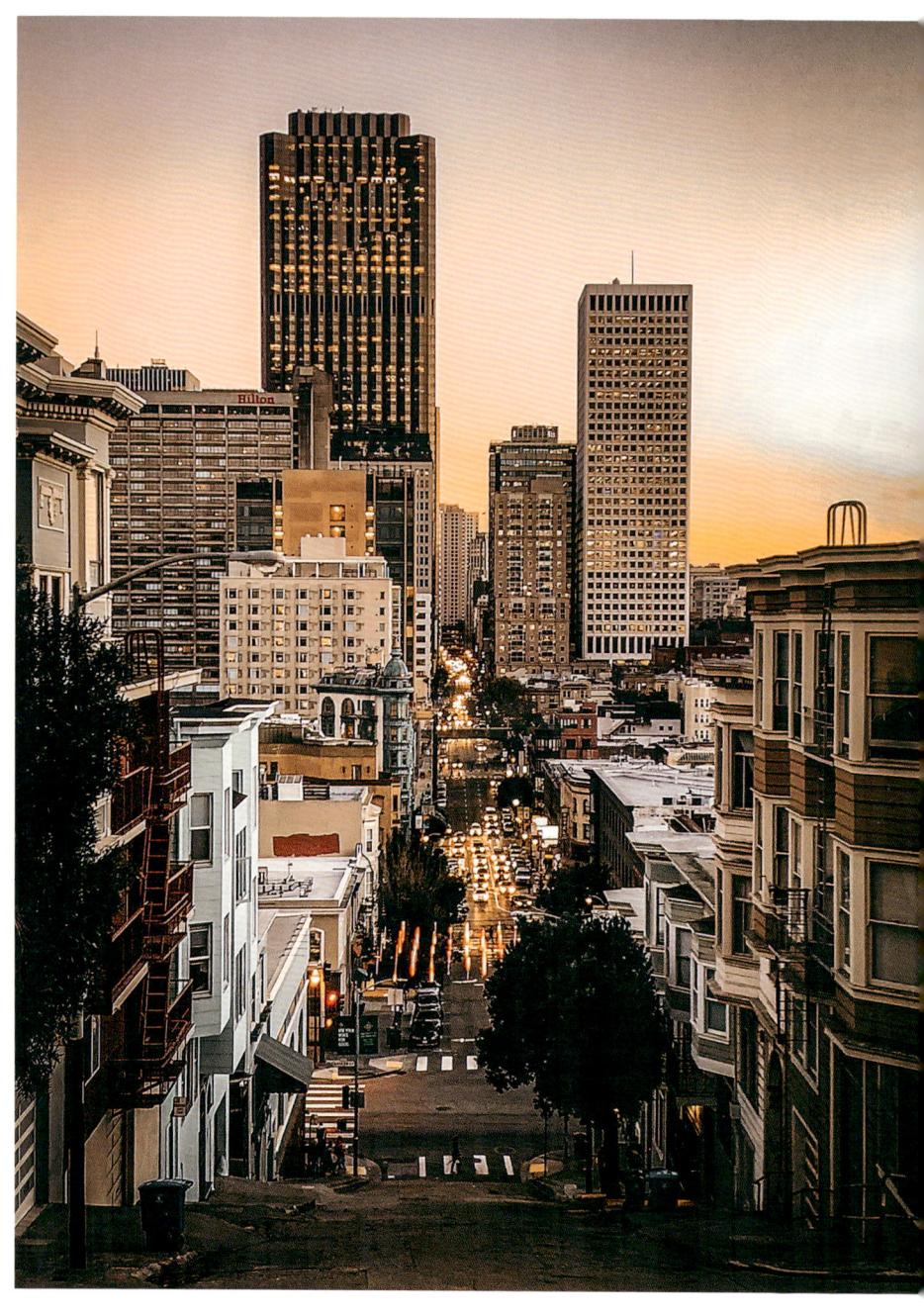

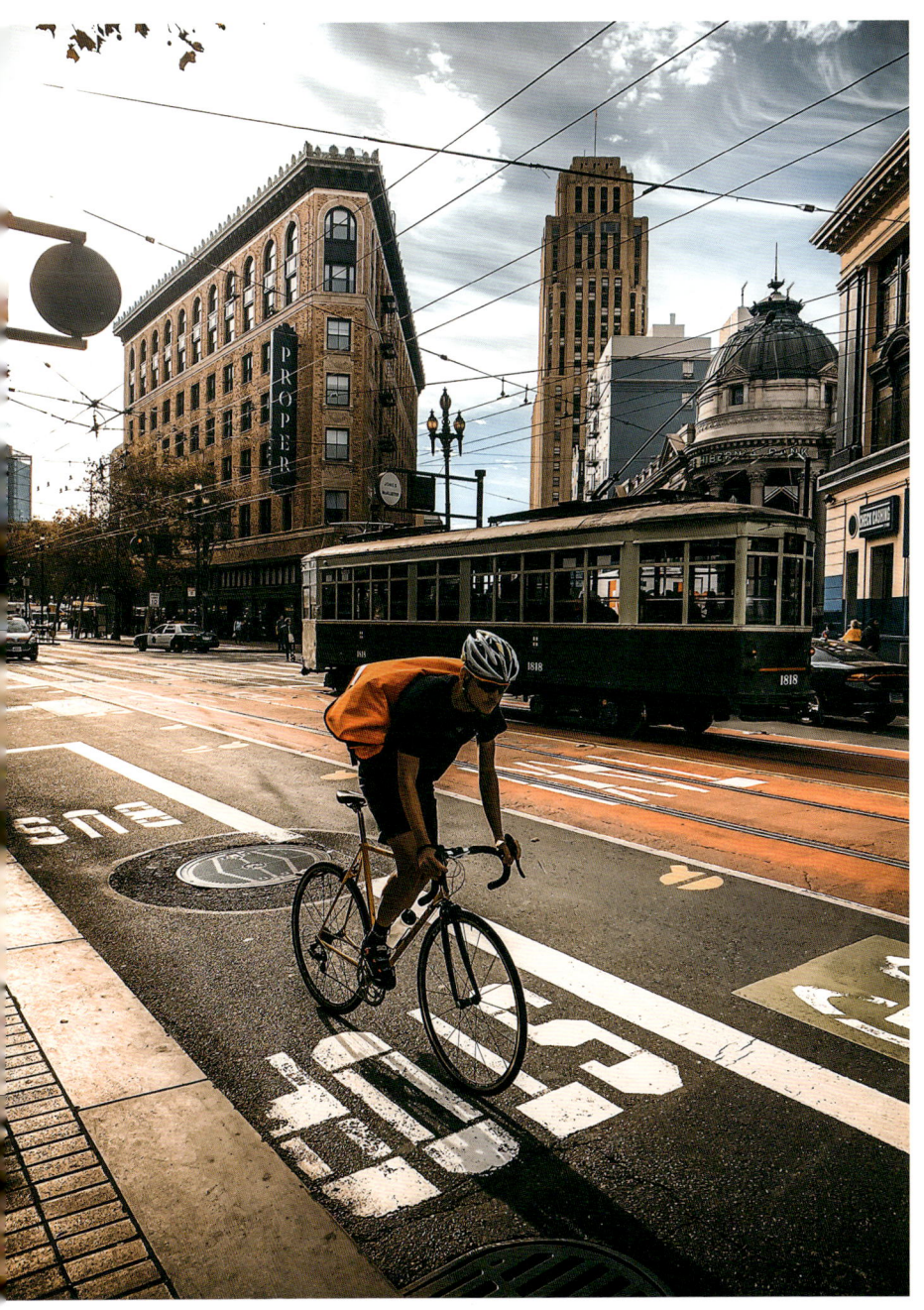

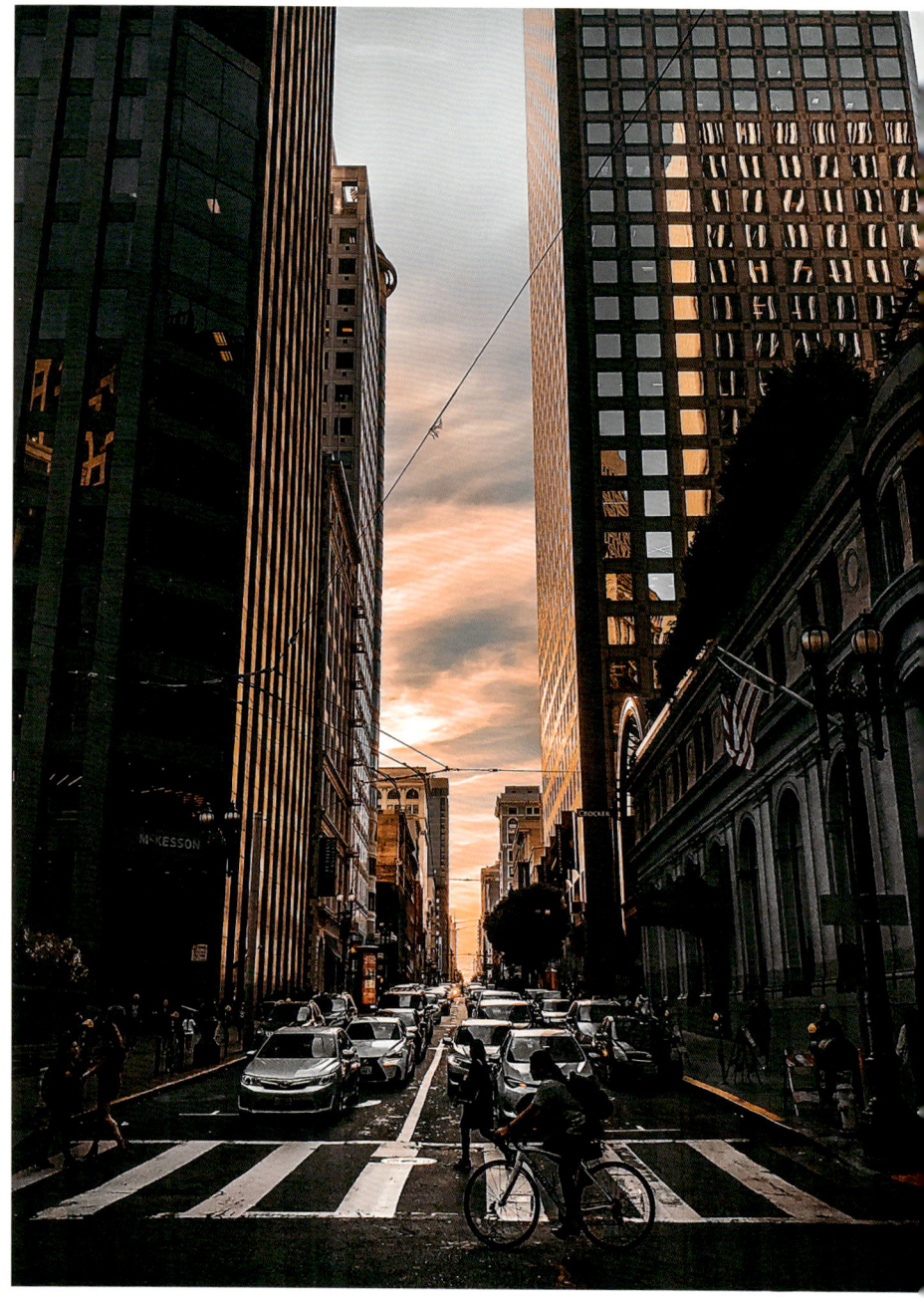

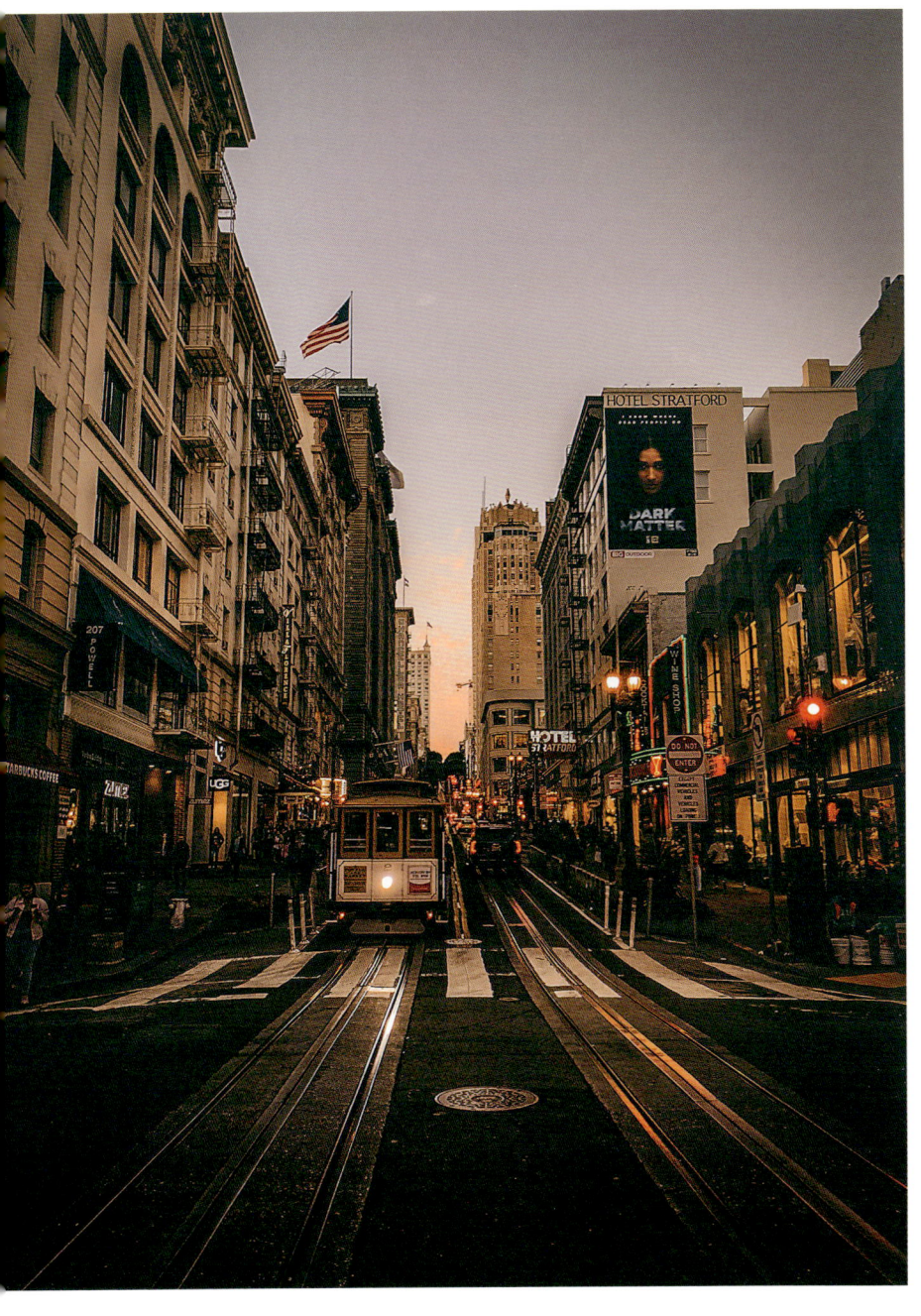

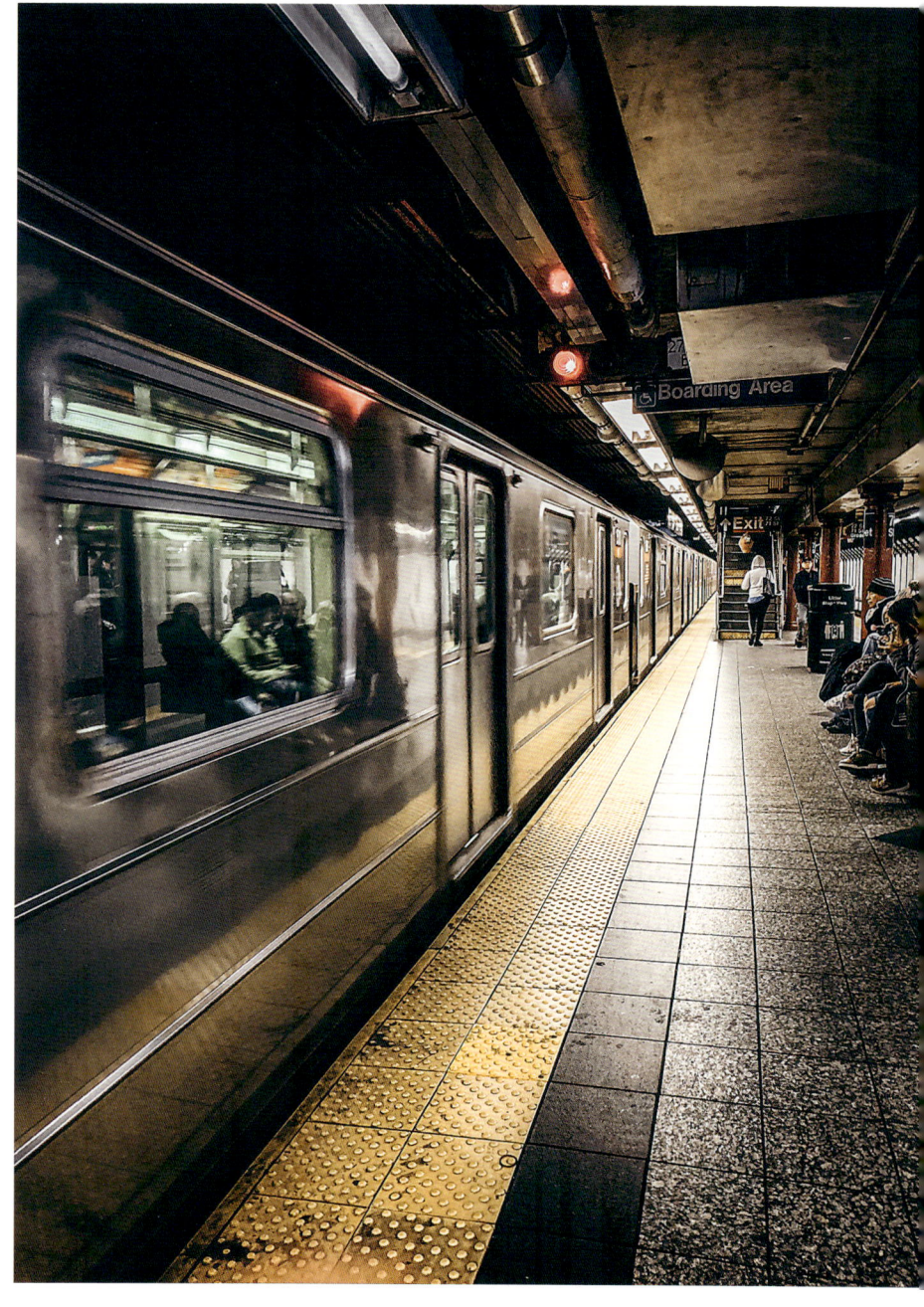

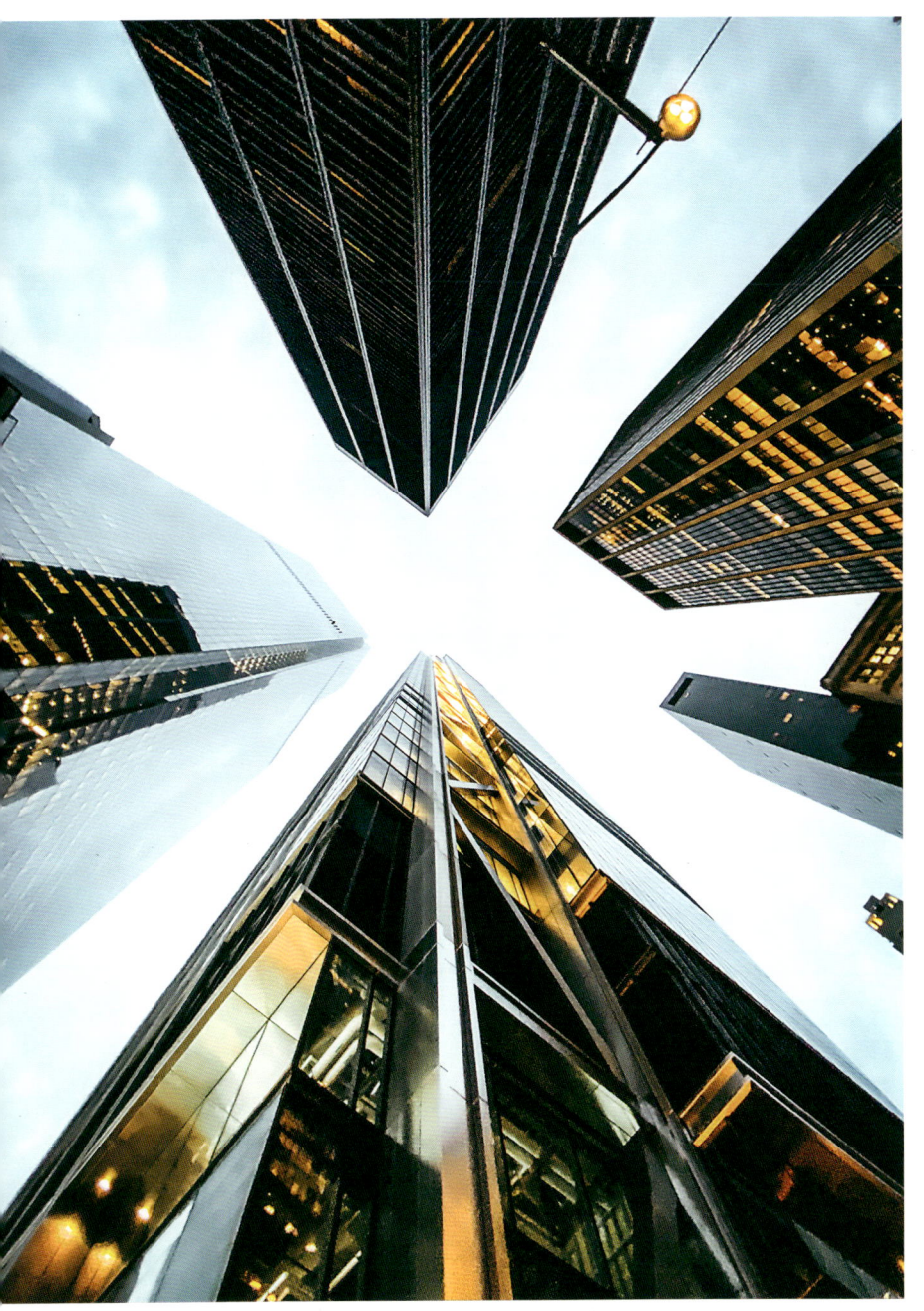

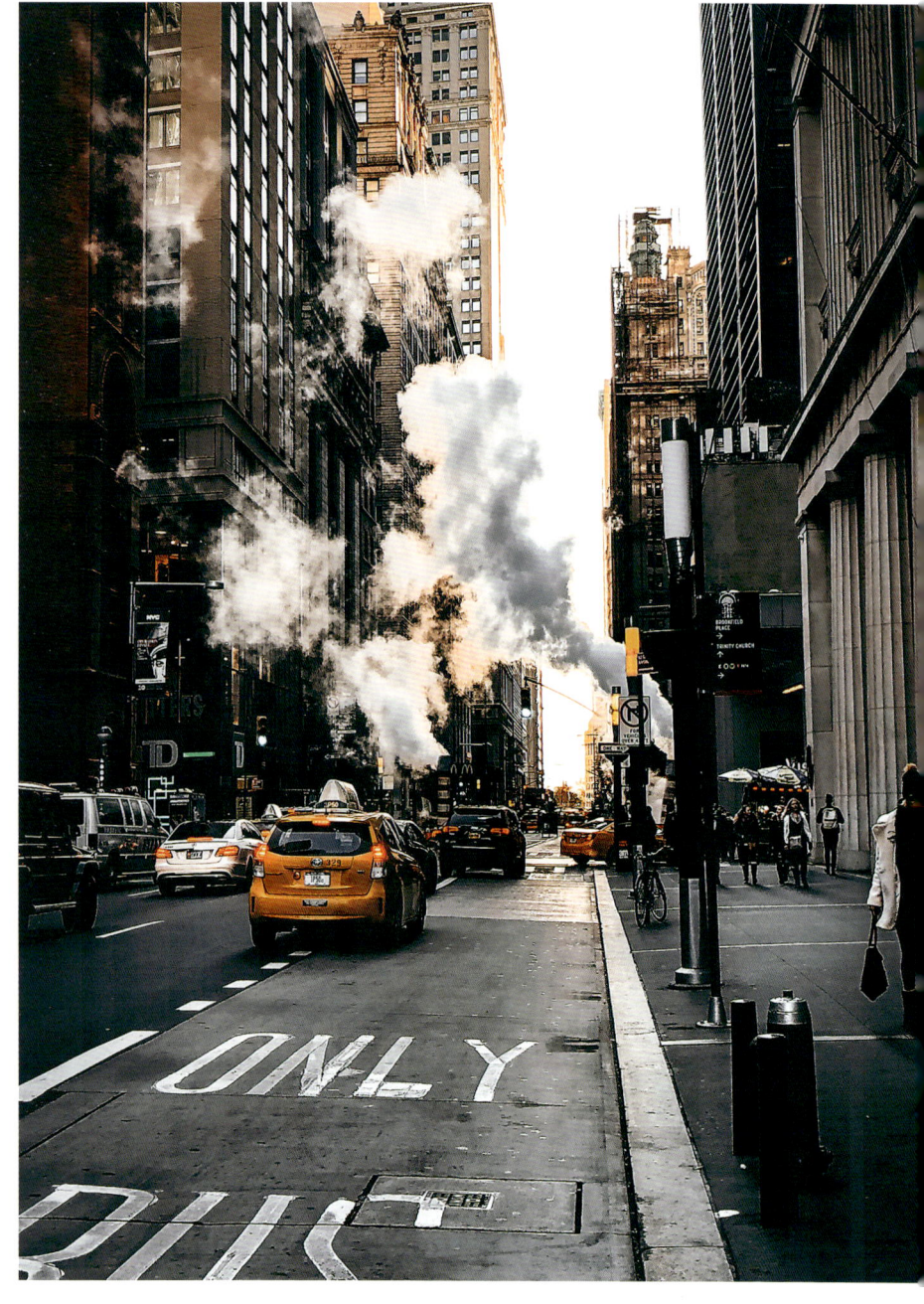

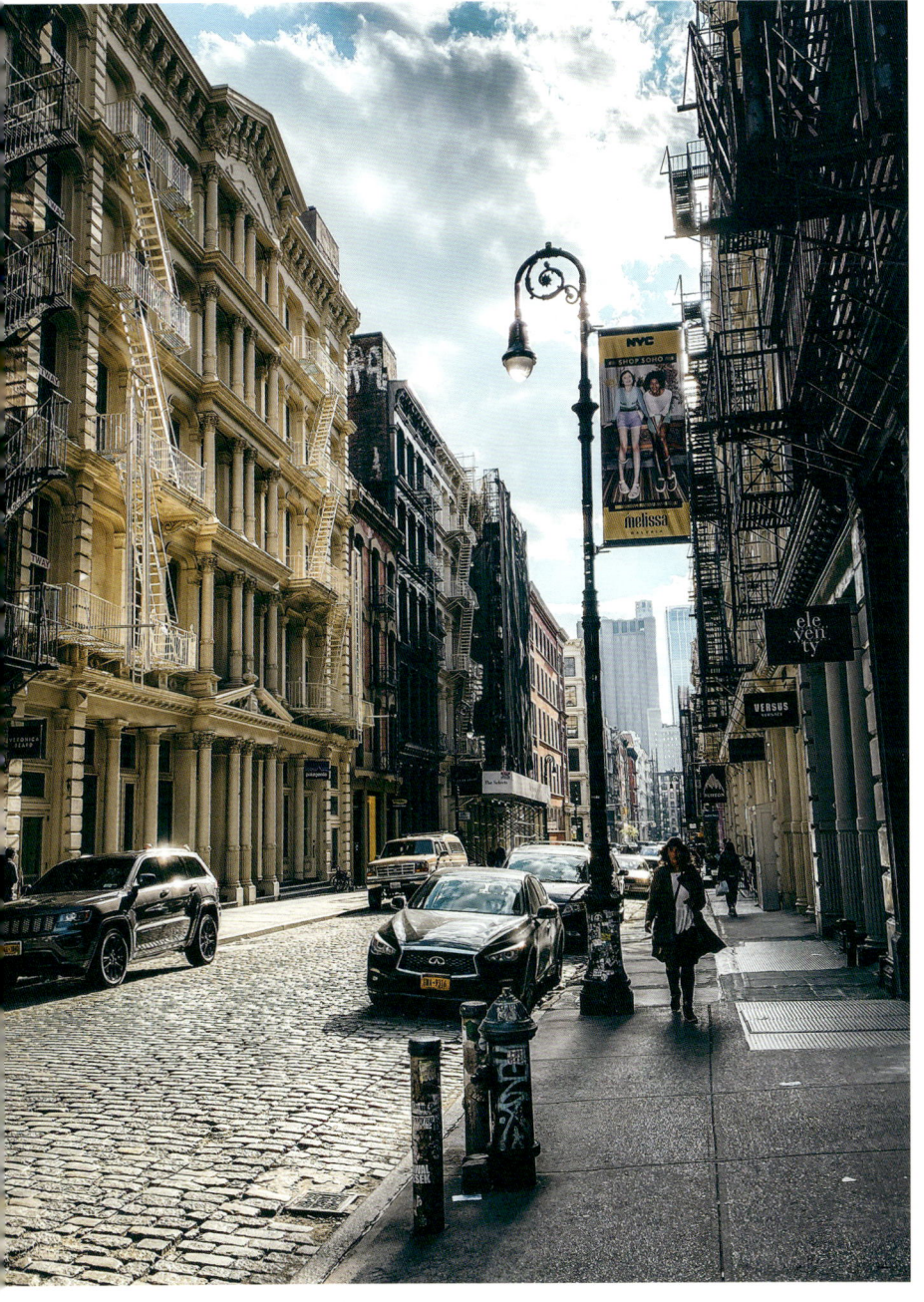

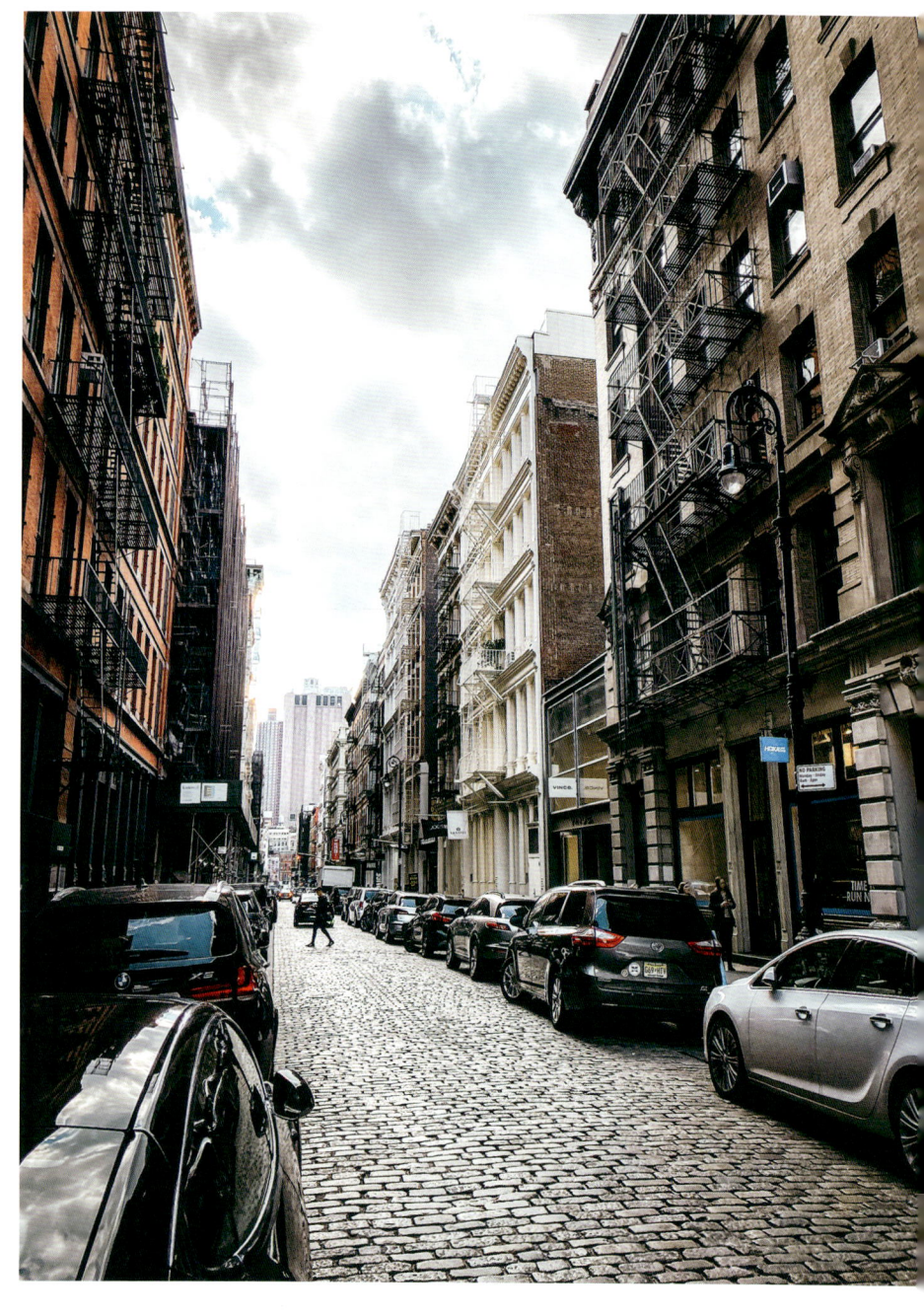

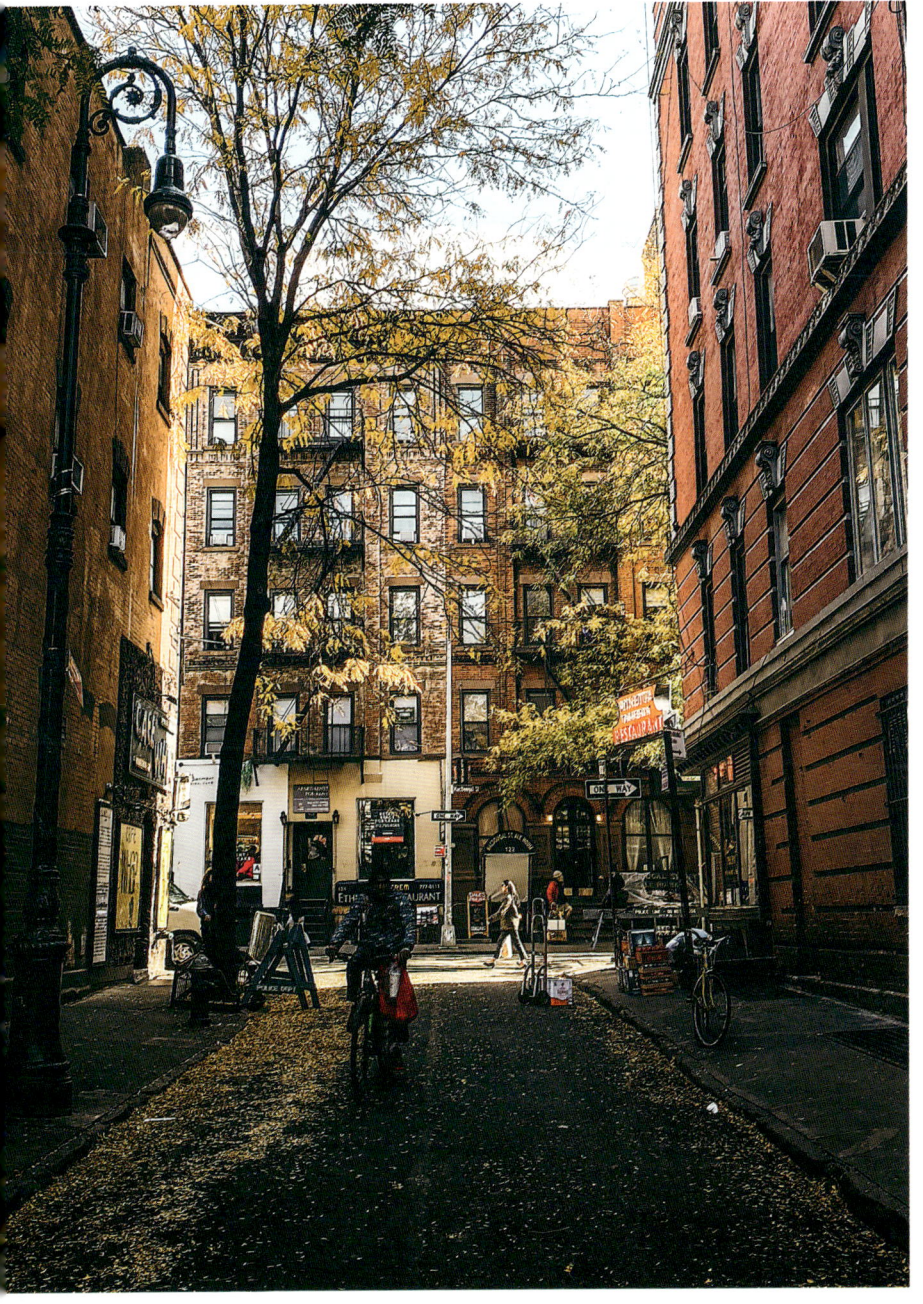

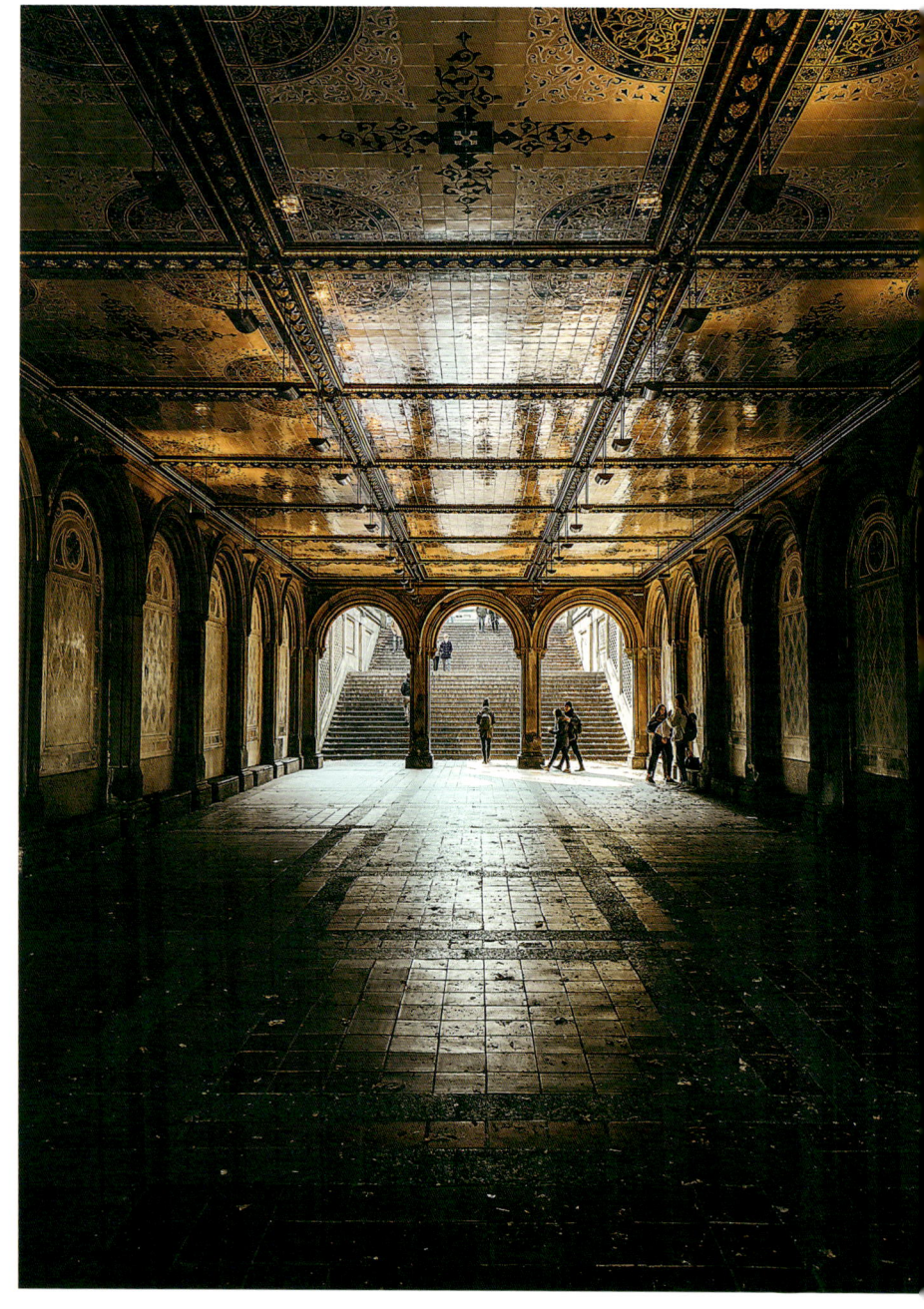

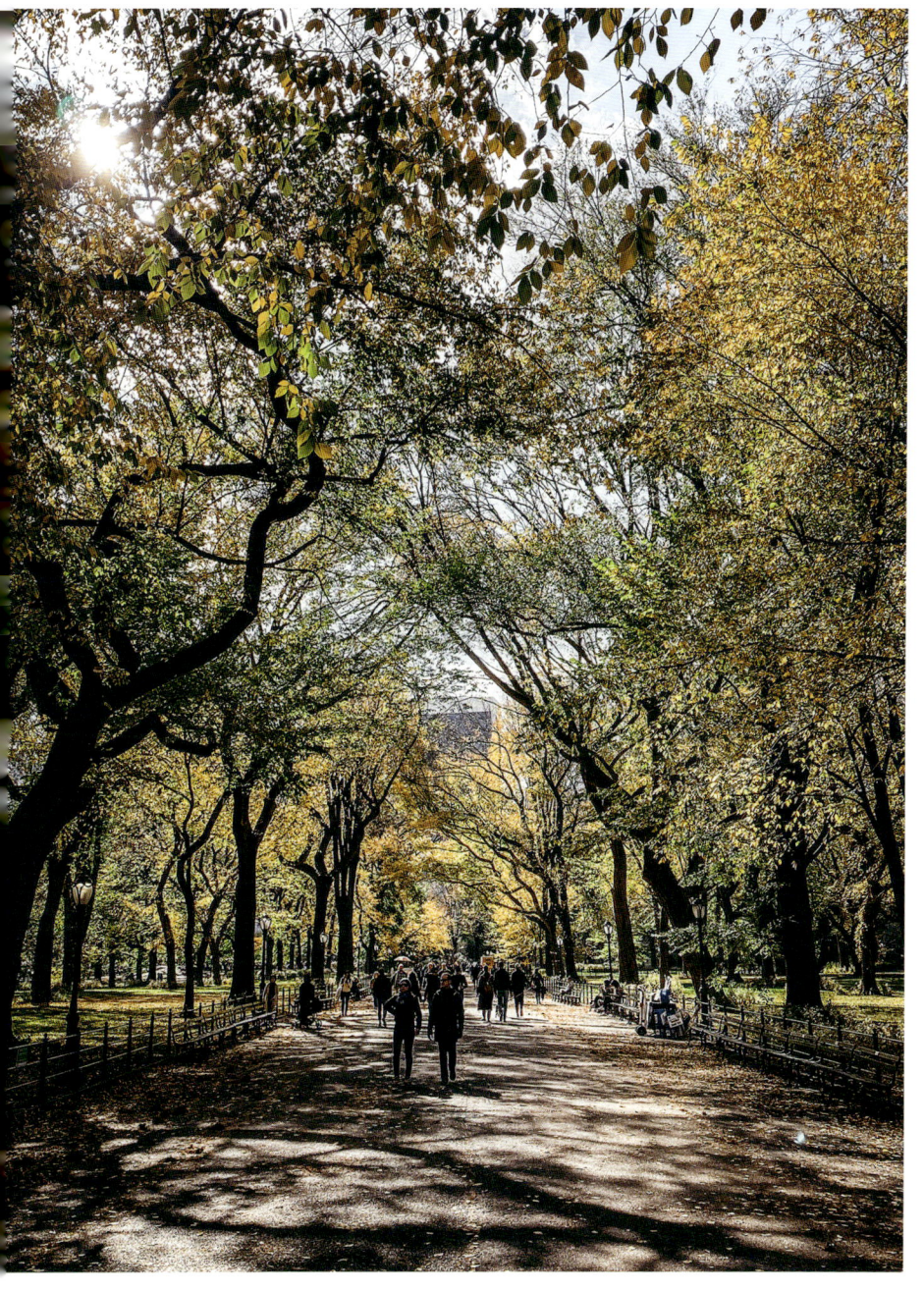

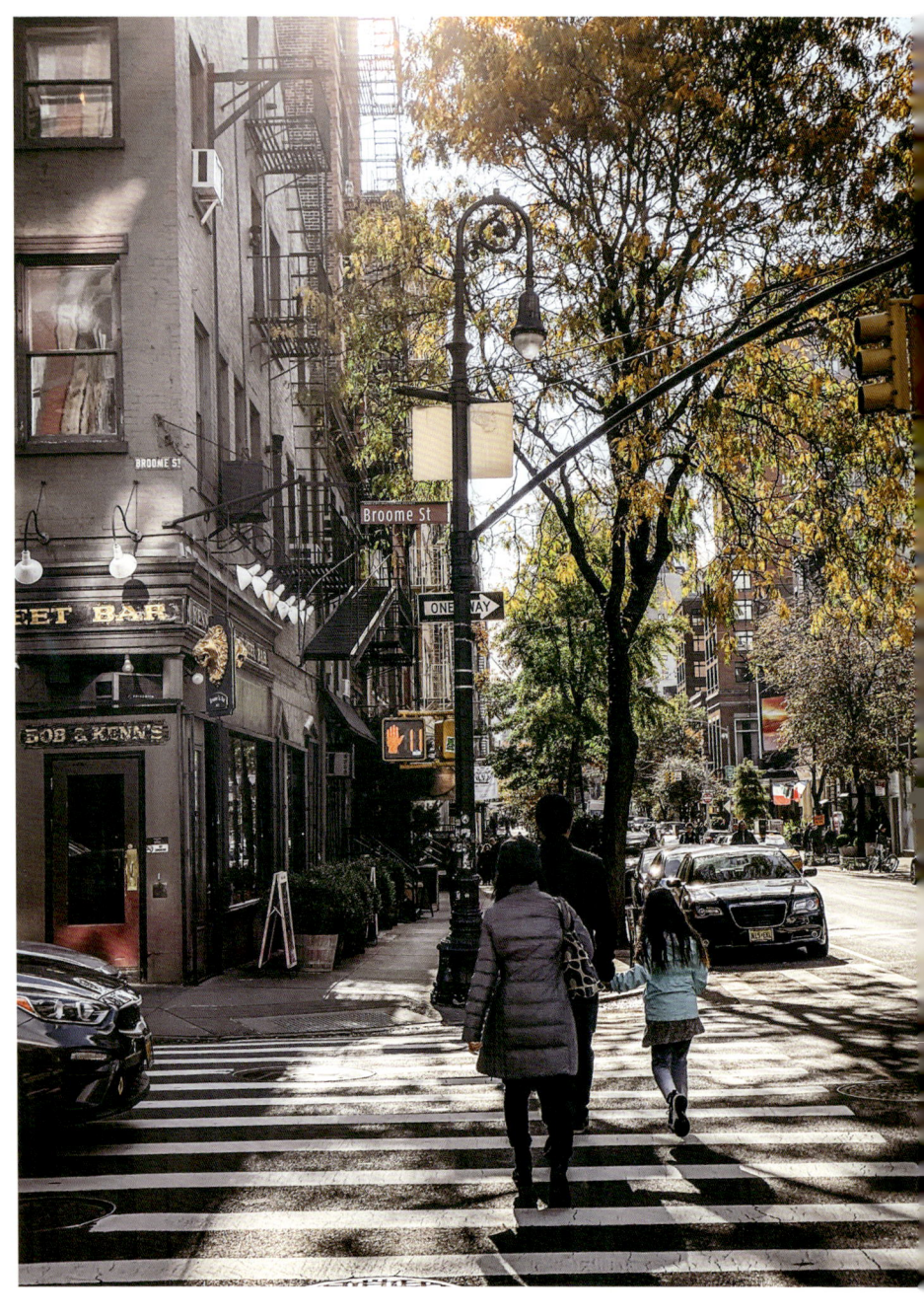

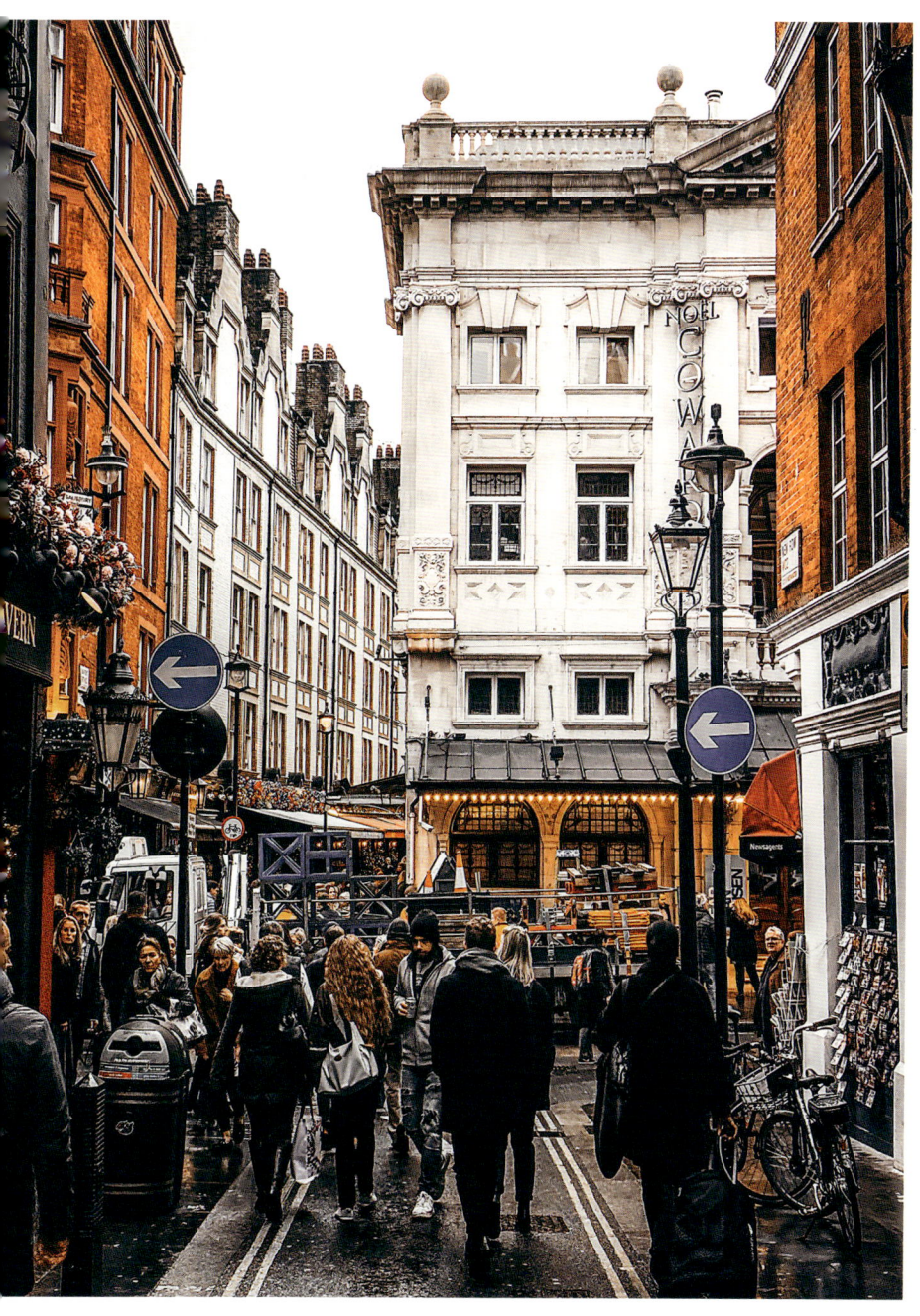

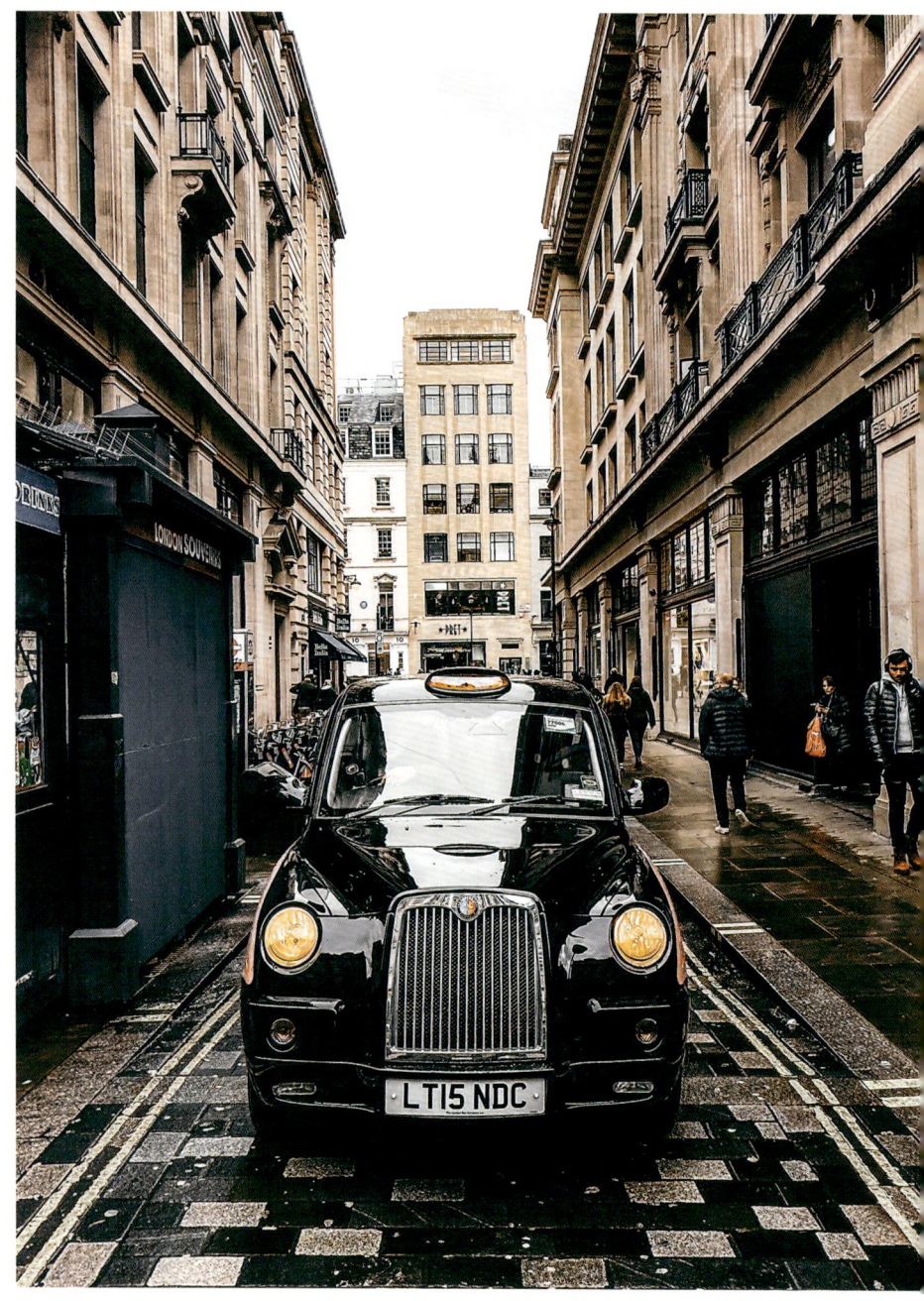

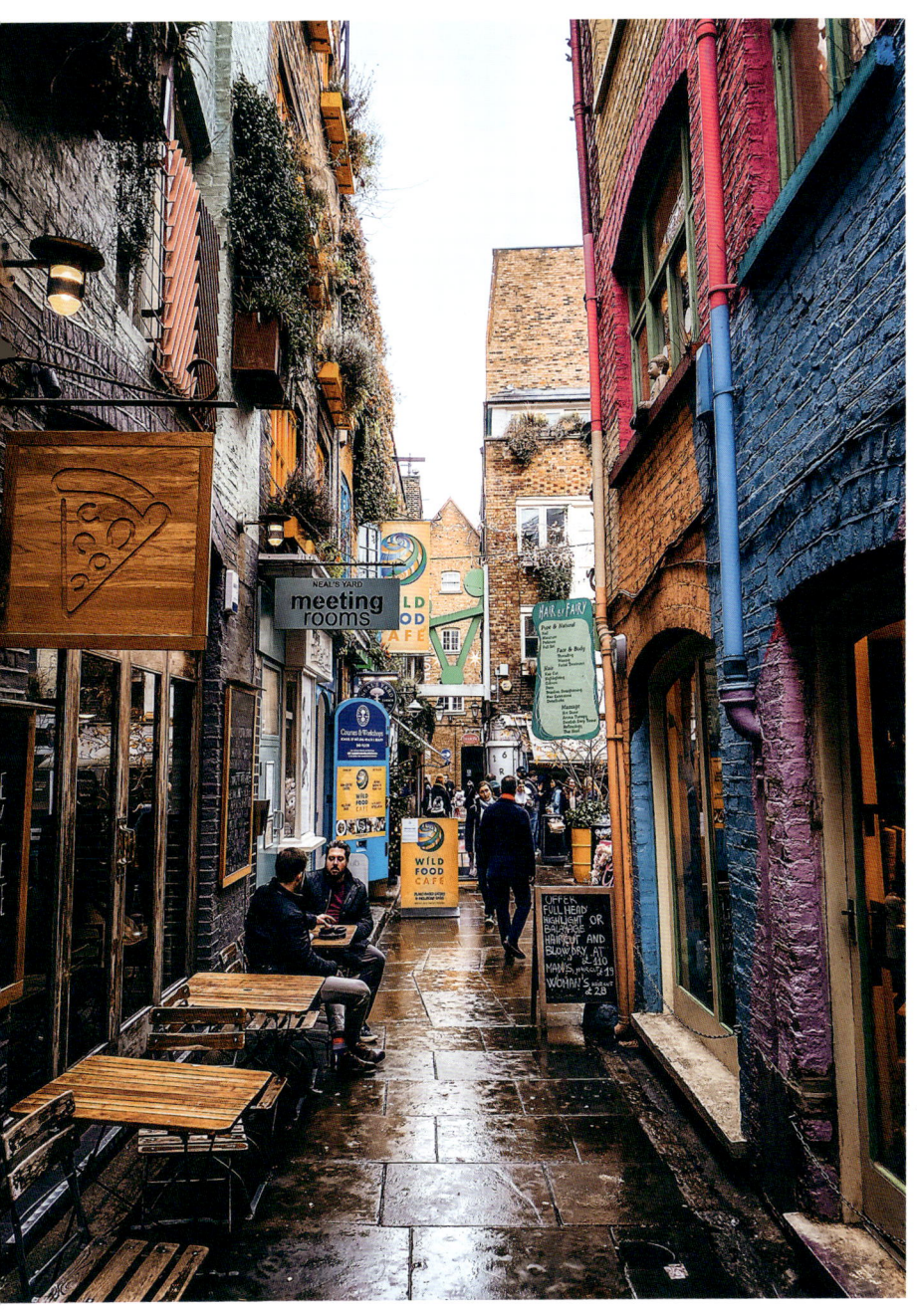

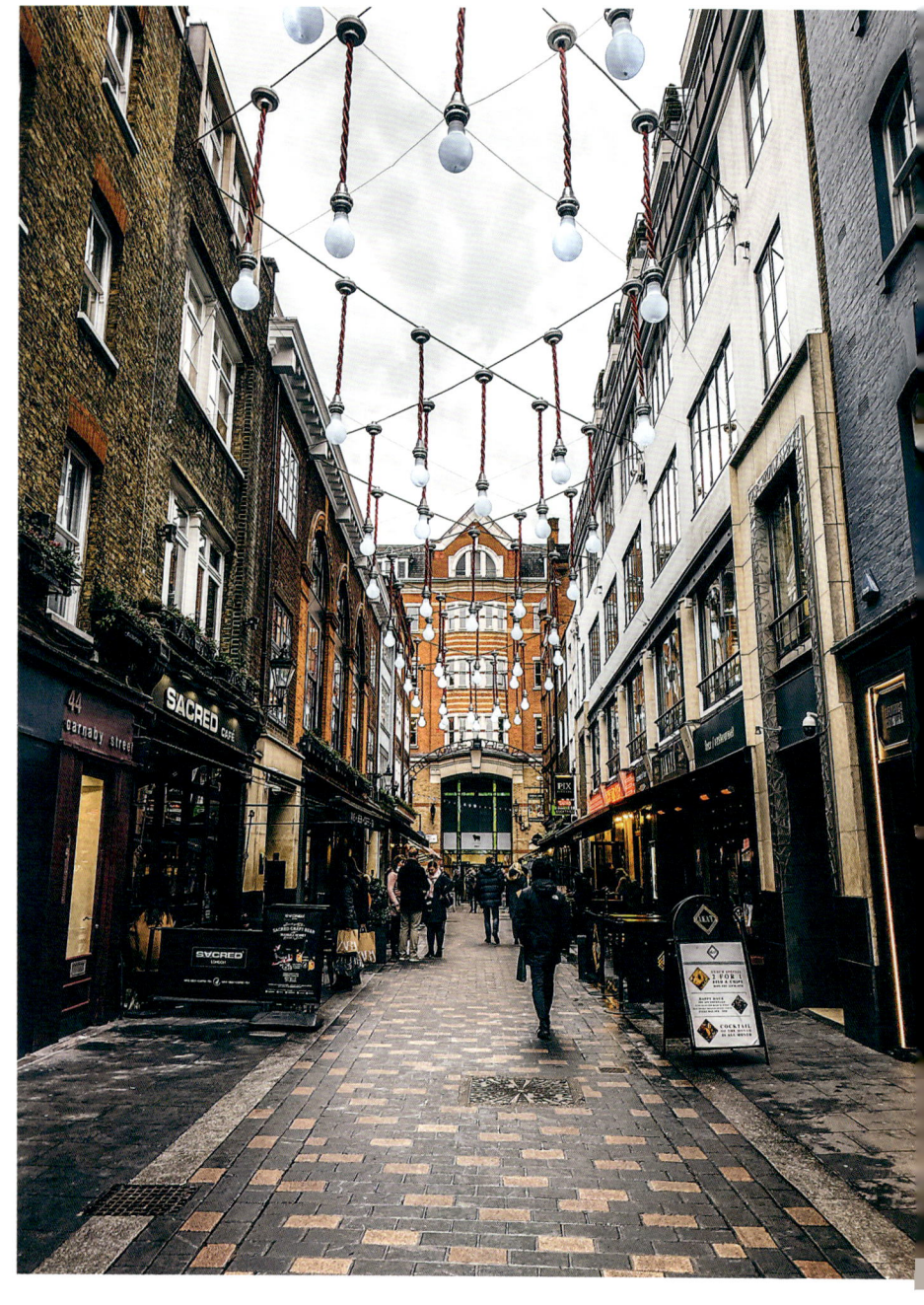

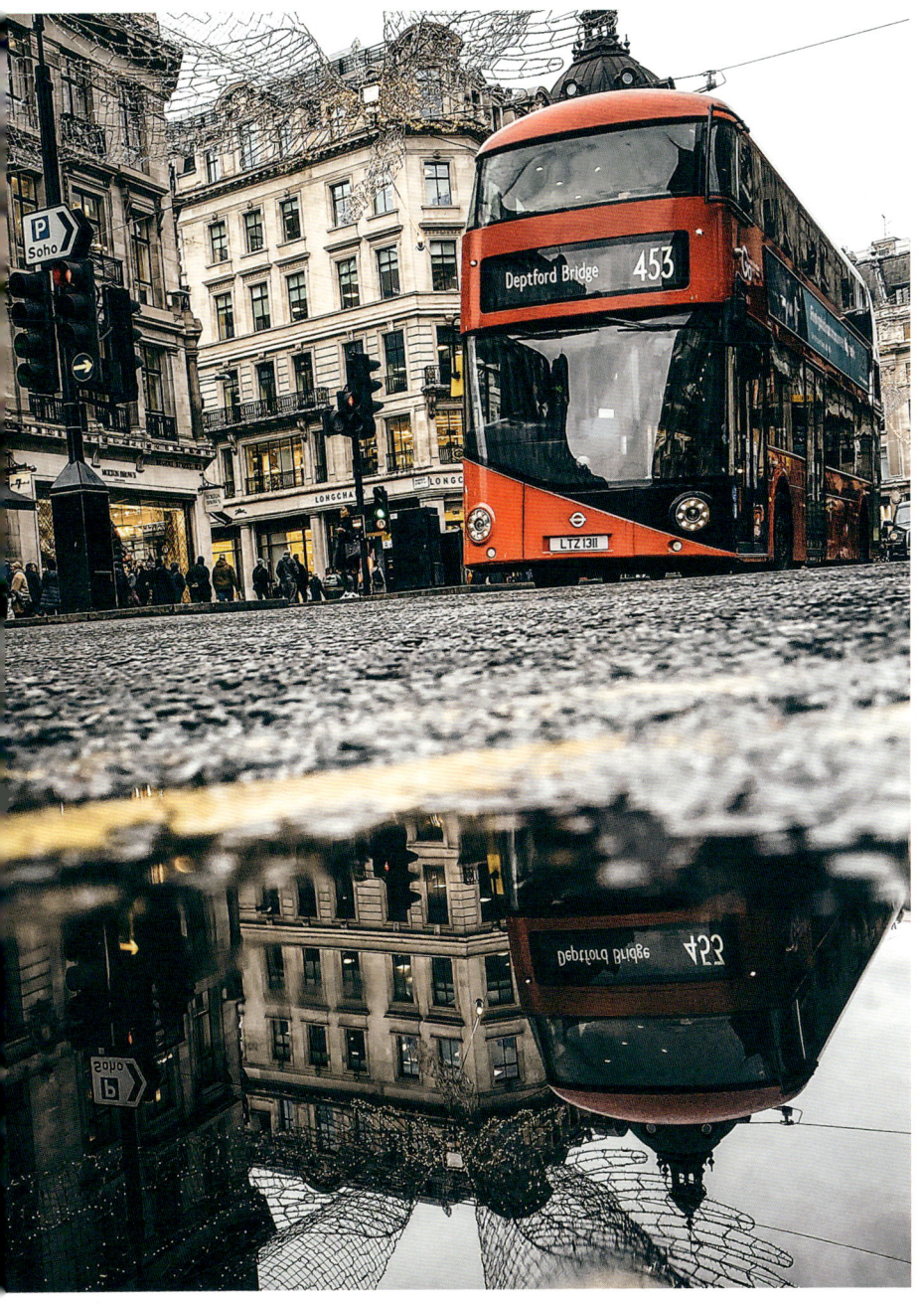

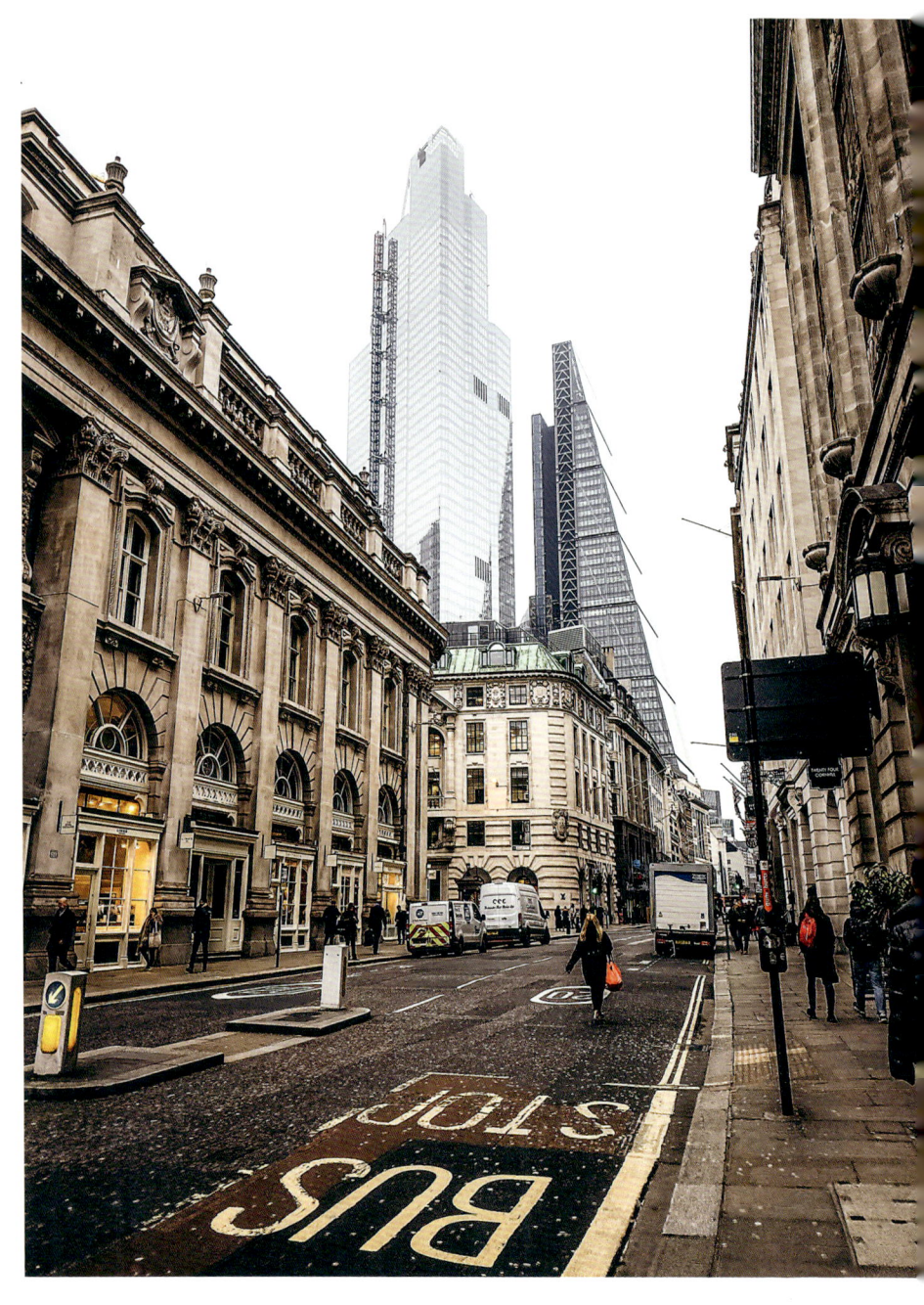

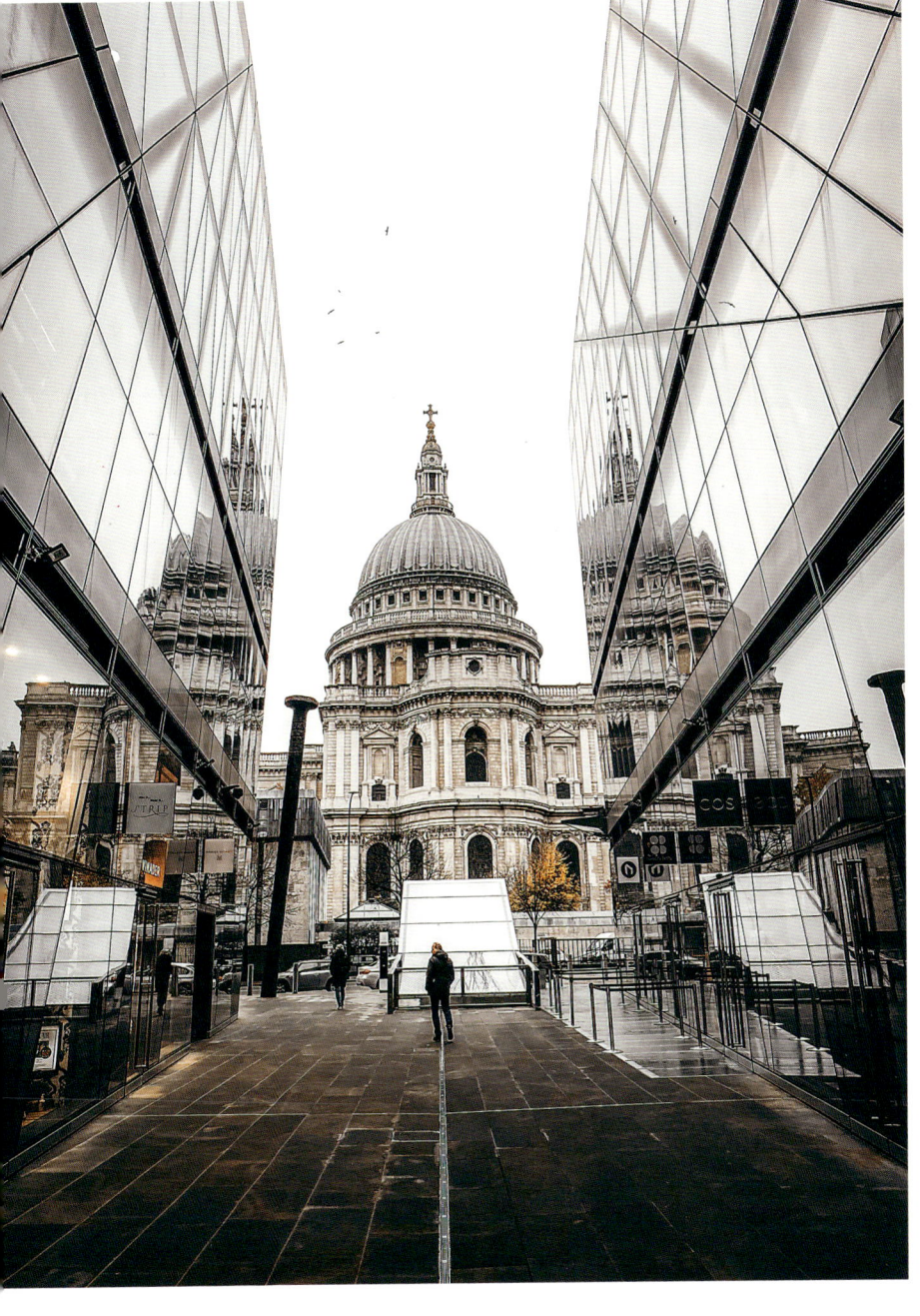

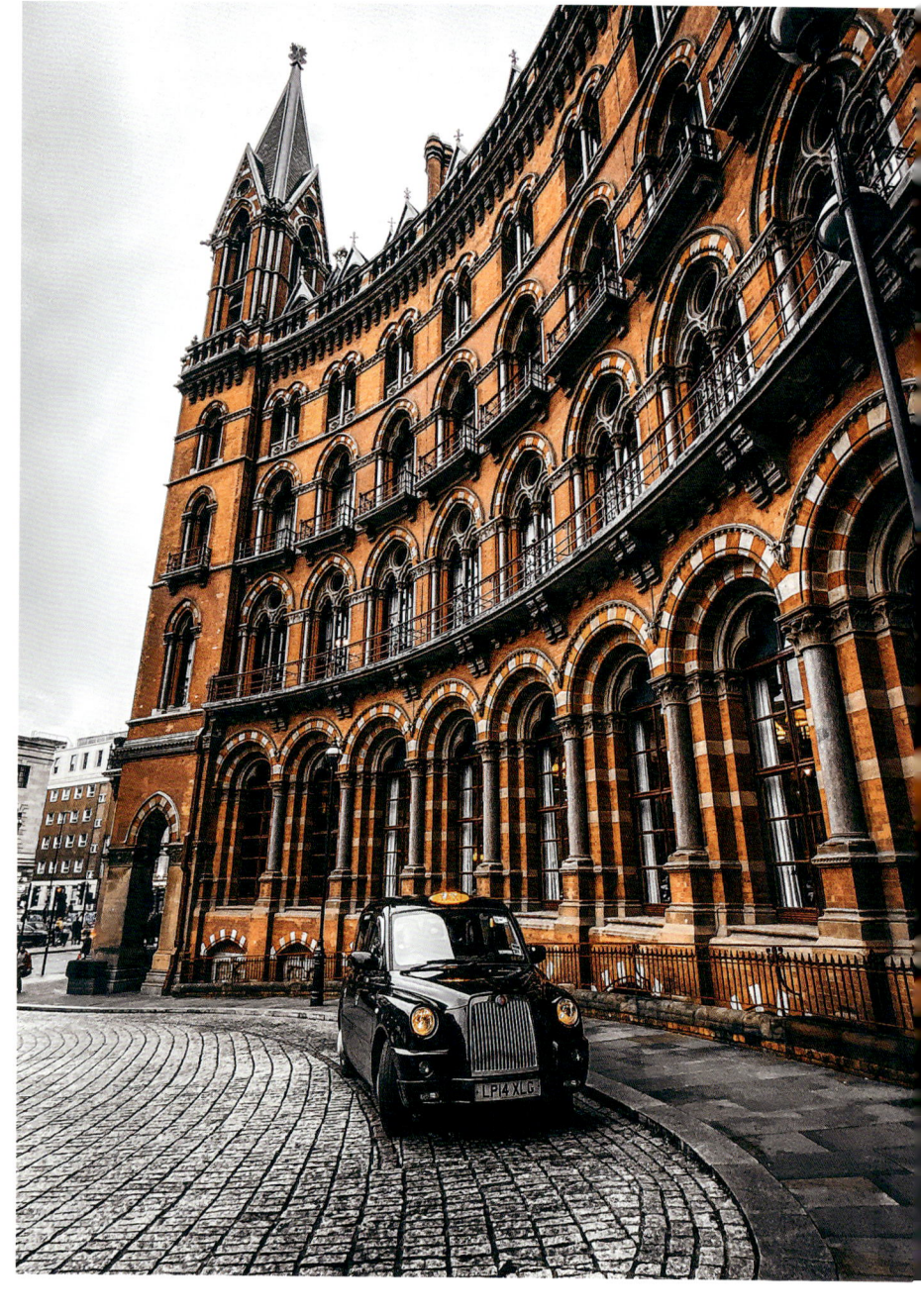

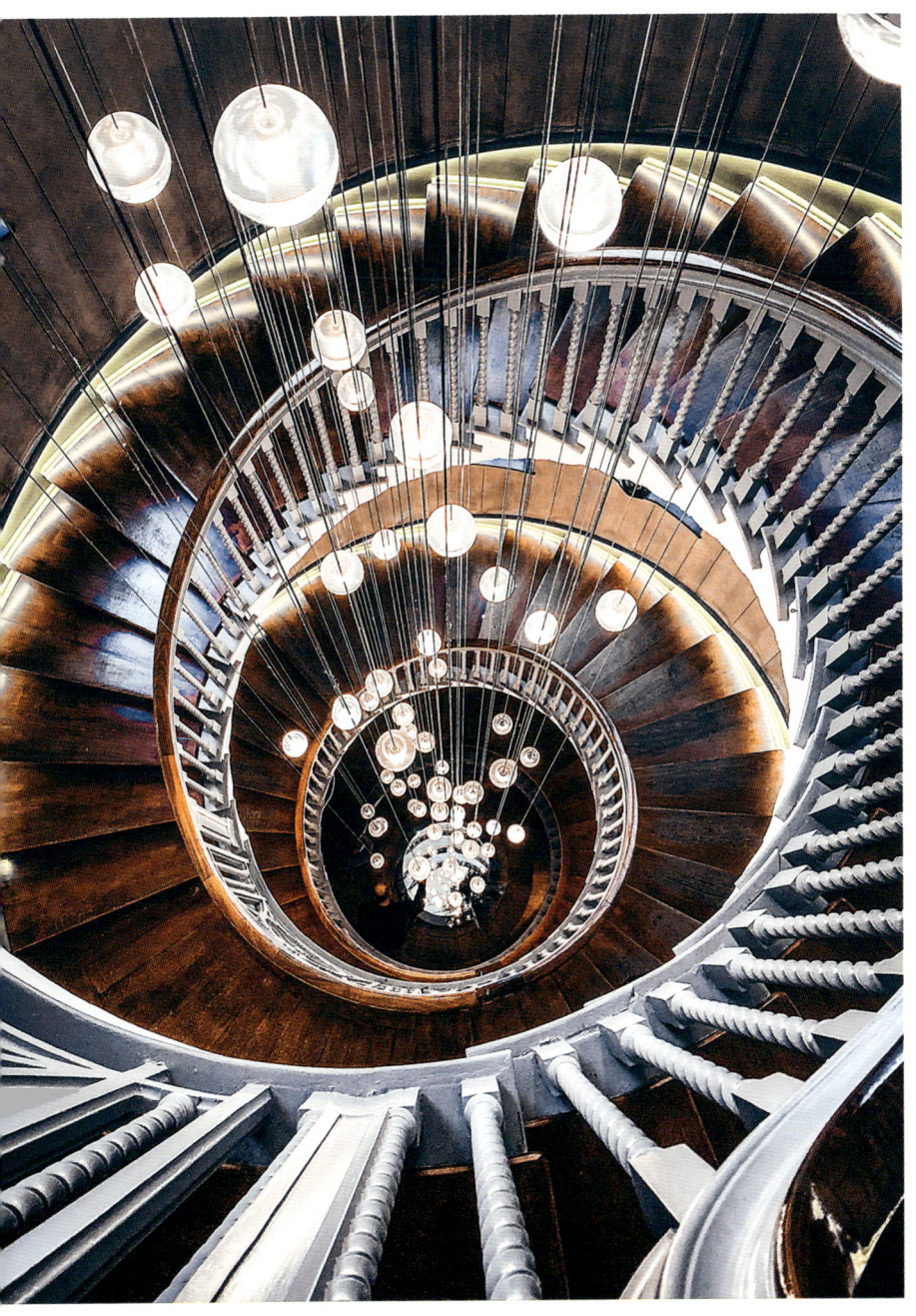

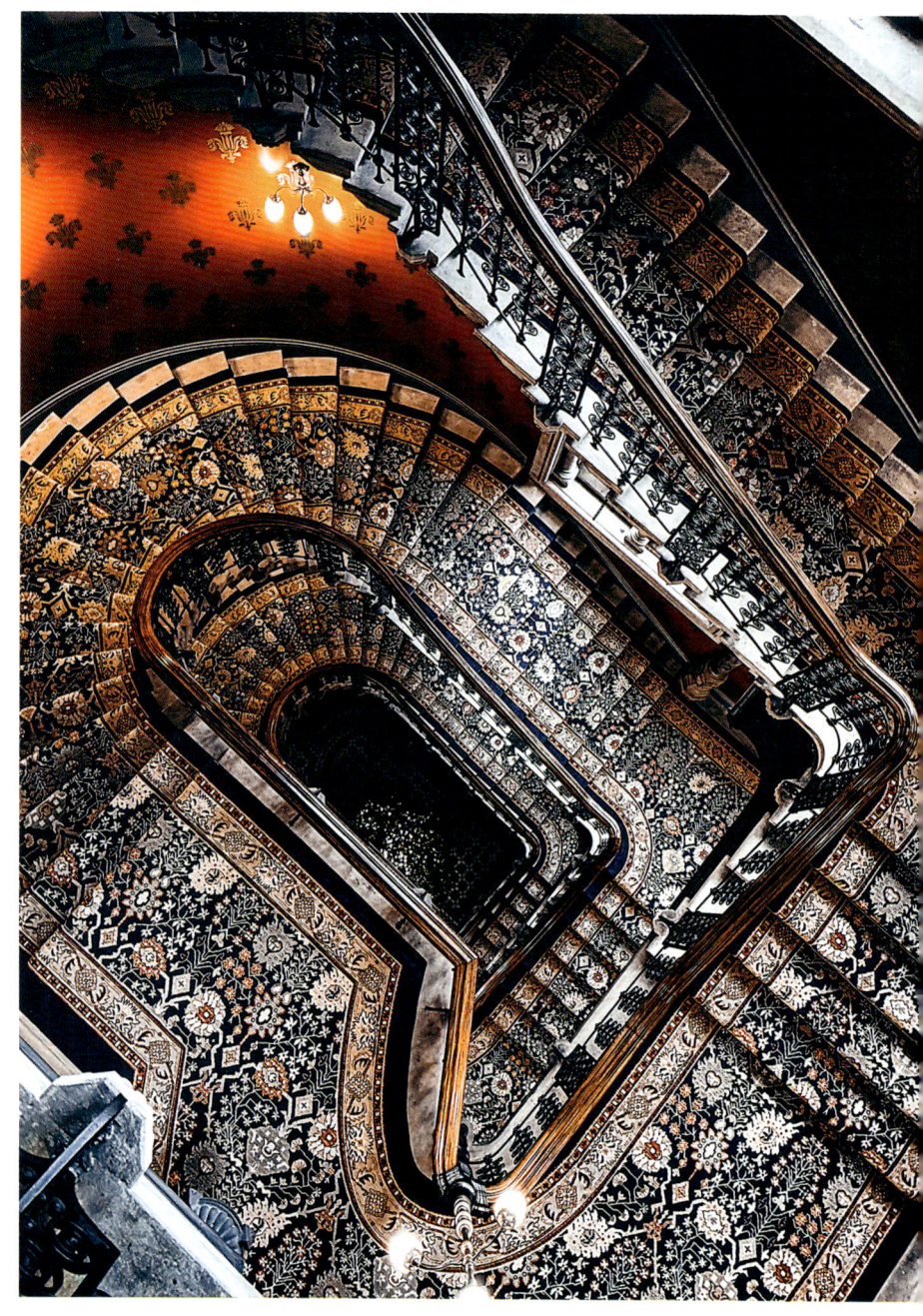

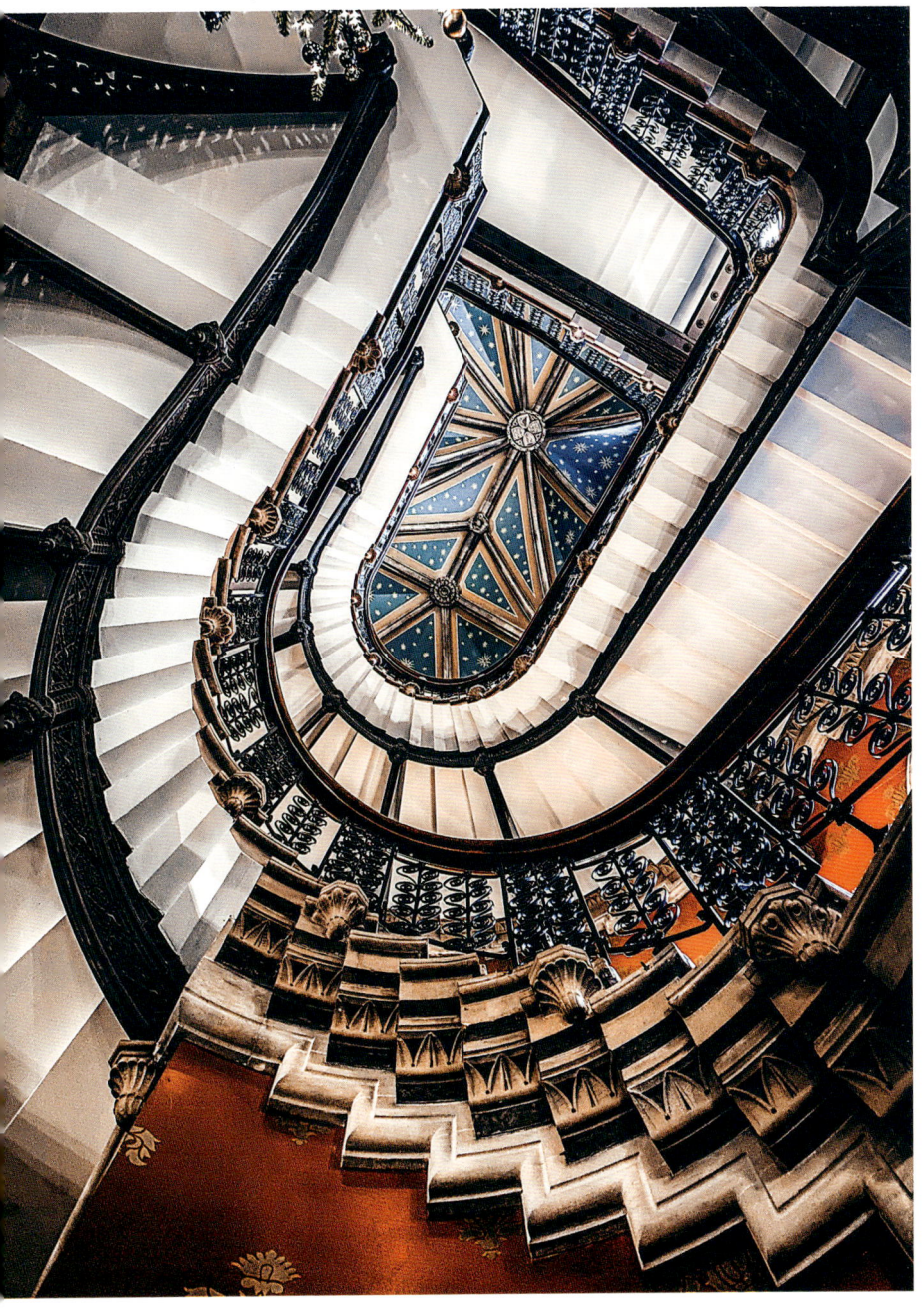

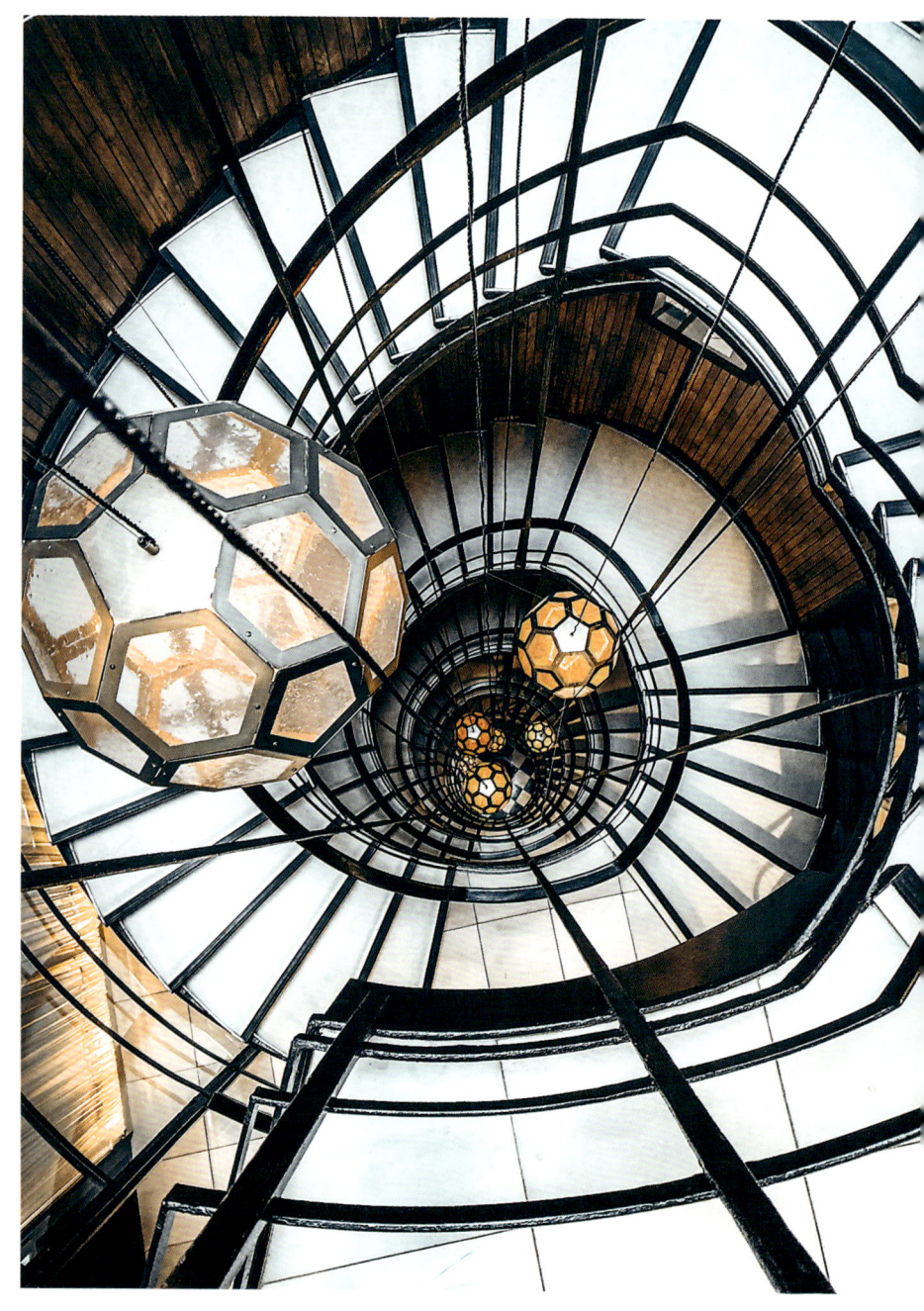

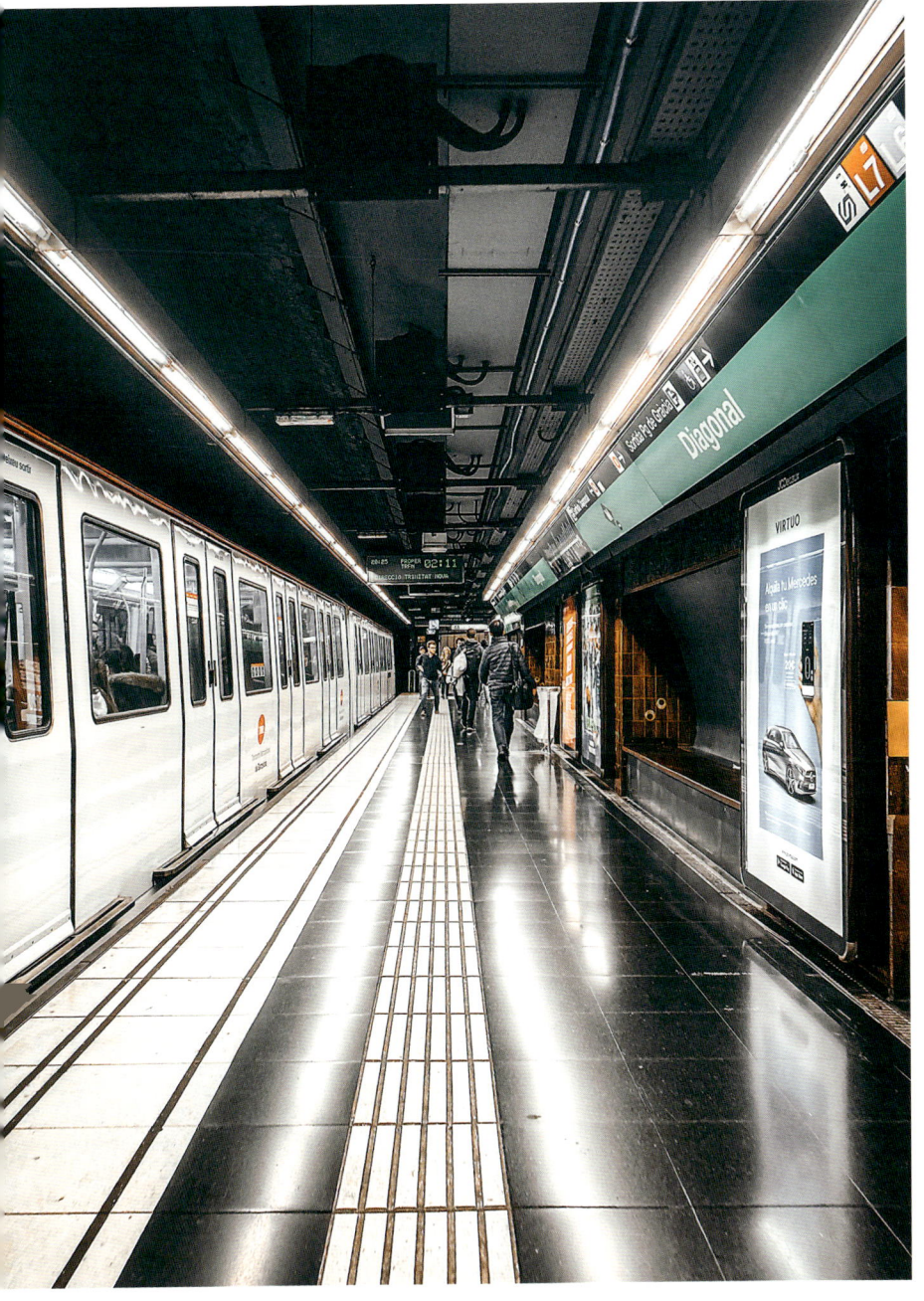

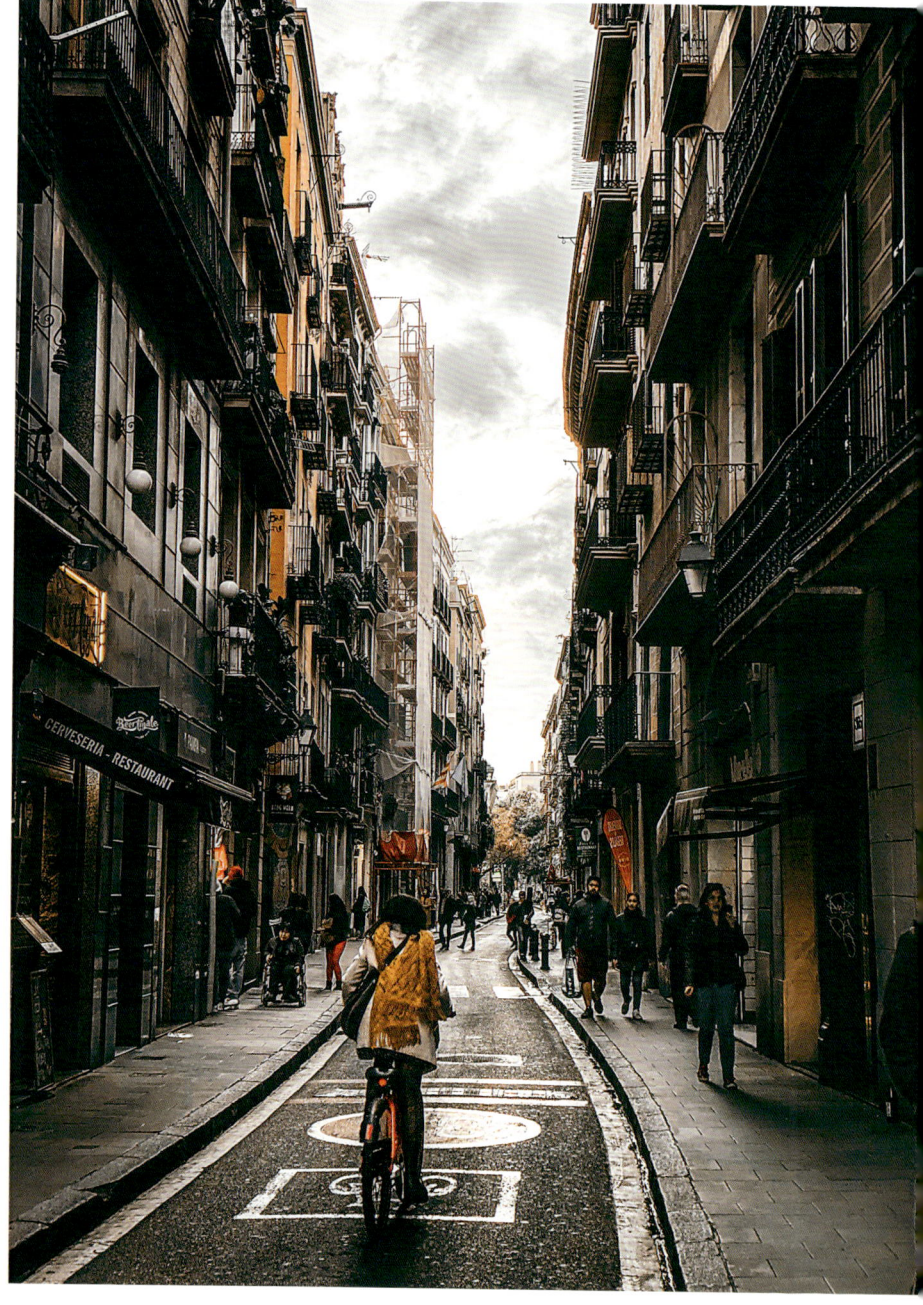

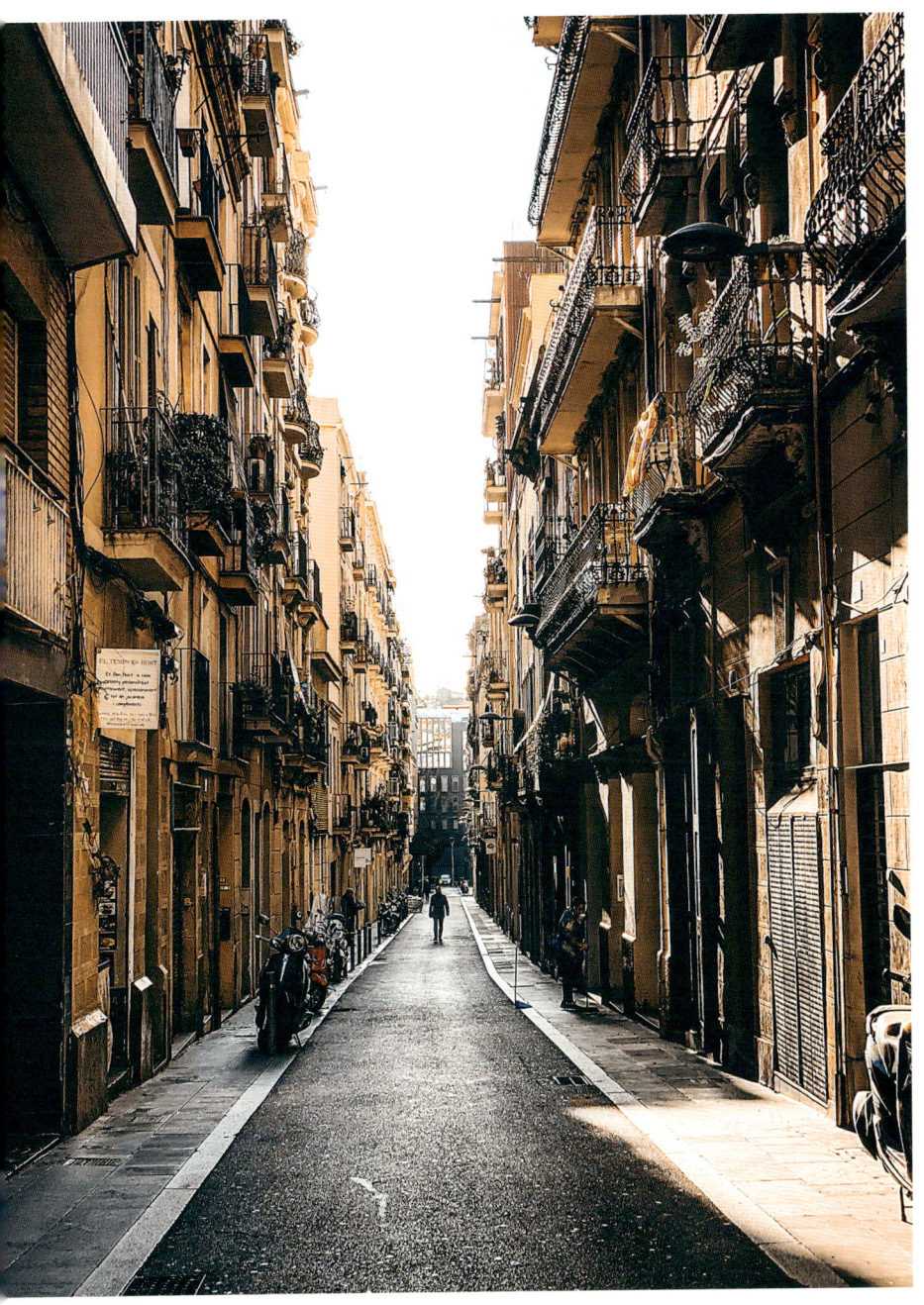

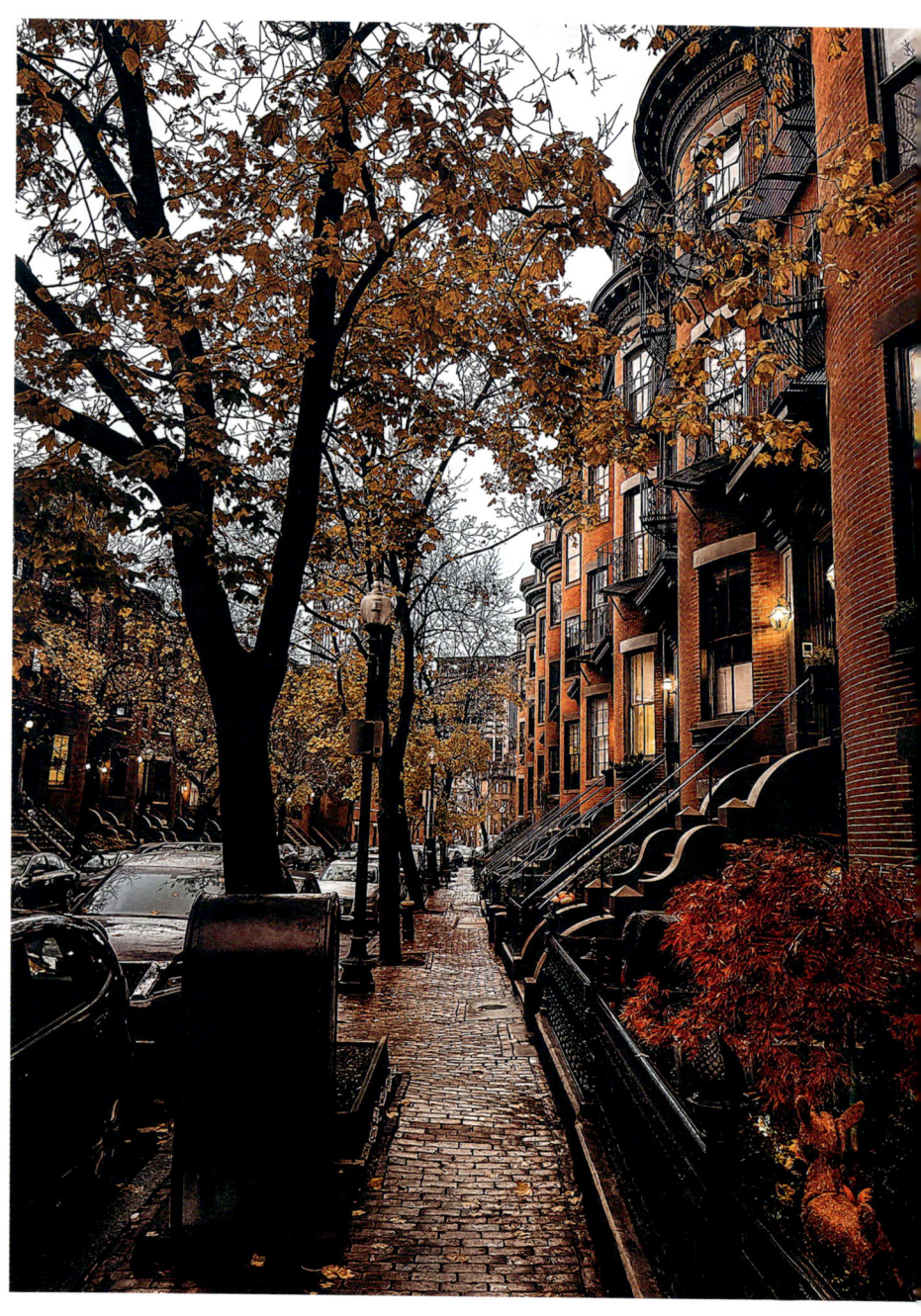

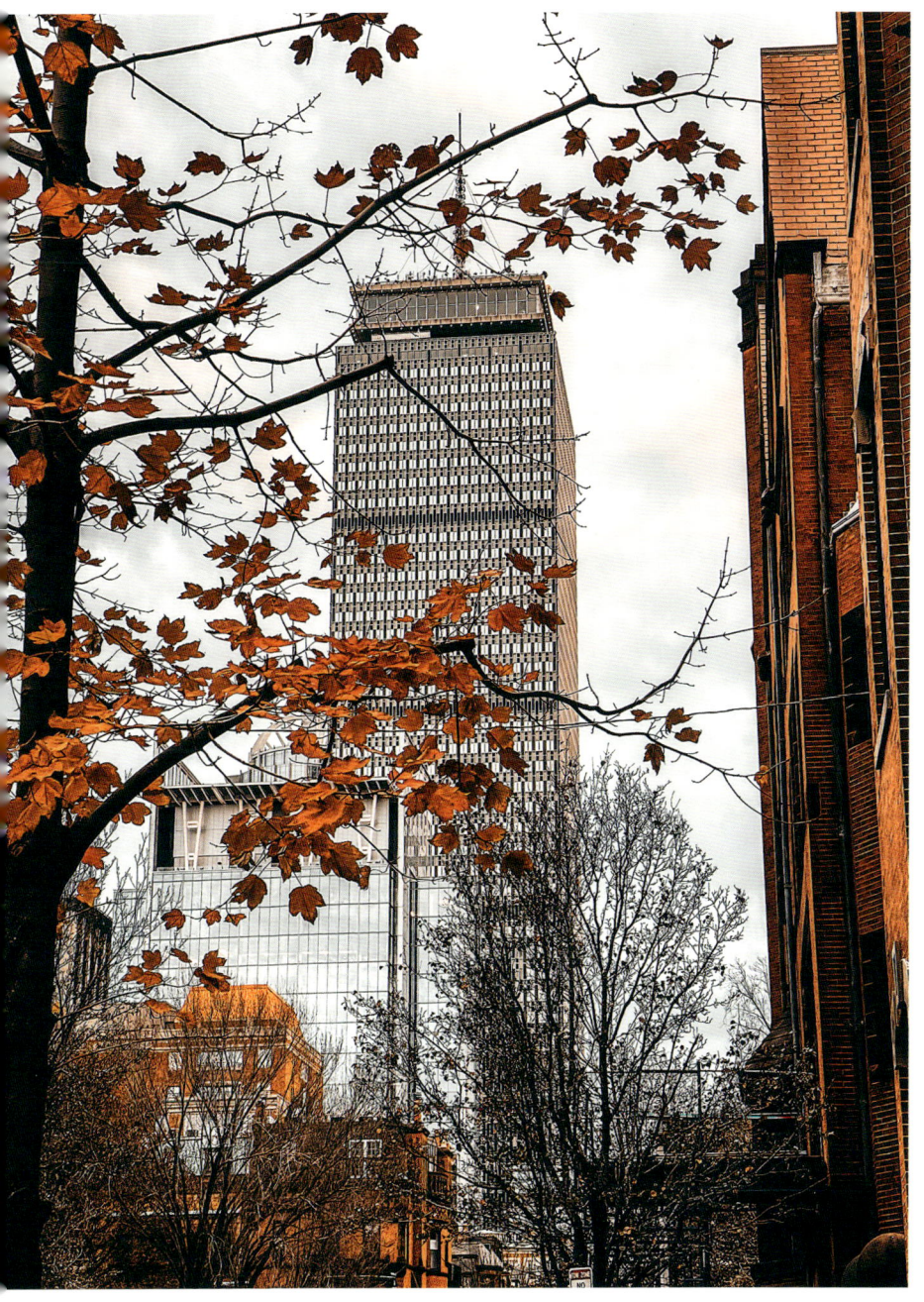

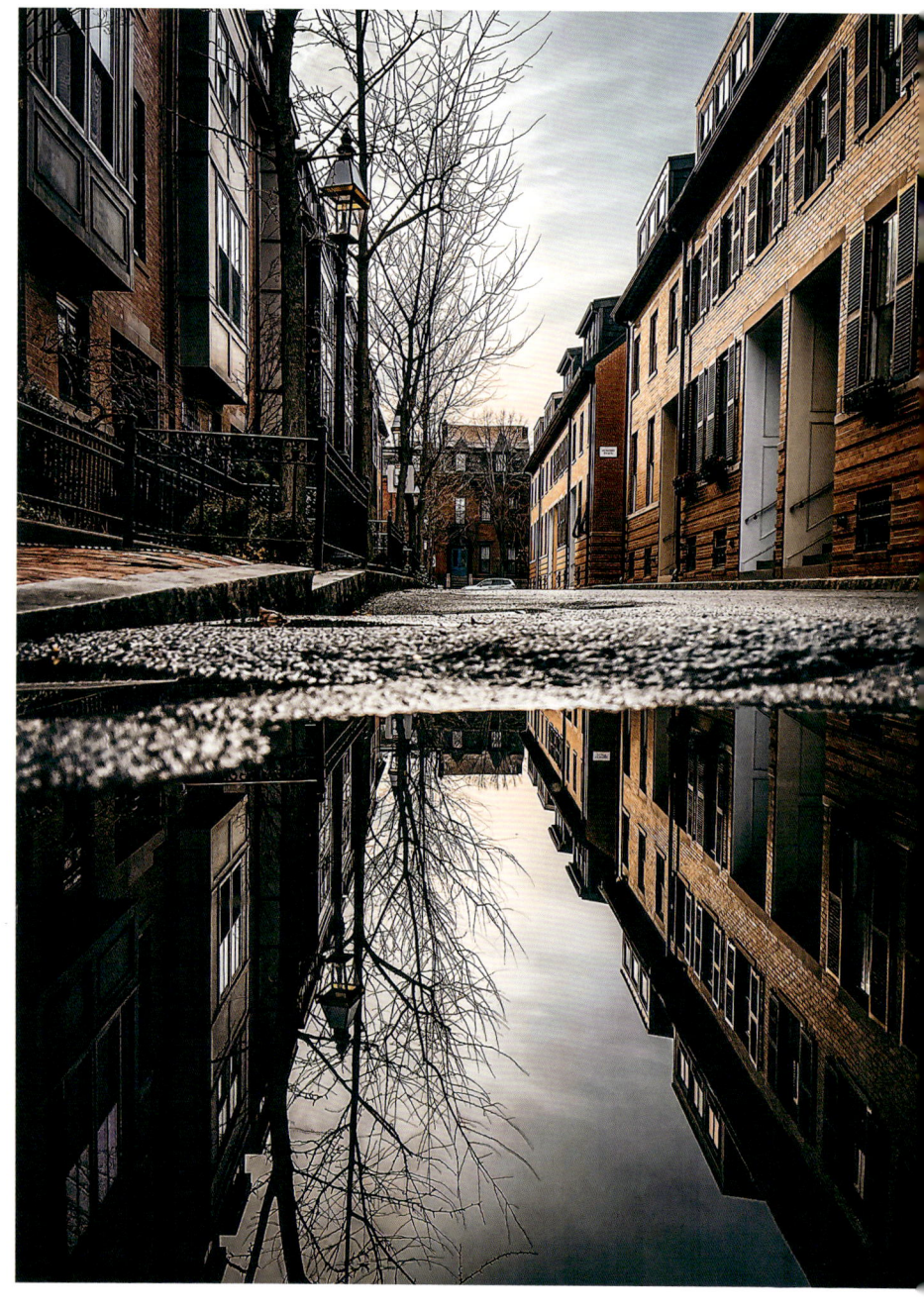

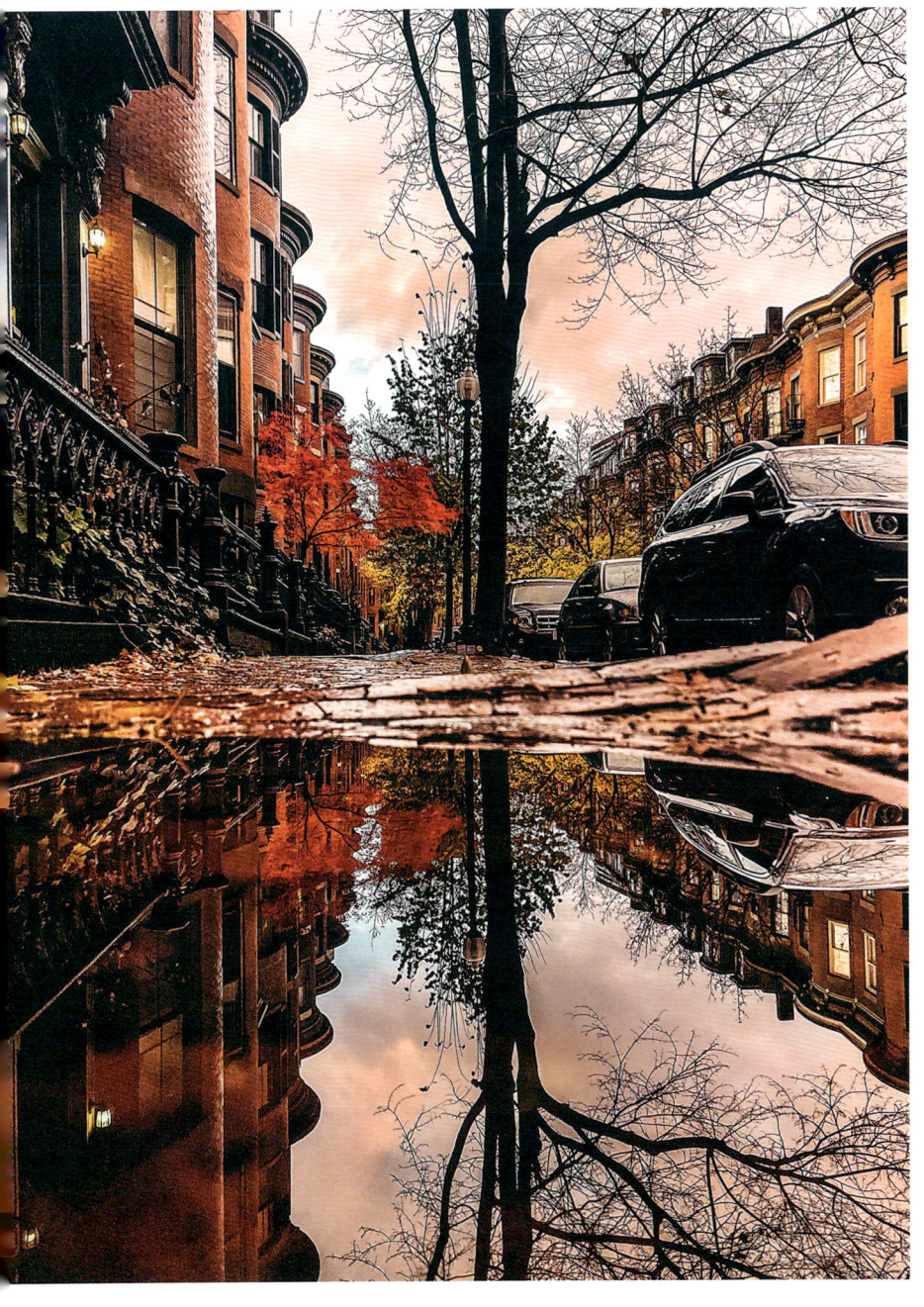

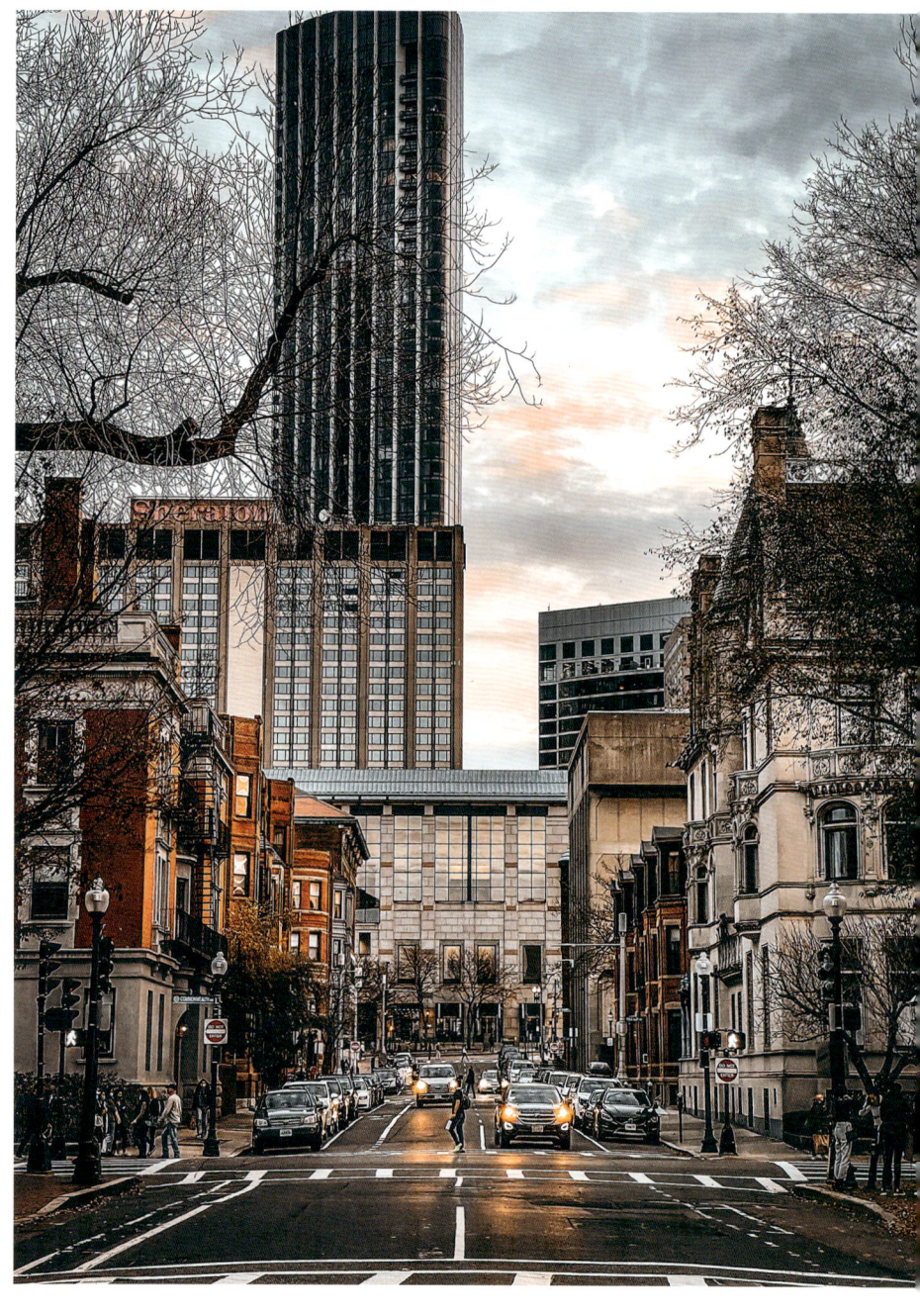

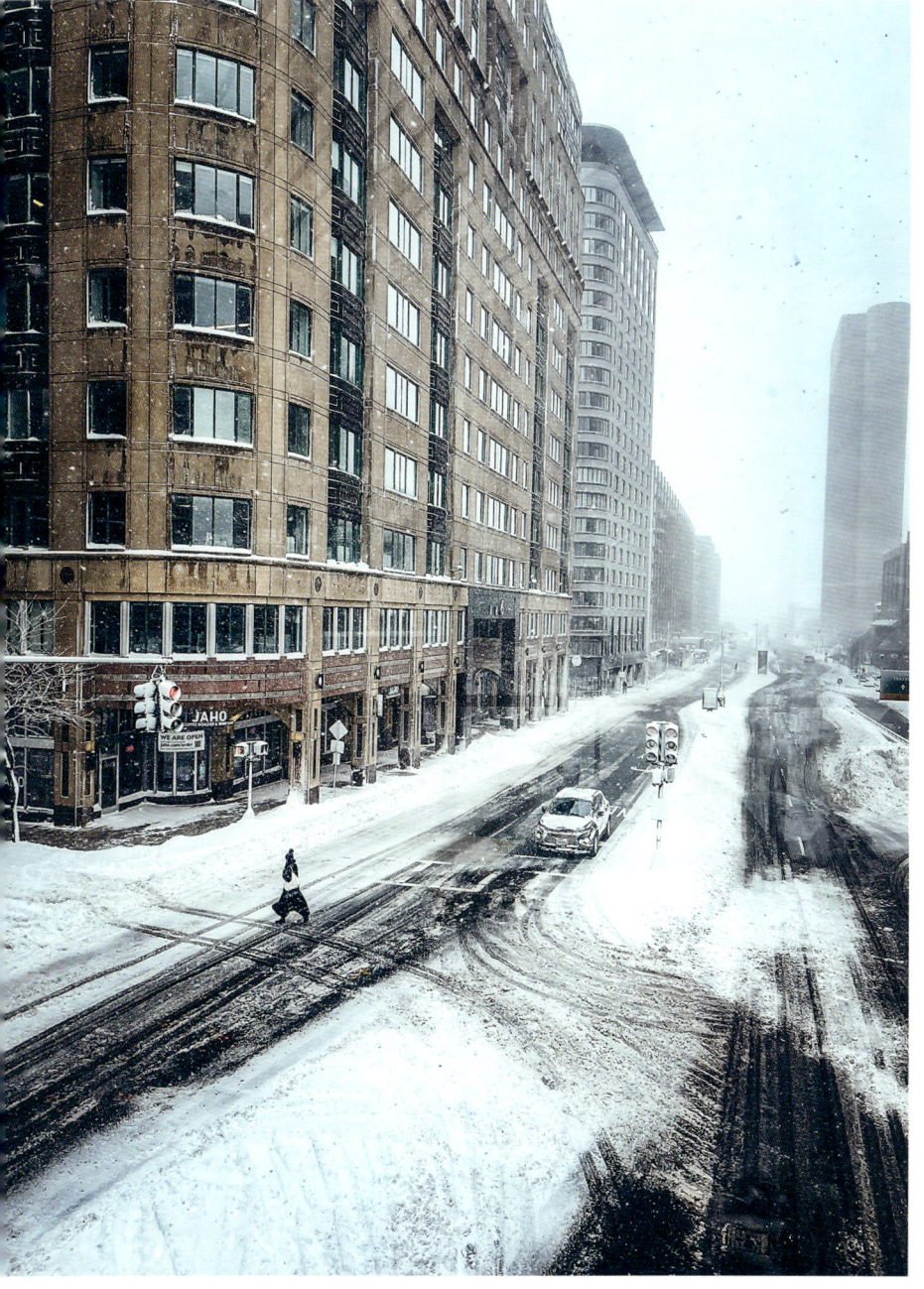

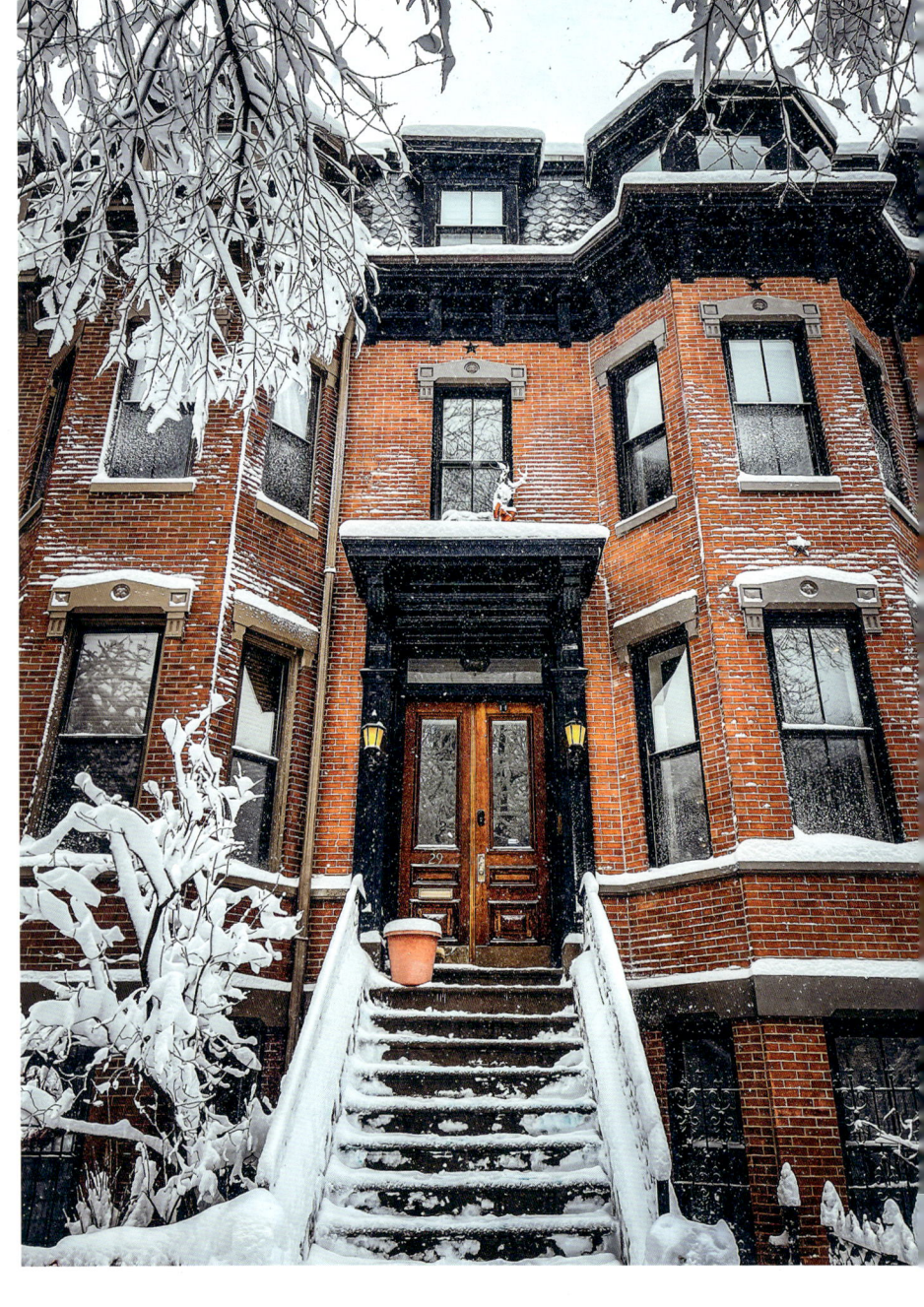

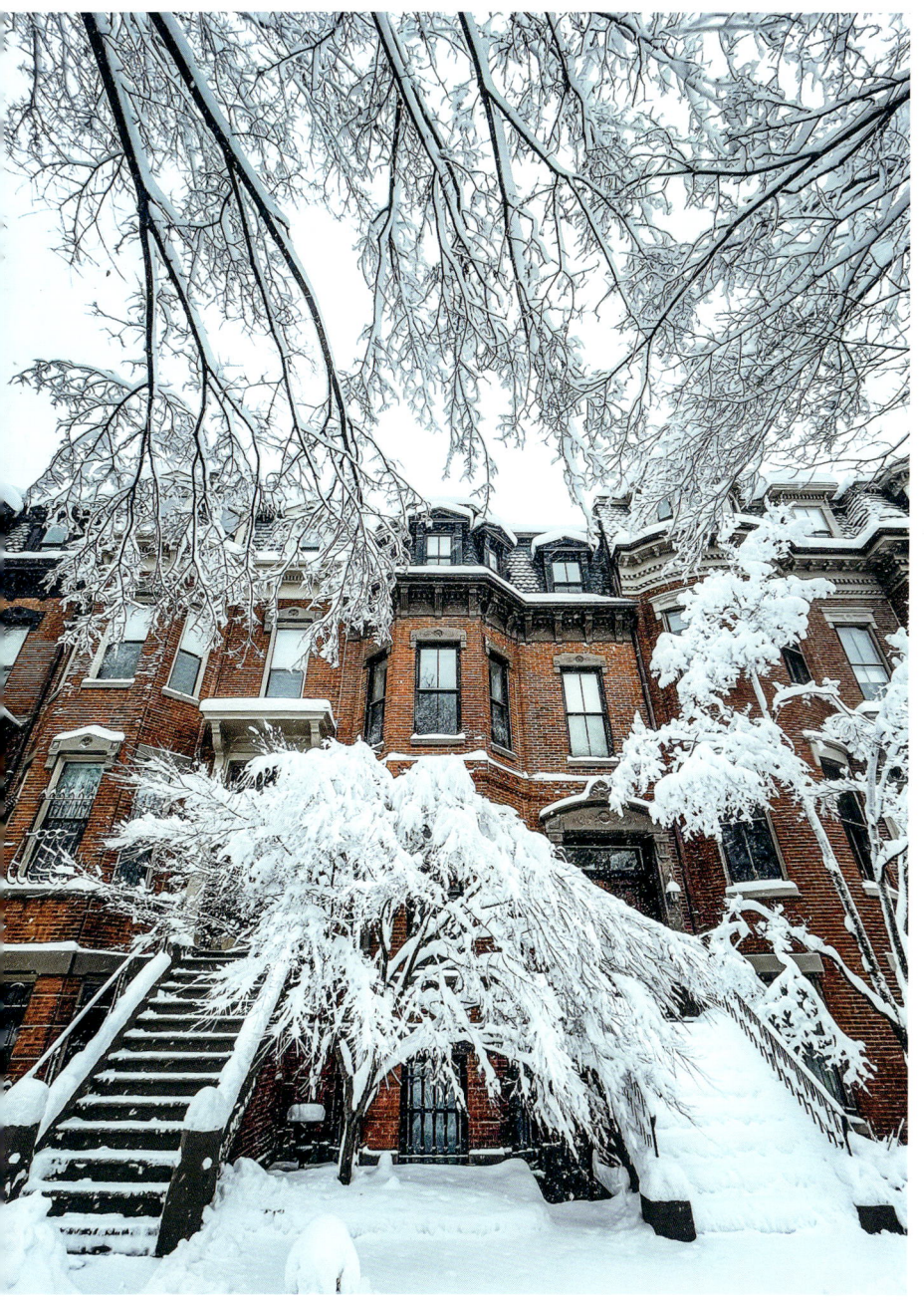

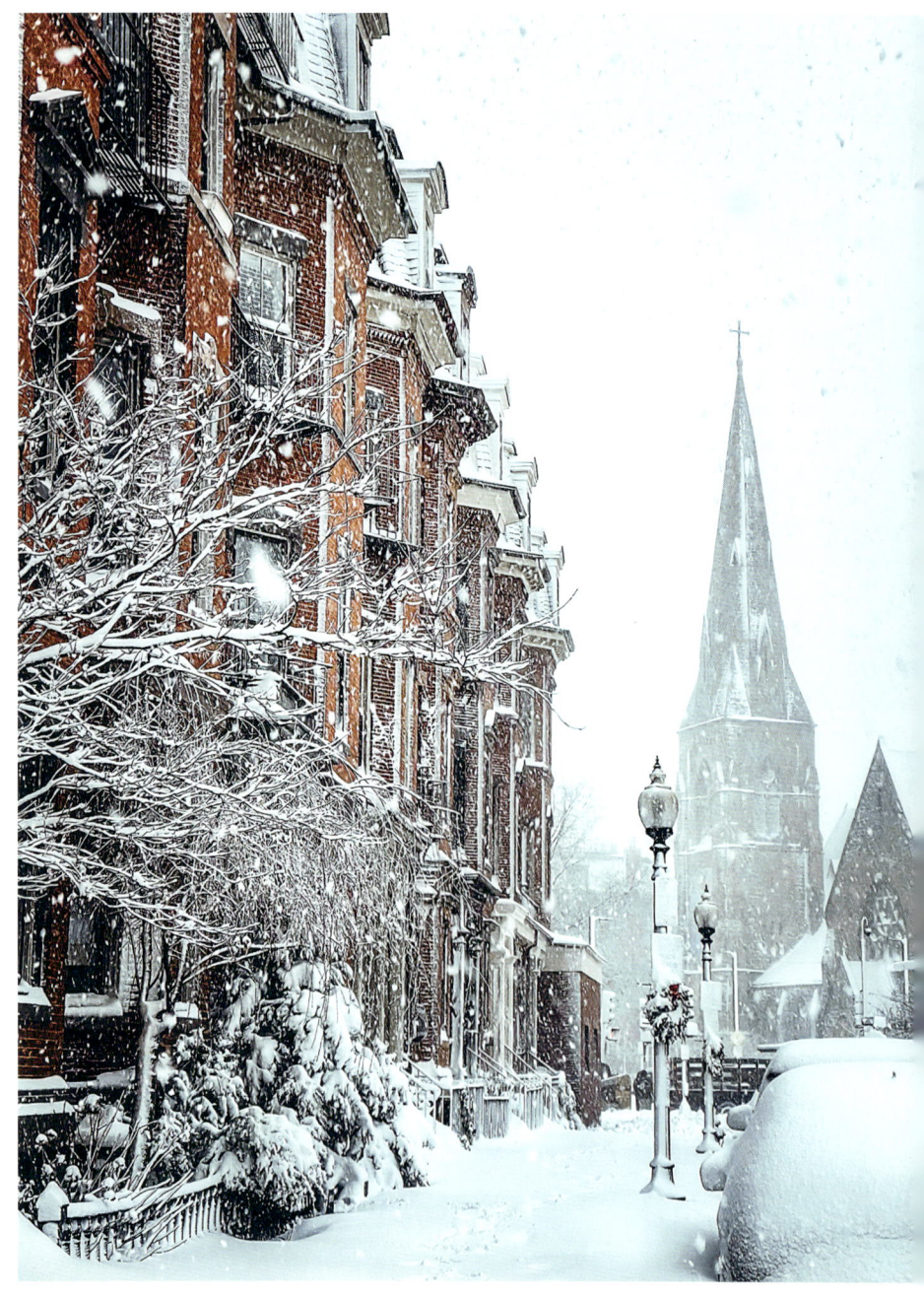

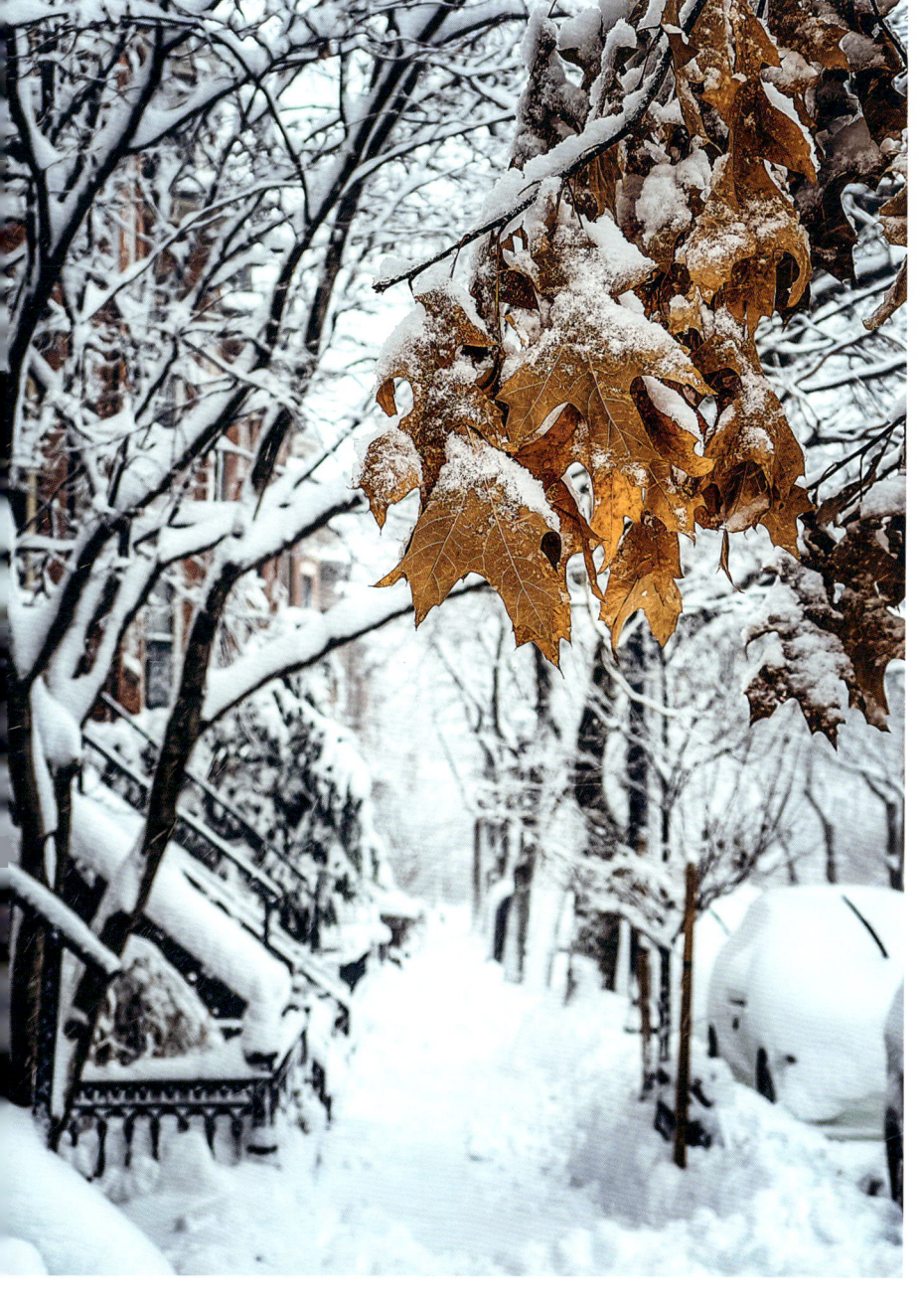

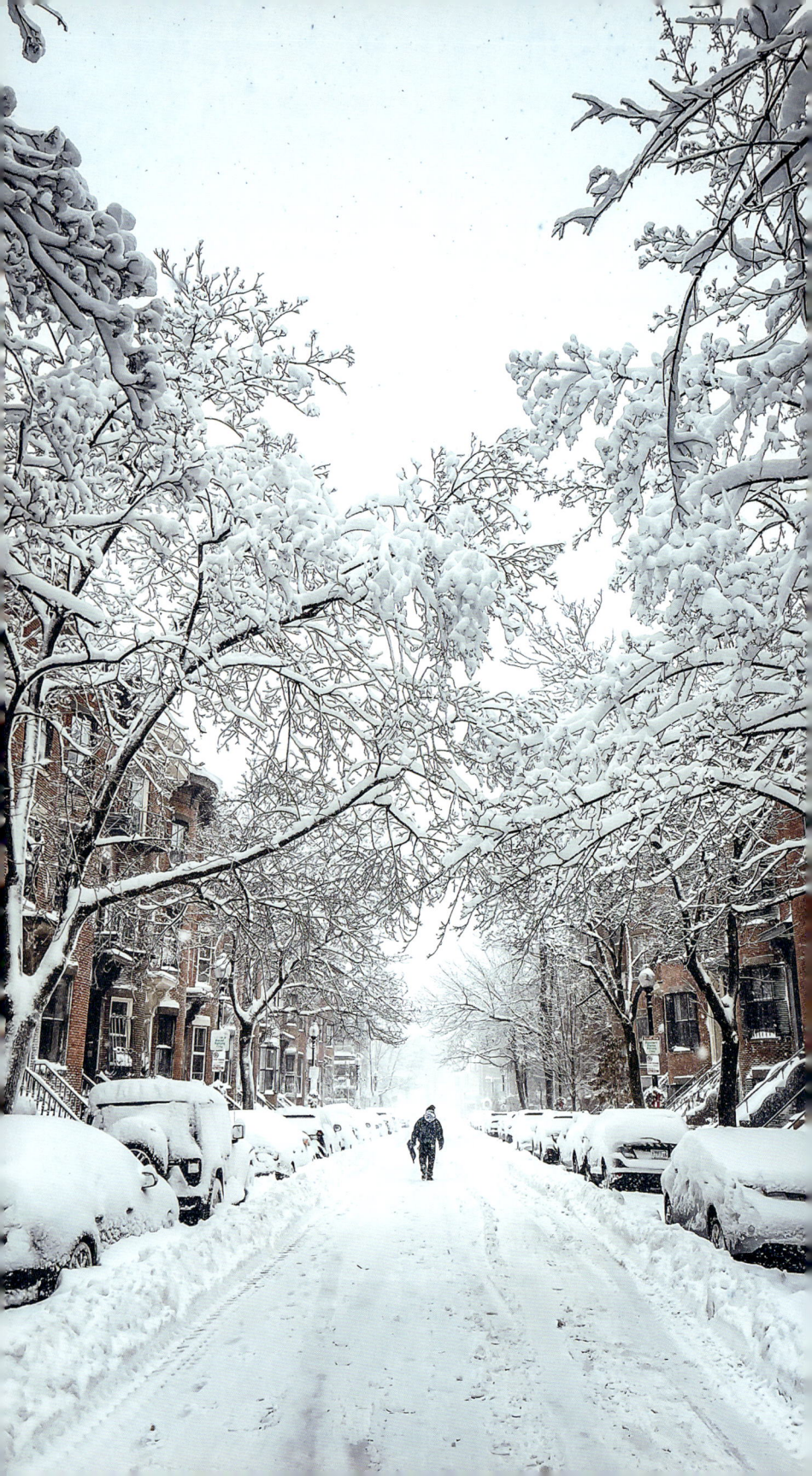

Throughout my photography journey, my wife Ele has always supported me, whether it's helping me choose between different versions of a shot, or exploring new sights during our travels around the world.

My mobile photography friends who have inspired me, taught me, and explored with me, in the rain, in the freezing cold, and at the break of dawn.

The innovative team at Moment. What an exciting journey it's been to test out new mobile lenses to enhance the shot; to write for their blog; and to teach mobile photography to groups of people from around the world in Japan.

NEAL KUMAR

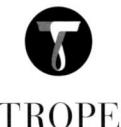

TROPE